PROPAGANDA AND AMERICAN DEMOCRACY

D1557169

Media and Public Affairs | Robert Mann, Series Editor

303.375 PROPA

Propaganda and American
democracy

JUN 2 2 2016

PROPAGANDA AND AMERICAN DEMOCRACY

Edited by NANCY SNOW

Louisiana State University Press
Baton Rouge

Published by Louisiana State University Press
Copyright © 2014 by Louisiana State University Press
All rights reserved
Manufactured in the United States of America
LSU Press Paperback Original
First printing

Designer: Barbara Neely Bourgoyne
Typefaces: GarageGothic, display; Miller, text
Printer and binder: Maple Press

Library of Congress Cataloging-in-Publication Data

Propaganda and American democracy / edited by Nancy Snow.
pages cm. — (Media and public affairs)
Includes index.
ISBN 978-0-8071-5414-4 (pbk. : alk. paper) — ISBN 978-0-8071-5415-1 (pdf) — ISBN 978-0-8071-5416-8 (epub) — ISBN 978-0-8071-5417-5 (mobi) 1. Propaganda—United States. 2. Propaganda, American. 3. United States—Politics and government. I. Snow, Nancy.
HM1231.P75 2013
303.3'750973—dc23

2013028475

The paper in this book meets the guidelines for permanence and durability of the Committee on Production Guidelines for Book Longevity of the Council on Library Resources. ♾

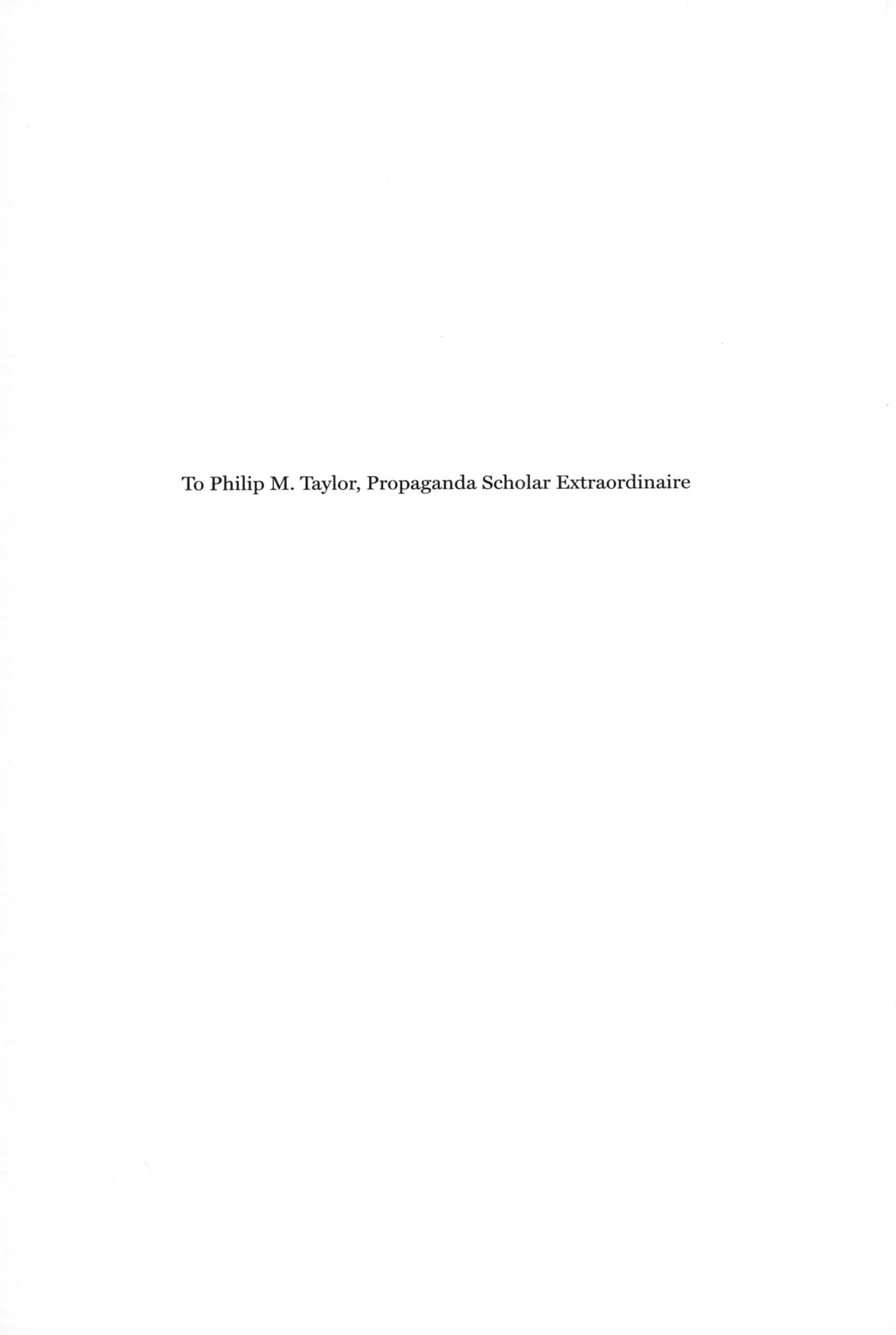

To Philip M. Taylor, Propaganda Scholar Extraordinaire

CONTENTS

★ ★ ★ ★

ACKNOWLEDGMENTS ix

Introduction 1
Nancy Snow

1. Propaganda in the Digital Age 9
Dan Kuehl

2. Good Propaganda or Propaganda for Good 29
Anthony Pratkanis

3. Propaganda and Public Discourse 75
J. Michael Sproule

4. Propaganda for War 94
Mordecai Lee

5. Pervasive Propaganda in America 120
Nancy Snow

6. Journalists as Propagandists 148
Asra Q. Nomani

7. Propaganda as Entertainment 168
Garth S. Jowett

8. Reforming the Worst Propaganda 184
Randal Marlin

CONTRIBUTORS 203
INDEX 207

ACKNOWLEDGMENTS

I would like to thank the man at the helm of this ship, Robert Mann, who invited me to tackle this subject as moderator of the 2012 Breaux Symposium at Louisiana State University. Bob holds many academic titles, but it is his commitment to scholarly and teaching excellence in political and persuasive communication that humbles my efforts here. Emily Tiller Wascom was extremely helpful with all her assistance, patience, and feedback as we corresponded from California to Louisiana, across two time zones, in preparation for the symposium. Both Bob and Emily made this project a joy. I also want to thank LSU Press, Alisa Plant in particular, for the opportunity to make this volume part of the press's outstanding series on media and public affairs.

Finally, I wish to acknowledge all of the contributors, many of whom I knew only through their works that had so influenced my own understanding of propaganda in a democratic society. All are highly regarded in their respective fields, and our Breaux Symposium gathering in March 2012 allowed us to meet in person to exchange ideas and hold conversation in a setting that is rare in the academy today. We listened and learned from one another in a spirit of intellectual enthusiasm that revived and renewed an interest in and dedication to propaganda studies in the United States.

PROPAGANDA AND AMERICAN DEMOCRACY

INTRODUCTION

NANCY SNOW

This edited volume grew out of a spirited discussion that brought together some of North America's leading minds on propaganda in a democracy. The 2012 Breaux Symposium at Louisiana State University, "That's the Way It Is: Media Propaganda and Its Impact on American Democracy," was designed to address a subject that is often alluded to in media and political conversation but mostly missing as a serious subject of inquiry in academic research and teaching.

The study of propaganda is well received overseas. For a variety of reasons, we tend to shirk it here in America, most probably due to our devotion to the idea that democracies are all about facts and the unvarnished truth. At the water's edge, propaganda in general and American propaganda in particular are closely monitored and discussed. Many of my international counterparts, both inside and outside the academy, are quick to ask why the United States doesn't have propaganda studies departments or propaganda research institutes. To these global citizens, the United States is a major purveyor of propaganda worldwide. I'm often inclined to think of Jeremiah 5:21: "Hear now this, O foolish people, and without understanding; which have eyes, and see not; which have ears, and hear not," more commonly expressed as "There is none so blind as he who will not see." We can continue to mistakenly link propaganda to just negative communication or what strictly despotic regimes do, but it will be at our own understanding deficit.

For this symposium we did something rather unprecedented for a group of scholars that is used to the formality of conference presentations. We faced each other around a table in order to elicit more engagement and exchange of ideas. What we discovered is that while we differ a bit on how we define propaganda uses and abuses, we have much more in common that unites us: we believe that the study of propaganda's role in American society is highly neglected and yet exceedingly needed in building a more discerning, critically conscious citizen. As editor of this volume and one who has worked at two foreign affairs agencies of the federal government, the U.S. Information Agency and the State Department, I strongly believe there is a national security dimension to the study of propaganda in American democracy. Citizens in a democracy need to be informed about the tools of persuasion and social influence that shape and manipulate their thoughts and actions. Without such tools, democratic nations are vulnerable to the social diseases of ignorance and misunderstanding that are consequences of an undeveloped critical consciousness and which, in turn, lead to strife, violence, and war.

It is no accident that our propaganda symposium occurred during a presidential campaign season. We the people don't necessarily point to a presidential contest as our best exemplar of George Washington's apocryphal outburst about lies and cherry trees. Rather, we live in a political age when fact-checkers are often dismissed as driven by personal or political bias. The Pew Research Center for the People and the Press, which has been tracking press reputation and credibility since 1985, reported in 2011 that 66 percent of Americans consider news stories to be often inaccurate, while 77 percent of Americans believe that mainstream news organizations tend to favor one political side over another. The press is deemed elitist and out of touch: 88 percent of Americans agree with the statement that powerful people and organizations often influence news organizations. Conversely, when Americans are asked about their individual news sources, the percentage saying that such sources are biased or inaccurate drops precipitously, to fewer than 30 percent. Fully 62 percent say that their own main news sources are accurate.[1] What these statistics present is a landscape of America where perceived sources for accuracy and independence are few. In a presidential election year, much less any year, are we now just tuning in to voices and pundits with whom we agree? Are we reading columnists whose opinions are our own in order to just reinforce our own truths? If that's our reality, then no amount of fact checking from organizations like FactCheck.org or PolitiFact.com is going to make a difference with many of us. This is why political consultants often advise their candidates to go for broke with campaign ads that come under attack. Instead of pulling an ad, more often we see campaigns redouble their efforts and attack the fact-checkers as too biased. In politics, effectiveness in getting one's message across trumps accuracy every time. Increasingly in this democracy where free speech reigns supreme, we all seem entitled not only to our own opinions but also to our own set of facts. This is all the more reason why such a book about the uses and abuses of propaganda is before you.

I cannot help but think of a propaganda scholar who would have written an introduction or foreword to this volume were he still here. Propaganda historian Philip M. Taylor, a professor of international communications at the University of Leeds, epitomized the public scholar who placed student learning at the center of his teaching. I became one of his mentees as a junior scholar in 2001 when I emailed him about his seminal book, *Munitions of the Mind.* It was right after 9/11, and I was fielding reporter questions based on a small book I had first published in 1998, *Propaganda, Inc.: Selling America's Culture to the World.* I wanted to thank Dr. Taylor for giving me historical insight into propaganda. I did not expect to hear back from him, much less so quickly. Academics often burrow down into their own research and aren't always so responsive to other scholars' work, especially scholars so far down the academic hierarchy. Nevertheless, first a virtual friendship developed and then a collaborative scholarly effort to shape understanding of propaganda across the great pond. We both understood that the United States and the United Kingdom have been at the forefront of democratic societies heavily immersed in and led by propaganda, both at war and in peacetime. Phil's final book was our coedited volume, the *Routledge Handbook of Public Diplomacy,* released two years before his passing in 2010. His introduction to *Munitions of the Mind* could very well serve as our main theme for *Propaganda and American Democracy*:

> This book attempts to place the conduct of propaganda during these events within a wider historical context. It retains its main thesis that propaganda is a much misunderstood word, that it is not necessarily the "bad thing" that most people think it is. As a process of persuasion, it is value neutral. Rather, it is the intention behind the propaganda that demands scrutiny, and it is that intention which begs value judgments, not the propaganda itself.[2]

Like Phil Taylor's observation, the contributors to this volume support the study of propaganda for what it is, both good and bad. We know it is used regularly to shape specific outcomes to targets of influence. We know it is, at times, a most abusive form of communication as manipulation, used as a methodological tool to conceal and not to reveal. It is proactive and reactive; its categories, according to French sociologist Jacques Ellul, include rational and irrational, integrative and agitative approaches. During the Second World War, American writer Gorham Munson described propaganda as a form of communication distinguished by presentation:

> Propaganda, this powerful instrument for insisting upon a cause in such a way as to win masses of men to its side and to dismay opponents of the cause, makes use of lies, of the true mixed with the false, and of truth. It is a method and an instrument equally available for hideous purposes, as in the instigation of pogroms, and for merciful purposes, as in the propaganda of Christian pacifism. It may appeal to the generous tolerant impulses of men or to their brutal instincts, their proclivities to hate and slay. One writer has made a homely comparison of propaganda to a garden hose. Through a hose may pass water from a cesspool or crystal-clear water or a mixed muddy stream. Propaganda may present the clear truth or a muddy mixture of truth and lies or a poisonous stream of prejudice; it is a method of presentation, not subject matter.[3]

The *New York Times* observed in an editorial on September 1, 1937, "What is truly vicious is not propaganda but a monopoly of it." At that time there was no television, Internet, Instant Messaging, e-mail, or smart phones, much less the omnipresent social networking sites, such as Facebook and Twitter. World public opinion and newspaper editors were concerned with total information control by government dictatorships. The U.S.-based Institute for Propaganda Analysis, whose life span was barely three years, left us with a forewarning that it is not propaganda itself that does the most harm, but a monopoly of its ill effects. "If American citizens are to have a clear understanding of conditions and what to do about them, they must be able to recognize propaganda, to analyze it, and to appraise it. They must be able to discover whether it is propaganda in line with their own interests and the interests of our civilization or whether it is propaganda that may distort our views and threaten to undermine our civilization."[4] If the IPA could publish that statement in 1939, what might it say today?

American president Barack Obama observed in response to growing anti-American protests in 2012, "In the age of the Internet, and the way that any knucklehead who says something can post it up and suddenly it travels all around the world, every country has to recognize that the best way to marginalize that kind of speech is to ignore it, or to speak out against it and use words to counteract those words and to affirm that we respect all religions."[5] He was speaking directly to the propaganda effects of our mass communication channels and the responsibility or lack thereof with which we use these channels. So perhaps we must heed again the words of Edward L. Bernays, who said there is propaganda and impropaganda. Bernays in his time was increasingly disturbed by the latter's use in political campaigns. Imagine what Bernays might say about all the possibilities for use and abuse of influence in the digital age.

This collection of essays about propaganda in an American democracy is the first collection of its kind to utilize the insights of professionals whose entire careers have been devoted to research and teaching in propaganda and persuasion. Dan Kuehl, a retired lieutenant colonel in the U.S. Air Force, writes about the impact of the digital age in propaganda campaigns. Dr. Kuehl served as the director of the Information Operations concentration program, a specialized curriculum on national security in the information age at the National Defense University in Washington, D.C. His approach to propaganda is as a professional military service member and educator whose student population consists of information warfighters. His definition of propaganda is very helpful to anyone whose understanding of the subject falls outside military circles. Kuehl's "take it for what it is" approach contrasts with that of Randal Marlin, whose final chapter explores what we can do as reformers to combat propaganda at its worst.

This volume includes renowned academics and authors in the study of modern propaganda. We may not have Lasswell, Bernays, or Lippmann on hand, but we do have contributions from scholars whose combined work in American propaganda study spans decades. Garth Jowett, whose text with Victoria O'Donnell is the most adopted book in propaganda and persuasion, presents propaganda in an entirely different context than the opening chapter by Dan Kuehl. Jowett's specialty is the history of propaganda effects associated with the entertainment field in America, most notably film. In his chapter, we look back at the 1940s Capitol Hill, where Hollywood and mass entertainment were coming under fire by the moralists in government who felt threatened by the content of the messages in entertainment and the men behind them. What we learn from this case study is that Americans in the twenty-first century are just as concerned about the effects of propaganda as entertainment, particularly its effects on young, impressionable minds. My own chapter on propaganda's pervasiveness is located in close proximity to Garth Jowett's chapter to underscore the number one position that the United States holds in both propaganda manufacturing and consumption.

Other chapters in this volume are by the leading minds in their respective fields. I sought out J. Michael Sproule, a specialist in human communication, specifically for his ability to explain propaganda as a form of discursive practice. There is no one better than Sproule to present a list of the seven deadly dangers in propaganda influence, inspired of course by the seven propaganda devices of the 1930s-era Institute for Propaganda Analysis. He reminds us of the power of our words to persuade and conceal our intentions. Like Garth Jowett, Anthony Pratkanis is a highly regarded leading mind in our "age of propaganda," from which his highly popular textbook is titled. Anthony Pratkanis is an expert on social influence, and he presents a practical guide to the good that propaganda can do, a point to which I will return in the conclusion of this introduction. Pratkanis helps the reader to get over any negative associations with words like persuasion and influence. Human beings persuade and are persuaded. We influence others and are influenced by others. Granted, much of what we confront on a daily basis as intentional communication has some ill intents, but it is not all so! Pratkanis comes from a background of social psychology and consults widely with business and government on methods and techniques of persuasion for social good. His chapter is a reminder that this field can make change for public good.

For this volume I asked a personal friend of twenty-five years to contribute her professional and personal voice. Muslim-American activist, academic researcher, and reporter Asra Q. Nomani has been at the heart of this debate. She lost a close, personal friend and colleague, Daniel Pearl, to propaganda at its worst. Asra Nomani's chapter is nothing short of a chilling reminder of the reality of our present condition. Propaganda is not always effective, but when it is, it can be deadly so. Nomani's personal account of her role as a journalist subject to and active in propaganda manufacturing leads to Mordecai Lee's scholarship on propaganda for war. Lee's academic specializations include the federal government's role as purveyor of propaganda in wartime. We Americans associate propaganda most closely with war, not only once it is under way, but especially as the primer paint for preparing the public to acquiesce to war. Human beings are naturally inclined to not want to kill complete strangers in distant countries. We have to be conditioned to accept that reality as based on a "war to end all wars," or as a war to strengthen democracy. Whatever the narrative frame is, you can count on propaganda campaigns to take the lead in the conditioning of the war mind.

I am thankful to our last contributor, Randal Marlin, who allows us some space to catch our collective breaths as we contemplate the future. Marlin, a protégé to none other than Jacques Ellul, whose book *Propaganda* is to many the definitive text on the subject, is a teacher, first and foremost. For over thirty years Marlin has taught a highly popular university course in Canada called "Truth and Propaganda." A political philosopher, Randal Marlin shares insights into the value of studying propaganda to diagnose its ill effects in order to reform it and (in the process) ourselves.

This brings me back to the legacy of Philip M. Taylor. There is a section of *Munitions of the Mind* where my friend pauses to contemplate his life's work. It is the words that follow that form the spirit of this volume. All of the contributors are driven to serve humanity through our work. We seek first to understand and then to teach others about what we have learned. We want our study of propaganda to have a meaningful impact and we wish to hear from other scholars and practitioners who wish to form a network devoted to expanding study and research in this subject area, particularly dialogue and research into propaganda uses for good. As Phil Taylor reminds us, we know whose narrative currently dominates our media and mindscapes. Let's work to tell our own stories:

Differences of opinion between people and nations are inevitable, but they can only remain a healthy aspect of civilized society if violence, war and terrorism are avoided. Since 9/11, we need peace propagandists, not war propagandists—people whose job it is to increase communication, understanding and dialogue between different peoples with different perspectives. A gradual process of explanation can only generate greater trust, and therefore a greater willingness to understand our perspective. And if this dialogue is mutual, greater empathy and consensus will emerge. We might not always like what we see about others but we need to recognize that fear, hypocrisy and ignorance are the enemies of peace and peaceful co-existence. The historical function of propaganda has been to fuel that fear, hypocrisy and ignorance, and it has earned itself a bad reputation for so doing. But propaganda has the potential to serve a constructive, civilized and peaceful purpose—if that is the intention behind conducting it. We must all become propagandists on behalf of those very characteristics that genetically and anthropologically link all people to the human species. Only then might we really begin to see an end to history. It may, however, be a long time coming.[6]

Notes

1. The Pew Research Center for People and the Press, "Press Widely Criticized, But Trusted More than Other Information Sources," September 22, 2011, http://www.people-press.org/2011/09/22/press-widely-criticized-but-trusted-more-than-other-institutions/.

2. Philip M. Taylor, *Munitions of the Mind: A History of Propaganda from the Ancient World to the Present Era,* 3rd ed. (Manchester, England: Manchester University Press, 2003), viii, http://www.questia.com/read/117223929.

3. Gorham Munson, *12 Decisive Battles of the Mind: The Story of Propaganda during the Christian Era, with Abridged Versions of Texts That Have Shaped History* (New York: Greystone Press, 1942), 17, http://www.questia.com/read/22838234.

4. Alfred McClung Lee and Elizabeth Briant Lee, *The Fine Art of Propaganda: A Study of Father Coughlin's Speeches* (New York: Harcourt, Brace, 1939).

5. President Barack Obama and First Lady Michelle Obama on ABC's *The View,* September 25, 2012.

6. Philip M. Taylor, *Munitions of the Mind,* 324.

1

PROPAGANDA IN THE DIGITAL AGE

DAN KUEHL

Propaganda seems to fit well into that old definition of obscenity: hard to define, but easy to identify. But not only is that trite, it's inaccurate, because it really isn't that easy to identify. While it is certainly easy to recognize simplistic and obvious examples—North Korean posters of the latest "great leader"—it is far more difficult to discern more subtle examples in things that we might not even categorize as propaganda.

Propaganda is defined via the eyes and ears of the audience. One individual or group may define it very differently than another. The thesis of this chapter is that although propaganda has been with us for thousands of years, its form and substance have changed significantly in the past few decades because of several synergistic developments. Some of those are political, with the rise of large, authoritarian states in the past century. More important has been the explosion of what are termed information and communication technologies (ICT), such as global television, the spectacularly rapid growth of the Internet, and the decreasing size, increasing capability, and expanding mobility of personal information devices. A critical connective thread is the ability of these technologies to capture, modify, and disseminate images, because the visual dimension is the most critical way through which propaganda creates its impact.

DEFINING PROPAGANDA

While few would dispute that the word itself has attained an almost universally pejorative meaning, it was not always so. An exhaustive analysis of how we have defined propaganda would require another book rather than this chapter.[1] But many of the definitions of propaganda yield useful insights, culminating in the current Department of Defense definition. The term, used for decades before in the Counter-Reformation, gained a new level of institutional prominence in 1622 with the Vatican's "propagation of the faith" (*Congregatio de Propaganda Fide*), which was certainly not a pejorative term, at least not to that community. In all of the thousands of pages in the massive 120 serial volumes of the American Civil War's fabled *Official Records*, the term appears only once, suggesting that in nineteenth-century America the word had not attained the widespread usage of today, although the use of what we would call propaganda has been widespread throughout recorded history.

The concept of propaganda and its use is far more important than the evolution of the term itself. The twentieth century has been the "century of propaganda," primarily because of two ravenous world wars, two enormously powerful and authoritarian political systems, and a steady stream of advances in ICT.

World War I was a breakout event for propaganda, as both Germany (and its allies) and Great Britain (and its allies, including the United States) made extensive use of it, both domestically and globally. Unlike in earlier wars, such as the U.S. Civil War and the German wars of unification, by WWI the marriage of new means of creating propaganda (photography, the print media, and even early movies) and the means of disseminating it (telegraphy and radio) opened a tremendous new battlefield for propaganda to paint "ourselves" in the best possible light and "them" in the worst.[2] British control of information connectivity[3] to the United States in 1915–1917 was a significant factor in shifting American public opinion toward entering WWI on the Allies' side. It was during and after this period that propaganda became a pejorative term as a result of how both sides used it to demonize the other side, often falsely. Radio as a stepping stone to the modern era of television enabled the dissemination of propaganda with much greater speed and over greater distances. The developments in radio during the 1930s set the stage for its use as a key propaganda medium during WWII.

If the regimes of WWI gave propaganda a bad name, then those of WWII cemented it. The Nazis and the Communists combined inherent political evil with the widespread and all-encompassing use of propaganda to support that evil. The Nazis had two men—Adolf Hitler and

Joseph Goebbels—who were geniuses in its use, and the Nazi regime put together an apparatus that established extremely close ties between policy and propaganda, especially internally and domestically.[4] They also had the benefit of an artistic genius filmmaker, Leni Riefenstahl, whose film *Triumph des Willens* (*Triumph of the Will*) about the 1934 Sixth Nazi Party Congress in Nuremberg is arguably one of the best propaganda films ever made.[5] The Communists also made use of propaganda globally throughout the Cold War. Sometimes it was crude—North Korean propaganda posters come to mind—and sometimes it was very insightful and leveraged the actions and missteps of their adversaries to make powerful points against the United States and its allies. Starting in the 1950s, both sides in the Cold War used the new medium of television as a weapon in their war of ideas, influence, and images, and this struggle for influence using electronically transmitted imagery continues today, over the Internet and its many variants.[6]

But what do we mean by the term? Two major schools of thought have emerged. One is that propaganda is essentially amoral, and its use and intended effects must be analyzed before a judgment can be rendered as to its morality. The great American broadcast journalist Edward R. Murrow once said that "truth is the best propaganda,"[7] and the late Phil Taylor,[8] along with this book's editor, argued that as a process of communication, propaganda must first be viewed as value-neutral.[9] Political communications scholar Harold Lasswell observed, "Propaganda as a mere tool is no more moral or immoral than a pump handle."[10] Even the United States Holocaust Memorial Museum uses a value-neutral definition of propaganda as "biased information spread to shape public opinion and behavior."[11] On the other side of this debate are George Orwell[12] and Jacques Ellul, who observed that propaganda is inherently immoral, regardless of who is using it or for what purpose, because propaganda possesses immutably evil characteristics designed for political control.[13] This is not the place to explore these two arguments—that has been done far more exhaustively elsewhere—but they help inform the debate over what we call propaganda.

Many of the definitions provide insight into the person or entity offering that particular definition. Every dictionary includes a definition of propaganda. All include propaganda's objective of influencing opinion, and many of them also tie this objective specifically to government.

George Orwell's deep suspicion of government led him to define propaganda as inherently evil, as noted above. Just before the end of the Communist era in Eastern Europe, the German Democratic Republic defined propaganda as "the systematic spreading and thorough explanation of political, philosophical, economic, historical, as well as scientific, technical, and other types of ideas."[14] While fairly straightforward, without alluding to lies, deceit, or manipulation, it drew a clear distinction between the nefarious aims of "imperialist" propaganda as contrasted with Marxist-Leninist propaganda, which only aimed to advance the historic cause of the working class.[15]

While this approach clearly hewed to the "ours is okay, theirs is bad" perspective on propaganda during the early years of the Cold War, in which both sides made widespread use of propaganda, it also argued that everyone uses it. NATO, in its 2011 guidance for military public affairs, defines propaganda as "Information, ideas, doctrines, or special appeals disseminated to influence the opinion, emotions, attitudes, or behaviour of any specified group in order to benefit the sponsor, either directly or indirectly."[16] It acknowledges that adversaries may use propaganda but does not allude to any Alliance use. The definition officially endorsed by the Department of Defense (DOD) in 2006, "Any form of communication in support of national objectives designed to influence the opinions, emotions, attitudes, or behavior of any group in order to benefit the sponsor, either directly or indirectly," was similarly value-neutral.[17] The basic approach used in all these definitions could be applied also to commercial advertising.[18]

The DOD's newest official definition of propaganda, promulgated in early 2010, has two subtle but important changes, highlighted here in italics: "Any form of *adversary* communication, *especially of a biased or misleading nature,* designed to influence the opinions, emotions, attitudes, or behavior of any group in order to benefit the sponsor, either directly or indirectly."[19] This change reflected a significant debate within the Pentagon, much of it spurred by the Pentagon's Public Affairs organizations. This effort clearly wanted to distinguish propaganda, with its negative connotations, from truthful and legitimate efforts to persuade and influence.[20] This approach stands Edward R. Murrow's famous dictim about "truth being the best propaganda" on its head. This definition appears intended to do several things. First, it declares that we certainly don't do propaganda, only the other adversarial side does. Next, it establishes that it is propaganda's nature to use information that is at least deceptive if not outright deceitful. Third, when combined with another terminology change that redefined "Psychological Operations" into "Military Information Support Operations," the DOD appears to be trying to distance itself as far as possible from any suggestion that its influence activities could be described as propaganda, especially as there is significant concern within other elements of the government—particularly the Congress—about those activities. While the State Department does not issue official definitions of terminology and activities—there is no official State Department definition for strategic communication or public diplomacy, for example—there can be little doubt that it would share this perspective.[21]

Regardless of how we define propaganda, it inevitably brings us to information designed to influence someone. It may be intended to convince you to purchase a commercial product, espouse a philosophy or ideology, or support or oppose a political cause, but it seems to always end with behavior. This chapter is not a "history of propaganda" since entire books have explored that. Rather, it explores some of the many ways humans have employed propaganda, even if at the time those activities took place the term propaganda did not yet exist.

We in the modern digital world often think of an "image" in a technological sense, a set of ones and zeroes translated onto a page or a screen and depicting a person, or event, or some other form of informational content. But if we expand its meaning to include any visual representation, it then becomes clear that images have been used as propaganda for thousands of years. In ancient eras we didn't have the connective means to transmit images over distance, so we moved the audience to the image. Stone carvings done by Mesopotamian empires such as the Assyrians are an example of this. The Assyrians used stone tablets, called orthostats, to depict their rulers in activities such as lion hunts, making treaties with other empires, and conquering and subduing enemies. Some of the depictions—captives beheaded, impaled on stakes, or being blinded—remain terrifying more than two millennia later. Their intent was to serve a political function emphasizing Assyrian power and the risks of opposing it; propaganda, in other words. The Persians did this also, but their images often emphasized a more peaceful and unifying message, an early form perhaps of propaganda emphasizing soft power.[22] The Romans, especially after the Republic became the Empire, raised propaganda to a monumental form. Two millennia later, visitors to Rome can still see Trajan's Column or the Arch of Constantine and see the depictions in stone of their conquests. Caesar Augustus is depicted in various statuary as a general, statesman, religious leader, and deity, each intended to create a different impression—influence and propaganda in stone.[23] Various forms of public punishment, from the Romans' use of crucifixion to the French Revolution's use of the guillotine, were conducted with a propagandistic intent.

Much of the art produced over the past several hundred years, of kings and battles and nobles, had a similar, if often understated objective, but it was with the rise of the Westphalian nation state that "art is propaganda," to use George Orwell's phrase, came into adulthood.[24] The American Revolution had it. Paul Revere's classic depiction of "The Bloody Massacre Perpetrated in King Street" was, as one commentator observed, "long on political propaganda and short on accuracy."[25] In the nineteenth century a unique form of visual propaganda emerged, the cyclorama or panorama, large circular paintings in which an audience was literally immersed while the painting was rotated around them. While many of them were indeed nothing more than entertainment, others were clearly intended to glorify some historical event, such as the battles of Gettysburg, Waterloo, or Borodino.[26]

Until about a century ago, most visual propaganda was of an isolated and individual scene or event, whether Assyrian orthostats, Michelangelo's frescoes in the Sistine Chapel, or the architectural propaganda of Rome.[27] The three great ICT developments of the twentieth century, however, totally remade the scope, reach, and techniques of propaganda. Radio enabled the delivery of audible propaganda over distances that would have been unimaginable to those striving to keep "within earshot" of a speech or oration. But the twin inventions of the motion picture and then television transformed propaganda. The invention of the motion picture and newsreel early in the twentieth century enabled the propagandist to influence audiences in ways never before possible. In the silent era the Russian filmmaker Sergei Eisenstein made what is still regarded as one of the greatest propaganda films, *Battleship Potemkin.*

Even though it was originally a silent film and thus had no dialogue, it was a brilliant bit of political propaganda.[28]

One of the most technically artistic and politically effective uses of the motion picture in propaganda was mentioned earlier, the German filmmaker Leni Riefenstahl's film of the 1934 Nazi Party rally in Nuremberg, *Triumph des Willens* (*Triumph of the Will*). Her film not only chronicled the Nazi event, her brilliant filmmaking techniques maximized the film's emotional appeal and impact by making viewers feel as though they were part of the event.[29] It also highlighted one of the most critical aspects of visual propaganda: not all audiences will be affected by the same image in the same way. It is both simplistic and obvious that German audiences were affected differently than non-German audiences: 100,000 storm troopers in massed ranks may have swelled German hearts with pride and power, but it is unlikely that British, French, Polish, or Czech audiences shared those sentiments—yet the visuals were the same.[30] It also emphasizes the critical point that if propaganda is to be effective, each individual use or product must be created and developed by experts, both in the use of the medium and in the analysis of the intended audience, which are different yet closely related skills. The combined impact of Riefenstahl—the visual expert—and Joseph Goebbels—the propaganda expert—made for one of the most compelling examples of visual propaganda ever created.[31]

The Nazi regime's use of and dependence on propaganda was utterly pervasive throughout its run, even to its last days, until it was overcome by what Churchill called "the Grand Alliance," one of whose members—the USSR—became the next great user of propaganda.[32] It is ironic that while the Germans were early users of television, they brought the audience to the medium, using it in theaters, which obviously limited its reach.[33] The Soviet use of television—indeed, that of all the wartime Allies—became an example of Murrow's comment about "this weapon of television," and by the early 1950s Germany had become a television battlespace, as all the occupying powers (the United States, Great Britain, France, and the USSR) created broadcasting entities there.[34] The Soviets made significant and effective use of the images from U.S. television news during the civil rights struggles of the 1960s: American statements about freedom and equality seemed hypocritical when contrasted with scenes of police dogs and water cannons being turned against protesters in Birmingham, an early example of the "say-do gap" in exposing apparent American hypocrisy.[35] In contrast, American television was able to use images of the charismatic and popular young President Kennedy, such as his famous speech in Berlin in which he made crystal clear the U.S. commitment to West Germany, saying, "*Ich bin ein Berliner.*"[36] But the development that would connect these early efforts to the television environment of today had not yet been invented, except in the fertile mind of Arthur C. Clarke. In the October 1945 issue of *Wireless World,* Clarke published his concept of communications satellites in geosynchronous orbit (approximately twenty-two thousand miles up) for broadcasting purposes. He hinted at the potential political uses of this in a short essay he published in 1962, "I Remember Babylon," in which the Communist Chinese planned to broadcast prurient and sensational material to morally undermine the West.[37]

It is live satellite television that provides the last development and link to today. Again, this is not the place for an exhaustive analysis of real-time 24/7 TV: it has been done elsewhere.[38] While the Vietnam War has often been described as the first television war, it was a war on tape delay, in which the images broadcast on our nightly news had to be transported by airplane to the United States. It was the Gulf War of 1991 that could have been called the first live TV war, made possible by interconnected satellite systems that created a global "network of networks." Many Americans remember watching the first bombs to fall on Baghdad in January 1991.[39] CNN's coverage of the war and its live broadcasts from downtown Baghdad were a key factor in CNN's rise to prominence in American TV and global communications. Al Jazeera and its many imitators and competitors around the world would have been impossible without global satellite television.[40] When Kennedy made his speech in Berlin, it was available on TV to a limited broadcast audience in Western Europe. When Ronald Reagan came to Berlin nearly twenty-five years later, his live audience was not only enormously larger, it reached across and into the formerly forbidden territory of East Berlin, East Germany, and the entire Communist Bloc. When Reagan spoke "to" Soviet Premier Mikhail Gorbachev, he was really speaking "to" a far larger audience: the millions to the east who were able to watch his speech and hear his words live, thanks to the nearly ubiquitous satellite dish that received the signal coming down from space. The Berlin Wall and the Iron Curtain couldn't prevent ideas and images from moving. This was the first of the three major ICT changes that have brought us the "new propaganda," and is the origin of what has been called "SOFT-WAR," emphasizing the use of television—indeed, the entire visual environment, including YouTube videos—as the critical means of influencing audiences.[41]

THE INTERCONNECTED AGE

There are many ways to describe the Information Revolution and to select a date or technology that initiated it. Gutenberg's printing press enabled the mass production of standardized information; Morse's telegraph enabled the distribution of information over continental distances; and Bell's telephone transformed the form of the information transmitted from symbols (dots and dashes) to actual human voice. Both Morse and Bell needed a wire, however, to connect sender to receiver. Marconi's wireless telegraphy eliminated the tyranny of the wire, and radio and then television expanded this to voice and then images.

One way to analyze the global information environment as described in current U.S. military doctrine as Information Operations is through this environment, which can be described as the interrelated and synergistic combination of connectivity (the ability to exchange information), content (the information itself), and the cognitive impact that results from humans using the content which the connectivity delivers to them. We have dramatic new ways in which information technologies are transforming how content is created, how people are connected, and how they impact propaganda on targeted audiences.[42] What has made all of this possible, of course, is the digital revolution and the transformation of virtually any kind of information—a visual image, a human voice, the precise location of a point in physical space—into a string of ones and zeroes. Each of the "three Cs" has been transformed by this revolution.

The first step in the use of propaganda remains unchanged: the content needs to be created. But the form of that content has changed a bit from Assyrian orthostats that required months and perhaps years to chisel from stone and even then represented just lifeless images frozen in time. Now, of course, the full capability of digital imagery creation is at the service of the propagandist. Leni Riefenstahl's *Triumph of the Will* was, after all, about a real event, and even though it was staged for the cameras, everything she filmed actually happened. What could she have done with the resources and capabilities of Industrial Light and Magic behind her? Perhaps her product was more influential precisely because everyone knew it was real, albeit theatrical. One of the weaknesses of old-style Stalinist-era Soviet propaganda was that all too often, changes to the photographic "evidence" could not change human memory (for example, photos of Comrade Stalin with three key Communists in front of a hydroelectric project that eventually became a photo of Stalin alone).[43] But current capabilities turn this on its head, led of course by the entertainment industry. The techniques used in the 1990s—Forrest Gump's meeting with President Lyndon Johnson, for example—are *so* 1990s! Modern technologies and techniques for creating content make it difficult for the eye and mind to distinguish between the real and the created. In the future, will we be able to trust our eyes, or will all photographic evidence become suspect?[44]

An additional aspect is size, or rather lack of it. The apparatus Riefenstahl used in the filming of *Triumph of the Will* necessitated her own private army of film crew and logistics train. When Peter Arnett and his crew set up at the Al Rashid Hotel in Baghdad to cover the war in 1991 they needed an entire satellite uplink truck. When Al Jazeera went to Baghdad in 2003 they were using equipment packed into suitcases. Now, less than a decade later, those capabilities can literally be held in the palm of one's hand. The content is captured not on film but digitally, which opens up vast capabilities for its modification, enhancement, or manipulation. Further, these operations do not require the capabilities or resources of MGM or Industrial Light and Magic (although the greater the resources the better the product), just a computer, which also keeps getting smaller and more portable. Whether this content is news, entertainment, or propaganda depends on the intended effect (and one's definition of propaganda), but the common thread is that the technology of creation grows more capable while getting smaller and more portable.

Nik Gowing of the BBC has written of this "virtual revolution" in which "citizen journalists" capture images and video of events using a nearly ubiquitous handheld device and weapon of propaganda, the cell phone camera.[45] Increasingly, the first images we see of events come from one of these small instruments with which to "bear witness," as Gowing suggests. A growing list of recent events and incidents shows how the handheld revolution has exploded. Gowing describes several in his book and associated videos. One of the most well-known such videos came from the streets of Tehran in June 2009, in which a Basij sniper's murder of a young Iranian woman, Neda Agha-Soltan, was captured in at least three different videos, each using small handheld cell phone cameras.[46] Another such video, also apparently shot with a cell phone camera, surfaced in early 2012. It showed U.S. Marine snipers urinating on several dead Taliban in Afghanistan.[47] Professor Cori Dauber of the University of North Carolina has analyzed the use and impact of these devices and concludes that the combination of small cameras and computers with tremendous video modification and manipulation capabilities essentially gives almost anyone the ability to produce propaganda with high video quality.[48] Sometimes it is the near-professional quality attainable by amateurs with modern software that gives the propaganda its credibility, and sometimes it is the grainy cell phone camera imagery, such as in the videos of the 2005 London subway bombings, which possessed a *cinema verite* quality, which suggests "I was there" credibility. There is no cookie-cutter answer—it depends on the audience and the intent.

But just having content is only the first part of the new propaganda. The ability to exploit global connectivity to deliver it to the intended audience is even more important. Fortunately for the propagandist, this has expanded even more rapidly and decisively with the explosive growth of the Internet. At the end of 2012, one Internet analysis estimated that more than 2.4 billion people were using the Internet out of a global population of approximately 7 billion, and many of these users pass along information to nonusers.[49] The cell phone videos cited above had impact only because of the Internet's ability to make them accessible to any of those 2.4 billion people, and from there to the rest of the planet's population. We've seen numerous examples of the phenomenon known as "going viral," as videos are passed from user to user in an expanding torrent of information. Defense and influence planners have yet to come to grips with the implications of a world in which anyone, anywhere, can contact anyone else, anywhere else, anytime, to exchange anything they wish.[50] Although there are obvious difficulties and frictions arising from this trend, it also offers an enormous advantage to those who support transparency of government, freedom of expression, political liberalization (in the classic sense), and the "forces of democratization" against the "forces of repression." The liberal democracies of the world function fairly well when the bright light of information shines on them. It's the regimes in places like Tehran, Pyongyang, Moscow, and Beijing (to name a few obvious ones) that find such trends politically challenging and even threatening.

The growth of global interconnectivity is enabling the "anyone anywhere" paradigm described above. In the case of the Neda Agha-Soltan video, the critical communications aspect of this incident was not her murder or the filming of it, but rather the posting of it to the Internet, where it went globally viral in a matter of hours.[51] The viewing tabulations numbered in the millions, and that counts only the direct links. Did the release and dissemination of the video bring down the Iranian regime? Of course not, but Tehran's strenuous efforts to close off access to the video inside Iran shows the threat it posed to the regime's control of the information environment. From this perspective, the most damaging aspect of the recent urinating incident was not the act or even the filming; it was the posting of the video to a location where it was accessible. The Marines do have a policy on the use of social media such as Facebook or Twitter, and the policy emphasizes that Marines are personally responsible for the content that they post.[52] The issue hotly debated online about whether "too much" was being made of the act misses the point—it wasn't the act or the filming that were damaging, but rather the releasing/posting of the video. Regardless of the means used to take them, videos as visual imagery have tremendous power. If the other side has them they can be used against you. If you don't have them they can't be used for you.[53] As CNN's Andrea Koppel once quoted Pope John Paul II, "If it didn't happen on TV, it didn't happen."[54]

On the other hand, few things in life are of unilateral benefit, especially with the political impacts of transparency. The WikiLeaks case provides an example. When its trove of diplomatic cables was released, some of them concerned the political situation in Zimbabwe, brutally ruled for decades by Robert Mugabe. For a while Mugabe had contended with a nascent political opposition movement, but not after WikiLeaks. Some of its cables revealed that the U.S. embassy had been tacitly supporting the opposition, and that faint touch of U.S. influence fatally harmed that opposition movement. While the "Arab Spring" has been hailed as an example of the power of transparency to strike at politically repressive regimes, we also know that those same regimes have used that same technology to gather intelligence on and track their foes.[55] Political groups, some of which the United States has defined as terrorists, use the first two Cs—connectivity and content—to create political cognition supporting their causes and objectives. The "Nashi" movement in Russia, which is young and politically supportive of Vladimir Putin, has a series of extremely well-made videos, edited to appeal to a young audience and designed to capture their youthful idealism.[56] At the same time, Russian information policies seem intended to "keep ours in and theirs out." These policies have their origins in Soviet-style information control objectives from the Cold War. An excellent example of the kinds of well-done products now available is a Hezbollah video, "Nasrak Haz el Deni" ("Our Victory"), a superbly produced four-minute film that hammers home the position that Hezbollah and Lebanon are one and the same. It is just one of many excellent pieces of propaganda video produced by radical Islamist movements such as Hezbollah.[57]

Another example concerns an incident that has come to be called "Collateral Murder." The real facts are simple: On July 12, 2007, a U.S. Army helicopter gunship fired on a group of individuals in Baghdad, killing and wounding several, including two Reuters employees. Soon after, the helicopter fired on a vehicle, killing and wounding several more people, including two children. American ground forces reached the scene, took the two wounded children to a U.S. military hospital for treatment, and retrieved weapons and ammunition from within the vehicle. With the exception of the journalists and children, this scene has been repeated often in Iraq and Afghanistan. Nothing new here, move on. Even the existence of gun camera film from the helicopter isn't new, because that is standard procedure, used to assess the effectiveness of both the weapons systems and the operation itself.

What is new comes from the confluence of at least three factors. Two have already been discussed: the use of digital technologies to capture, store, and modify the informational content itself, and the exploitation of global connectivity to disseminate that content. The third change, however, links to our third "C," cognitive effect, because the reason this incident has become notorious is its use as political propaganda by the organization WikiLeaks.[58] Their "facts" about the incident are quite a bit murkier and closely fit the definition of propaganda. In short, WikiLeaks released an unedited thirty-seven-minute video of the event, and a heavily edited seventeen-minute version. Viewed more than 7 million times on YouTube in just its first week (a number well over 13 million now that continues to grow), the incident made national news, in which the length of the video shown shrank to merely a few seconds, capturing only the most sensational imagery.[59] There isn't space here to dig deeper into the details of the incident or the corrective analysis. The point to emphasize is how WikiLeaks, an unofficial and nonstate group with a political agenda of weakening what it sees as abusive U.S. power and influence, was able to use the technologies of content and connectivity to successfully create cognitive effects and achieve propaganda value. The integrated use of these technologies to achieve maximum propaganda effect has become a trademark of insurgent operations over the past decade, and as the "Collateral Murder" example has shown, an effective response to such operations requires speed, flexibility, decision-making at the lowest levels, and the willingness to tell "most" of the story fast instead of waiting to tell "all" of the story later—conditions that military and governmental bureaucracies are not noted for.[60] "They" are better at it than "we" are—and that is a sobering assertion in a world increasingly dominated by the use of visual imagery disseminated globally and almost instantly to achieve propaganda effects on targeted audiences.

CONCLUSION

Propaganda has always been about creating influence. We've seen multiple forms of propaganda's content, from silent stones to moving pictures to bits and bytes, and we've watched an explosive evolution of the means of connecting propaganda's makers to its receivers.[61] The most powerful and effective forms of propaganda have always been centered on the uses of images, regardless of the physical form which those images took. As we watch people—one, ten, a million—being affected by these new forms and delivery mechanisms of propaganda and observe their effect on the cognitive processes of those audiences, we see propaganda's payoff: changing beliefs, attitudes, and eventually behaviors.

While many of propaganda's principles have not changed, the means by which the propagandist employs those principles is undergoing nearly constant change. It's a growth market. Get ready for more change.

Notes

I would like to thank several people for significant contributions to this piece and for their suggestions, especially Professor Cori Dauber of the University of North Carolina; my former colleague on the faculty of the Industrial College of the Armed Forces, Dr. Anne McGee; Chuck de Caro, creator of the term SOFTWAR; Matt Armstrong, executive director of the U.S. Advisory Commission on Public Diplomacy; Larisa Breton of Full Circle Communications; and Professor Russ Rochte, of the National Intelligence University. I also want to thank unnamed numbers of my students, whose comments and contributions during class have added to my thinking. If I've made any mistake, it is my own.

1. Googling "define 'propaganda'" yielded more than 15,000,000 hits in February 2012. Not all of them were definitions, of course, but many were compilations of definitions, which hints at the scope of this task.

2. A fascinating example of this is a recent book by Frederick A. Sharf, Anne Nishimura Morse, and Sebastian Dobson, *A Much Recorded War: The Russo-Japanese War in History and Imagery* (Boston, Mass.: Museum of Fine Arts Publications, 2005), which analyzes the use of visual imagery, including photography and the brand new field of cinematography, especially by the Japanese. There is even a Russian photograph of members of a captured Japanese cinematographic unit—a picture of one side's combat camera unit taken by the other side's combat camera unit.

3. This is based on how I describe the information environment for my students, as a combination of "3Cs": Connectivity, or the ability to exchange information; Content, or the information itself, in whatever form it exists; and Cognitive impact. For more on the two sides' influence struggle during World War I, see Jonathan Reed Winkler, *Nexus: Strategic Communications and American Security in WWI* (Cambridge, Mass.: Harvard Univ. Press, 2008), and Jonathan Reed Winkler, "Information Warfare in World War I," *Journal of Military History* 73, no. 3 (July 2009): 845–867.

4. The United States Holocaust Memorial Museum in Washington, D.C., opened an excellent temporary exhibition in 2009, State of Deception: The Power of Nazi Propaganda, which examines the Nazis' use of propaganda during three periods: seizure of power, consolidation of power, and the war, www.ushmm.org/propaganda/. While the temporary exhibit in Washington closed in October 2012, segments will be used in a traveling exhibition across the United States.

5. The professional debate over the film's impact and effect remains vigorous today. See, for example, Martin Loiperdinger and David Culbert, "Leni Riefenstahl, the SA and the Nazi Party Rally Films, Nuremberg 1933–1934: 'Sieg des Glaubens' and 'Triumph des Willens,'" in *Historical Journal of Film and Television* 8, no. 1 (1988): 3–38. The debate

over Reifenstahl herself is active, including: Exactly how much of a Nazi was she? Or was she just an artist whose work was used by the regime?

6. One of Edward R. Murrow's great insights was "This weapon of television could be useful." This is from Murrow's speech to the Radio and Television News Directors Association Convention in Chicago, October 15, 1958. The speech has a lengthy list of wonderfully quotable and thought-provoking insights, but it was his prescient characterization of television as a "weapon" that is most useful to the world of the early twenty-first century.

7. Edward R. Murrow, director of the U.S. Information Agency, congressional testimony, May 1963. The entire quote is: "American traditions and the American ethic require us to be truthful, but the most important reason is that truth is the best propaganda and lies are the worst. To be persuasive we must be believable; to be believable we must be credible; to be credible we must be truthful. It is as simple as that."

8. Philip M. Taylor, *Munitions of the Mind* (Manchester, England: Manchester Univ. Press, 2003), 2.

9. Nancy Snow and Philip M. Taylor, "The Revival of the Propaganda State," in *International Communication,* vol. 3, *Politics and Communication,* ed. Daya K. Thussu (Thousand Oaks, Calif.: Sage Publications, 2012).

10. J. Michael Sproule, *Propaganda and Democracy: The American Experience of Media and Mass Persuasion* (Cambridge, UK: Cambridge Univ. Press, 1997), 69.

11. United States Holocaust Memorial Museum, Online Learning Module, "Mind Over Media: Are You More Powerful Than Propaganda?," http://mindovermedia.whatscookin.com/learn/.

12. See, for example, George Orwell's *Animal Farm* (1945) and *Nineteen Eighty-Four* (1949), for his most dystopian views.

13. Jacques Ellul, *Propaganda: The Formation of Men's Attitudes* (New York: Vintage Books, 1973). Herein Ellul argues that propaganda is "necessary for democracy."

14. Gerhard König, *Kleines Politisches Wörterbuch: Neuausgabe 1988* (Berlin: Dietz Verlag, 1988), 17–18, 795–797.

15. For more of the propaganda of the GDR, see the German Propaganda Archive at Calvin College, http://www.calvin.edu/academic/cas/gpa/kpwb.htm.

16. NATO Military Public Affairs Policy, MC 457/2, February 2011, http://www.nato.int/ims/docu/mc0457-2_en.pdf.

17. Joint Publication 1-02, *Department of Defense Dictionary of Military and Associated Terms,* the official dictionary of standard and approved terminology, is frequently updated as new terms are introduced or old terms redefined.

18. The best-known examples of these (in the United States) occur every Super Bowl Sunday, in which advertisers pay exorbitant amounts of money to broadcast commercial propaganda lasting less than a minute per bit. For a compilation of the very best ones, go to http://www.superbowl-commercials.org/; for my personal all-time favorite, go to http://www.youtube.com/watch?v=Pk7yqlTMvp8 (EDS's "Herding Cats" from 2000).

19. Joint Publication 1-02, *Department of Defense Dictionary of Military and Associated Terms,* November 8, 2010, as amended through January 15, 2012, http://www.dtic.mil/doctrine/new_pubs/jp1_02.pdf (accessed on February 16, 2012). The source for this defi-

nition is Joint Publication 3-13.2, *Joint Doctrine for Psychological Operations,* January 7, 2010. Since the publication of JP 3-13.2, the DoD has even redefined the term "Psychological Operations" out of existence, replacing it with a less-than-inspiring term MISO, or "Military Information Support [to] Operations." The origins of this change seem to be nothing deeper than then-Secretary of Defense Robert Gates's dislike of the term. Such are the origins of many internal Pentagon actions.

20. Memo, Robert T. Hastings, Principal Deputy Assistant Secretary of Defense for Public Affairs, recommending changes to the "DOD Dictionary of Military and Related Terms (JP 1-02)," March 10, 2009.

21. This is related to an oft-cited but misunderstood piece of law, the Smith-Mundt Act of 1948. For an analytical and detailed examination of it, see Matt Armstrong's "MountainRunner" blog site at http://mountainrunner.us/smith-mundt/. Smith-Mundt's origins were as much concerned with protecting the early post-WWII broadcasting industry as they were with protecting the American populace from the baleful influences of U.S. propaganda.

22. Catherine P. Foster, "Royal Art as Political Message in Ancient Mesopotamia," a presentation at the University of California Berkeley, http://orias.berkeley.edu/summer2009/foster.pdf.

23. See http://www.vroma.org/~bmcmanus/augustus2.html for various depictions of Augustus.

24. George Packer, ed., *All Art Is Propaganda: Critical Essays by George Orwell* (Boston, Mass.: Houghton Mifflin Harcourt, 2008).

25. See the webpage of the Boston Massacre Historical Society, http://www.bostonmassacre.net/index.html, for a wealth of information on both the event and Revere's engraving. The recent HBO series on John Adams opened with an episode on Adams's role in defending the British soldiers. It has a thorough comparison of the facts as contrasted with the depictions. For the larger issue of propaganda in the American Revolution, the classic work is Carl Berger's *Broadsides and Bayonets: The Propaganda War of the American Revolution,* rev. ed. (San Rafael, Calif.: Presidio Press, 1978). Also see Gladys Thum and Marcella Thum, "War Propaganda and the American Revolution: The Pen and the Sword," in *Readings in Propaganda and Persuasion: New and Classic Essays,* ed. Garth S. Jowett and Victoria O'Donnell, 73–82 (Thousand Oaks, Calif.: Sage Publications, 2006).

26. See the Cyclorama of Jerusalem at http://www.cyclorama.com/. If you visit the website at http://www.bourbakipanorama.ch/de/index.html you can watch the painting scroll across your computer screen. The main webpage emphasizes the painting's role in establishing the modern Swiss view of its role as a humanitarian nation—in other words, propaganda.

27. Of course, there have been visual displays intended to influence "the masses," from Roman triumphs to Aztec or Inca displays in the Americas, but even for these the audience had to be in the direct physical proximity of the propaganda vehicle.

28. To watch the *Battleship Potemkin* go to http://www.youtube.com/watch?v=CKgHVzQbis.

29. Directors commonly use several techniques today that Riefenstahl used, such as moving cameras on stable dollies. If you compare the long-lens shot of Luke, Han, and Chewbacca walking between the assembled ranks toward Princess Leia in *Star Wars* to the

long-lens shot of Hitler and his henchmen walking between the assembled ranks of storm troopers . . . well, George Lucas knew a good visual when he saw one, as he admitted.

30. See the microfilm project *Leni Riefenstahl's Triumph of the Will*, edited by David Culbert (Frederick, Md.: University Publications of America, 1986); see also David Welch, *Propaganda and the German Cinema, 1933–1945*, rev. ed. (London: I. B. Tauris, 2001).

31. See Joseph Goebbels's "Principles of Propaganda," http://www.psywarrior.com/Goebbels.html. The literature on Nazi propaganda is beyond extensive; two examples are David A. Welch, "Reconstructing the Means of Communication in Nazi Germany," and Kenneth Burke, "The Rhetoric of Hitler's 'Battle,'" in *Readings in Propaganda and Persuasion: New and Classic Essays*, ed. Garth S. Jowett and Victoria O'Donnell, 121–148, 149–188 (Thousand Oaks, Calif.: Sage Publications, 2006).

32. Ian Kershaw, *The End: The Defiance and Destruction of Hitler's Germany, 1944–45* (New York, Penguin Press, 2011). It seemingly has a reference to Nazi propaganda on every page.

33. The United States Holocaust Memorial Museum in Washington, D.C., has an example of German television in its wonderful exhibit on Nazi propaganda.

34. There has been significant research on this issue and period; see, for example, James Schwoch, *Global TV: New Media and the Cold War, 1946–69* (Chicago: Univ. of Illinois Press, 2009).

35. It is an oversimplification, but every parent knows the danger of falling into the "do as I say, not as I do" trap!

36. There is a well-known myth that Kennedy's choice of words—in German—was incorrect and that he was actually calling himself a pastry, but this is itself incorrect. No one who was in Berlin that day—or West Germany—failed to understand and be affected by what Kennedy was saying, regardless of the grammar.

37. I must here pay homage to Arthur C. Clarke, one of the most brilliant writers of the twentieth century. The list of his stories that later became the foundation for later works is legion. "Superiority" (1951) could be a lesson in the RMA debate between the "technology is superior" versus "technology doesn't matter" camps; "The Sentinel" (1951) was the basis for *2001: A Space Odyssey*; and *Dial F for Frankenstein* (1964) was the basis for Skynet in the *Terminator* movie series!

38. The term "CNN Effect" comes from a path-breaking article by Warren P. Strobel, "The CNN Effect," in *American Journalism Review* 18, no. 4 (May 1996): 33–37. See also Steven Livingston, "Clarifying the CNN Effect: An Examination of Media Effects According to Type of Military Intervention," published by the John F. Kennedy School of Government's Joan Shorenstein Center on the Press, Politics, and Public Policy at Harvard University; and Margaret Belknap, "The CNN Effect: Strategic Enabler or Operational Risk" (Carlisle, Pa.: U.S. Army War College, 2001). See also Bruce Hoffman, *Inside Terrorism*, rev. ed. (New York: Columbia Univ. Press, 2006). He describes the three pieces of technology needed to broadcast live international events—just in time for the 1972 Munich terrorists to exploit those developments.

39. I was one of the Air Force planners who created in August 1990 the concept for the air campaign, and I remember watching the CNN broadcast from Baghdad go blank. This

was important because it was an indicator that one of the very first strikes in Baghdad, on what we called the "AT&T Building" (it had no connection to the American telecommunications giant AT&T), was successful. We knew that a successful strike would sever the link to the television signal. I also remember a broadcast the next morning in which CNN's Peter Arnett described what he saw in Baghdad that morning and which became a real-time assessment of the first strikes' impact, what we termed "bomb damage assessment" (BDA). I clearly recall Arnett describing one building as having "melted," which is a pretty good BDA.

40. In many ways, Al Jazeera itself was merely an imitator of CNN, albeit a very good one with a mostly BBC-trained staff. Just as the Gulf War of 1991 was CNN's launching pad to success, it was the Gulf War of 2003 that was Al Jazeera's. In 1968 it was said that "the whole world is watching," which referred to both street protests at the Democratic National Convention in Chicago and Soviet tanks rolling through Prague during the USSR's suppression of Czech protests. Of course, by 1991 (the First Gulf War) and 2001 (the 9/11 Terror Attacks) the whole world really was watching. For more background, see Todd Gitlin, *The Whole World Is Watching: Mass Media in the Making and Unmaking of the New Left,* rev. 2nd ed. (Berkeley, Calif.: Univ. of California Press, 2003).

41. "SOFTWAR" was coined by Chuck de Caro, a technical advisor for several hit television programs, such as *NCIS,* who even played himself in the *JAG* television series. SOFTWAR refers to the "hostile use of global visual media to shape another society's will by changing its view of reality."

42. My students over the years have come to know this model as "Dan's 3Cs," for Connectivity, Content, and Cognitive Impact.

43. David King, *The Commissar Vanishes: The Falsification of Photographs and Art in Stalin's Russia* (New York: Metropolitan, 1997). Also see Philip M. Taylor, "The Bolshevik Revolution and the War of Ideologies," in *Readings in Propaganda and Persuasion: New and Classic Essays,* ed. Garth S. Jowett and Victoria O'Donnell, 111–120 (Thousand Oaks, Calif.: Sage Publications, 2006). Although copies of the old photo always existed, and it was impossible to hide the alteration from experts, that didn't lessen the propaganda value of the new photos.

44. In criminal trials, for example, how will we be able to verify the authenticity of photographs upon which guilt or innocence may hang?

45. Nik Gowing has a ten-minute video discussion on this, http://www.youtube.com/watch?v=8TgERpVtAgI. See also his entire study, "'Skyful of Lies' and Black Swans: The New Tyranny of Shifting Information Power in Crises," http://reutersinstitute.politics.ox.ac.uk/?id=445.

46. Robert Tait and Matthew Weaver, "How Neda Agha-Soltan Became the Face of Iran's Struggle," *Guardian,* June 22, 2009.

47. "Video Shows What Appear to Be U.S. Marines Urinating on Bodies," CNN Wire Staff, January 11, 2012.

48. Cori Dauber, *YouTube War: Fighting in a World of Cameras in Every Cell Phone and Photoshop on Every Computer* (Carlisle, Pa.: U.S. Army War College Strategic Studies Institute, November 2009).

49. Internet World Stats, http://www.internetworldstats.com/stats.htm.

50. The fact that the world is not yet fully to this point, nor is it likely to be there anytime soon, does not change the direction of this trend.

51. For a discussion of the Internet significance of Neda Agha-Soltan's death in Iran, see Ian Black, "Film About Iranian Protest Victim Neda Agha-Soltan Beats Regime's Censors: Jamming and Power Cuts Fail to Prevent Documentary Going Viral," *Guardian*, June 4, 2010.

52. See http://www.marines.mil/News/SocialMedia/Guidance.aspx.

53. Cori Dauber, "The Importance of Images to America's Fight Against Violent Jihadism" (Carlisle, Pa.: U.S. Army War College Strategic Studies Institute, January 24, 2012); Cori Dauber, "The Impact of Visual Images: Addendum" (Carlisle, Pa.: U.S. Army War College Strategic Studies Institute, March 6, 2012.)

54. Andrea Kopple, CNN Saturday Morning News, April 25, 2005, http://edition.cnn.com/TRANSCRIPTS/0504/23/smn.01.html.

55. Manuel Manrique and Barah Mikhail, "The Role of New Media and Communication Technologies in Arab Transitions," Fride Policy Brief, no. 106, May 2011, http://fride.org/publication/965/the-role-of-new-media-and-communication-technologies-in-arab-transitions. For another perspective, see Ivan Watson, "Cyberwar Explodes in Syria," CNN, November 22, 2011, http://www.cnn.com/2011/11/22/world/meast/syria-cyberwar/index.html.

56. Anselm Waldermann, "The Nashi Movement: Russian Youth and the Putin Cult," *Spiegel Online International* (November 2, 2007), http://www.spiegel.de/international/world/0,1518,514891,00.html.

57. For the basic video go to http://www.youtube.com/watch?v=Mci094ltPyo&feature=related and note the Al Manar logo in the corner for what amounts to commercial propaganda—a video about the making of the video. See the Shia TV site, http://www.shiatv.net.

58. WikiLeaks, http://wikileaks.org/. I hasten to add that the inclusion of the organizational webpage does not constitute even tacit support for their operations or intent. In many ways I find that what they have done has been reprehensible and damaging, and their political agenda seems to be focused on "damage the United States" instead of "search for truth." In fact, the lack of discussion of this by the very same media that uses WikiLeaks's information is troubling.

59. Larisa Breton and Adam Pearson, "Contextual Truth-Telling to Counter Extremist-Supportive Messaging Online: The WikiLeaks 'Collateral Murder' Case Study," *Small Wars Journal* (November 6, 2010), http://smallwarsjournal.com/jrnl/art/contextual-truth-telling-to-counter-extremist-supportive-messaging-online.

60. Cori Dauber, "The TRUTH Is Out There: Responding to Insurgent Disinformation and Deception Operations," *Military Review* 89, no. 1 (January/February 2009): 13–24.

61. Several years ago one of my students observed in class, "You keep talking about a war of ideas, but isn't it a war of images?" Yes, indeed.

2

GOOD PROPAGANDA OR PROPAGANDA FOR GOOD

ANTHONY PRATKANIS

> Our culture knows little of the use and the abuse of power; but we have to use power in global terms. Our idealists are divided between those who would renounce the responsibilities of power for the sake of preserving the purity of our soul and those who are ready to cover every ambiguity of good and evil in our actions by the frantic insistence that any measure taken in a good cause must be unequivocally virtuous.
>
> —REINHOLD NIEBUHR, *The Irony of American History*

One of the great ironies of American life is that our culture is founded on the use of persuasion and influence, yet we feel uncomfortable discussing and wielding these devices.[1] We know that as social animals it is our nature to influence each other and that such influence can be used as a tool to build great things. We also feel that it is much better to persuade, discuss, cajole, and negotiate then it is to use raw power to coerce and to destroy those who disagree. But yet, we feel uneasy about the use of influence, so much so that we often call its deployment by the pejorative term *propaganda*. Perhaps we feel this way because we also know that much bad and evil—from consumer rip-offs to cultic manipulations to genocides—can result from propaganda.

These conflicting feelings over the morality of influence—the need to use influence and the fear of the responsibility of its use, the potential for good and for evil—can produce in us the tension state of dissonance. We seek to escape this aversive state and commonly take one of Niebuhr's two solutions by becoming either a partisan or a purist in the use and nonuse of influence. Either way, we frequently avoid talking about some key matters.

The partisan resolves the moral dilemmas of the use of influence by ignoring them and pretending that the dilemmas do not exist. The partisan believes: "My cause is right, therefore my means are right. Whatever I do is fair; what my adversary says is propaganda." The partisan's worldview is marked by naive realism—a sense that one's own construal (perception and understanding) of the world is real—and a failure to correct for the subjective nature of one's own interpretation of events.[2] There is no gnawing doubt of uncertainty to spark a conscience. The partisan is fundamentally autocratic in nature and denies that there might be differences in the morality and goodness of specific uses of influence. A world of partisans is a world of Talibanism—each group and faction secure in its own belief that it is right, using whatever means possible to advance its cause. Propaganda might makes propaganda right.

The purist resolves the moral dilemmas of the use of influence by rejecting the use of influence in an attempt to remain pure and innocent—never to be blamed because no responsibility has been assumed. The purist believes: "All is propaganda. I am above it all." The purist's worldview is also marked by naive realism, but of a utopian nature. The purist would like to believe that "truth" falls naturally and intuitively into one's mind, and of course has already done so in the mind of each purist. Any form of influence is morally equivalent to any other form of influence, and all forms are merely manipulation. There is no difference between the use of influence in a dictatorship or a democracy. The purist—be it the libertarian on the right or the anarchist on the left—is laissez-faire in nature. Evil comes about through the system, and propaganda is the handmaiden of that system. Get rid of that system and its propaganda—whether it is the government, capitalism, meat-eating, white male hegemony, the illuminati, or some such corrupting influence—and the world would naturally come to see things as the purist does. The purist denies that humans are social animals unable to exist without the use of influence and pays a steep price for this denial. As the psychotherapist Rollo May has so eloquently argued, the fruits of innocence are often cynicism, alienation, and ultimately violence.[3] If everything is manipulation and thus the use of influence is forsaken, then the human being lacks empowerment to accomplish goals. Powerlessness corrupts, leaving a choice of learned helplessness and withdrawal or the adoption of the violence of the autocrat.

As long as the debate remains at the extremes—partisanship versus purity—there can be no understanding of what is "good" propaganda or a third way that describes an effective but ethical use of influence. Either my propaganda is good and yours is bad, or I am pure and innocent and all propaganda is bad. But what is this middle ground? When can influence be founded on a good moral basis?

In the early 1930s, Kurt Lewin and his students began to answer this question through their experiments designed to distinguish the effects of democratic, autocratic (partisan), and laissez-faire (purist) leaders.[4] Lewin's democratic leaders directed influence by encouraging group discussion and mutual influence in terms of what the group will achieve and how it will conduct its affairs. The hallmark of this influence is deliberative persuasion—a process that encourages thought, reflection, and critical analysis. In contrast to the naive realism of the purist and partisan, the democrat is marked by realistic empathy—understanding the worldview of others whether or not there is sympathy or agreement with that perspective.[5] Influence then becomes a means of resolving conflicts that occur as a result of differing perspectives and values. This middle-ground approach to the use of persuasion and influence has been championed by Phil Zimbardo, who teaches how to use influence effectively (and thus replaces the purist's sense of helplessness with self-efficacy) and at the same time raises ethical concerns about the use of influence (and thus replaces the partisan's means-justify-the-ends with a sense of responsibility for how persuasion is used).[6]

The fundamental disagreement between partisans and purists over the use and nonuse of influence can be seen throughout history and is at the heart of contemporary debates. Plato, using the mouthpiece of Socrates, attacked the Sophists and called their use of persuasion trickery and manipulation. Similarly, in the 1950s, Carl Rogers debated B. F. Skinner over the control of human behavior. Rogers believed in human freedom and the immorality of taking away this freedom. Skinner believed that all behavior was controlled, and that we should therefore control it for best results as determined by his rational planners (akin to philosopher kings) of *Walden Two*.[7] Even the democratic use of influence has been attacked by purists, as seen in William Graebner's criticism of Lewinian democratic and participatory persuasion as engineered consent and manipulation.[8] In discussions on the use of nonviolence, this debate has ranged between purists such as Leo Tolstoy and John Howard Yoder, who advocate passive, nonviolent nonresistance practiced for its own sake and middle-grounders such as Martin Luther King, Gene Sharp, and Krishnalal Shridharani, who seek to use nonviolence as a strategic influence tool for social change even if that means using coercion to obtain one's goals.[9]

The debate continues today over key issues of childrearing (laissez-faire parenting versus autocratic spankings); information campaigns during international conflicts such as psychological warfare; public diplomacy (America should use exchange campaigns versus should engage in one-sided pro-America publicity); psychological operations; interrogation of terrorists (purity versus torture); and political campaigns (apathy of the purist versus anything goes). In these debates, the middle ground of using influence effectively but morally is often neglected perhaps because there is not a clear understanding of what it means to use "good" influence. Defining and fleshing out the meaning of "good" propaganda and influence is the central task of this chapter.

Before addressing this issue, a brief note on nomenclature: Propaganda has been defined in a wide variety of ways but typically is either neutral in nature (propagate a belief, persuade, change attitudes and beliefs) or negative (manipulation, deceit, brainwashing, distortions).[10] In *Age of Propaganda,* Elliot Aronson and I defined propaganda as a subset of persuasion (which also includes debate, discussion, dialogue, dialectic, argument, speech, and negotiation, along with other forms).[11] Specifically, propaganda refers to the techniques of mass persuasion that play on our prejudices and emotions to secure the "voluntary" acceptance of a belief or course of action. In this article, I do not mean to limit the principles that emerge to just a narrow definition of propaganda (mine or anyone else's) but instead seek to apply it to all forms of influence, whether it be the use of power (control of critical resources), deception, or social influence (appeals rooted in our human nature). In other words, I don't want us to get bogged down in terminology because I think we need to talk.

WHAT IS GOOD?

> Antigone: Ah Creon, Creon, Which of us can say what the gods hold wicked?"
>
> —SOPHOCLES, *Antigone*

Antigone, the daughter and sister of Oedipus, speaks these words to Creon, the new King of Thebes. Creon has just passed a law sentencing to death anyone who attempts to bury the son of Oedipus, who has led troops against Thebes. Antigone wishes to bury her brother. Fundamentally, this is a debate over the nature of good propaganda—the integration propaganda of Creon (who is attempting to unite Thebes against its enemies), the agitation propaganda of Antigone's rebellious brother, or the reconciliation propaganda of Antigone's plea for love not hatred of others.

Throughout history, philosophers have attempted to answer Antigone's question: "What is good, just, and moral conduct and behavior?" Their answers have ranged from Aristotle's pursuit of the good life to John Stuart Mill's utilitarian ethics of the greatest good for the greatest number to Kant's categorical imperative of doing one's duty to Hobbes's social contract, among others.[12] One problem with these general approaches is that it is often not clear how to apply these theories to specific uses of influence. For example, how does one determine whether one ad versus another has the greater good—surveying consumers about their level of satisfaction, analyzing the impact of the ad on society, or through other means? Similarly, Kant's categorical imperative, while condemning an outright lie, allows one to create a misleading inference for a good cause (say, to protect a Jew from a Nazi). On the other hand, U.S. commercial law would disagree with Kant and deem an ad that creates a misleading inference (no matter the cause) to have the capacity to deceive and thus not an acceptable form of commercial speech.

Similarly, researchers and scholars from a range of disciplines—social psychology, rhetoric, communications, public relations, philosophy, and marketing, among others—have attempted to answer the Antigone question as it concerns influence—what is good and moral influence?[13] My approach is to take six of these answers and argue, debate, and discuss with them to answer Antigone. My inquiry is based on a science of social influence and a social influence analysis.[14] I develop general rules for good propaganda—The Ten Commandments of Good Influence and Propaganda—and an approach to applying these rules. I invite you to argue, debate, and discuss my commandments to create a process similar to that found in case law whereby unique instances are used to improve and develop the rules.[15]

The Ten Commandments of Good Influence and Propaganda

1. Influence others as you would have others influence you.
2. Good influence and propaganda require good ends and good means.
3. Thou shall not lie without a very good reason; deceive only to promote the welfare of others or in the face of extreme injustice and without polluting the communication environment and your reputation.
4. Let your influence be valued as a legitimate influence attempt.
5. Know and respect facts; base your influence on the facts.
6. Thou shall not pander and demagogue to human weakness, telling people what they want to hear, especially for your own gain.
7. Do not play on prejudices and emotions for gain, but use them to increase thought and understanding.
8. Practice realistic empathy and not naive realism. Listen. Respect alternative views.
9. Thou shall be responsible for negative, unintended consequences of your influence.
10. You are responsible for the influence environment.

BOB CIALDINI'S TRUTHFULNESS: BUNGLERS, SMUGGLERS, AND SLEUTHS

Bob Cialdini, the leading social influence researcher of the twentieth century, proposes an ethical theory of influence based on three types of influence agents: bunglers, smugglers, and sleuths.[16] Bunglers of influence fumble away the chance to use legitimate influence whereas sleuths approach an influence opportunity like a detective, looking to find ways to use the influence inherent in the situation. Of most importance for understanding good and bad propaganda is the smuggler—an influence agent who illicitly smuggles deceptive information into a situation to gain an unfair advantage. The smuggler is the agent of bad influence. According to Cialdini, smuggling creates a triple tumor for organizations and influence agents, resulting in (a) a poor reputation for the smuggler, (b) expensive turnover costs for organizations that use it, and (c) high surveillance costs for cheating employees in a culture of smugglers. In a nutshell, Cialdini's theory of ethical influence is based on the principle of "honesty is the best policy."

Cialdini's approach can be illustrated by the actions of the Federal Trade Commission against Encyclopedia Britannica, Inc.[17] In order to induce sales, *Encyclopedia Britannica* smuggled in the use of the scarcity tactic. Specifically, sales agents for Britannica led consumers to believe that they were being offered the encyclopedia at a reduced price and that this reduced price was available for a limited time only. In fact, all prices for the encyclopedia were the same and had not changed over the last dozen years or so. In Cialdini's framework, the *Encyclopedia Britannica* sales agent was a smuggler engaged in illicit, bad influence. In contrast to the smuggler, the bungler would not have found a way to use scarcity to make a sale whereas a sleuth would have found a legitimate example of scarcity (e.g., there is, after all, only one *Encyclopedia Britannica* in the world). The FTC (consistent with the Cialdini analysis) ordered *Encyclopedia Britannica* to stop misrepresenting its regular prices as reduced prices available for a limited time only.

Cialdini's anti-deception, anti-smuggler's blues is consistent with state and FTC laws and regulations prohibiting advertising with the capacity to mislead and deceive. Indeed, the case law and academic research on advertising deceptiveness and misleading inference can be used to provide specificity to the vague concept of smuggler.[18] Deceptive advertising laws serve multiple functions, including (a) ensuring free and fair markets needed for a capitalist system, (b) protecting consumers, and (c) preventing the pollution of the communication environment to the extent that consumers cannot trust the veracity of any given message. In other words, deception can damage social relationships and undermine the ability to communicate.

Despite its relevance to advertising deception, the smuggler versus sleuth distinction falls short as a criterion for distinguishing good from bad propaganda because it is simultaneously too exclusive (does not include other ethical principles that might be used to evaluate propaganda) and too inclusive (includes as unethical uses of influence that might be viewed as ethical). In terms of exclusion, imagine a sleuth who legitimately used scarcity to sell a product which was not needed or destroyed the environment or caused a person long-term harm or was made in a way to oppress workers or put the consumer in long-term debt at high interest rates or created a false social contagion leading to an economic bubble. I suspect that most of us would find at least one reason in this list to condemn the sleuth and, if not, could come up with our own rebuking reason.

In contrast, consider these two experiments conducted by Richard Miller, Philip Brickman, and Diana Bolin.[19] In their research, second graders were told by their teachers that they were excellent in math and fifth graders were told that they were the neatest, tidiest class in the school. Relative to controls who received lectures on the value of math or tidiness, the second graders showed a dramatic improvement in math and the fifth graders became neat and tidy. When I ask my students if this experiment demonstrates the ethical use of influence, there is universal agreement that it does, and in fact many students are puzzled that I would even ask such a question. Of course, the experimenters and teachers smuggled in the altercast of math and tidiness excellence—in other words, they lied. The grade-schoolers were randomly assigned to these experimental treatments and had not previously shown any special math or tidiness abilities. Social influence tactics such as altercasting, expectations, and the self-fulfilling prophecy often use smuggling to good effect.[20] The reaction of my students to these experiments indicates that there are at least some times when smuggling is seen as a good thing. However, would they have the same reaction if the teachers had used altercasting to create the best Nazi?

What are the boundary conditions of good and bad smuggling?[21] Seth Godin's claim that all marketers are (and should be) liars provides a useful contrast for identifying the boundary conditions on lying.[22] According to Godin, effective and appropriate marketing consists of creating stories about products; these stories do not need to be true, just authentic (that is, just believable to the consumer). Stories create the consumer experience that results in customer satisfaction. The stories work, in part, because consumers lack the time to check things out for themselves. For example, he praises Riedel glassware for creating overpriced stemware that in blind taste tests offers no advantage but when wine experts know that they are drinking out of a Riedel glass, they believe the wine to taste better. In other words, Riedel smuggled in an expectation of "better taste" and that expectation comes to create a perceived reality which wine drinkers enjoy. Godin also applauds the storytelling of Porsche for selling its Cayenne for $44k more than the VW Toureg (which is essentially the same car) and cereal makers for taking advantage of stories that fat-laden granola is health food.

I have no doubt that storytelling is an effective social influence tactic and that one's credibility and effectiveness is enhanced by telling people what they want to hear and believe as opposed to speaking the truth.[23] But is Godin's smuggler who creates reality ethical? Godin's marketers smuggle in a much different manner than Miller, Brickman, and Bolin's teachers. The teachers have a legitimate role to influence students—it is not only their right but their obligation to do so; marketers have no similar legitimacy. The teachers seek to promote the welfare and potential of others; the marketers potentially cause harm for personal profit as consumers pay more for goods and eat unhealthy granola when they could be eating healthy food. The teachers appeal to the better angels of their students; the marketers take advantage of the vulnerability of their targets (who lack the time for extended analysis) and instead appeal to what Fromm called false idols—things that appeal to baser passions.[24] I wonder how much Seth Godin would appreciate it if I told him an untrue but authentic story that resulted in his paying large portions of his income for a product that ultimately killed him?

In his insightful analysis of when to negotiate with evil, Robert Mnookin provides a useful principle for separating the good from the bad smuggler.[25] Mnookin describes the actions of Rudolf Kastner, who negotiated with Adolf Eichmann to save Hungarian Jews from the death camps. Kastner was a superb negotiator, highly skilled in bluffs and lying, who used these skills as best he could to win release of condemned Jews. Was he right to smuggle deceit into the negotiations? Mnookin answers yes because Kastner's deception was designed to promote the welfare of others and did not further damage the social fabric and pollute the communication environment. I believe this is a good rule for identifying when smuggling is a good thing. The teachers had a good purpose; Godin's marketers do not. The legitimacy of the teacher role for using pro-social influence helps mitigate the damage that a falsehood might do to the social fabric. In Katsner's case, the social fabric was so damaged that lies were expected and there would be little additional damage to the communications environment and his reputation.

I summarize what we have learned about good propaganda from our discussion of smugglers in Commandments 1, 2, 3, 4, and 10.

INSTITUTE FOR PROPAGANDA ANALYSIS (IPA): TABOO TACTICS

The Institute for Propaganda Analysis (IPA) in New York has a unique status in the history of propaganda—it was the first organization to systematically attempt to prevent the negative effects of propaganda.[26] The approach of the IPA was to designate a now familiar list of influence devices as taboo and unwarranted: glittering generality, name-calling (innuendo and projection), transfer device (association), testimonials, just plain folks, card stacking (information control), and bandwagon (social consensus).[27] The IPA sponsored monthly newsletters (from October 1937 to January 1942) that analyzed propaganda from a wide variety of sources and produced educational materials with an emphasis on identifying and condemning the use of these devices.[28]

In addition to the IPA efforts, there have been other attempts to declare specific influence and propaganda tactics off-limits and out-of-bounds, including Henry Lee Ewbank and J. Jeffrey Auer's taboo tactics for debates, Charles Sandage and Vernon Fryburger's unethical advertising techniques, Vance Packard's hidden persuaders, Wayne Minnick's list of unethical deceptions, Eleanor MacLean's deceptive practices used in news and journalism (although ironically she uses these techniques to advance her own political views), various proposals for dealing with hate speech, and Henry Conserva's expansion of the IPA taboo devices to eighty-nine techniques.[29]

As Sproule notes, the IPA was successful in institutionalizing the progressive era's criticisms of propaganda that arose after World War I.[30] (I learned the IPA list of devices in my first term in college in 1975.[31]) The IPA devices are particularly good at identifying the demagoguery of extremists, such as Father Coughlin. Such demagogues, prominent at the time of the IPA, tell people what they want to hear as a means of securing power and influence for themselves. The list of IPA devices is a roadmap for demagogues who seek to pander to a target audience.

The blacklisting of taboo tactics also has its uses in consumer protection (although the list of banned devices differs from those suggested by the IPA). FTC regulations and state laws have banned specific influence tactics when those tactics are harmful to consumers and/or free markets. The classic example is bait and switch laws, which prohibit the sale of nonexistent goods (thus preventing unwarranted phantom fixation and lowballing). As just one example of taboo tactics and consumer protection, the state of Wisconsin has a number of statutes designed to prevent the misuse of influence, such as preventing the abuse of the use of "free" by requiring solicitors to provide clear disclosure of the terms and nature of any free gift,[32] reducing lowballing by requiring full disclosure of any costs the consumer must incur to obtain free goods,[33] reducing the false manufacture of credibility by requiring sellers to disclose their name and to avoid using fictitious names,[34] and limiting illegitimate uses of the scarcity tactic.[35]

Despite the relevance of taboo tactics for education, identifying demagogues, and consumer protection, the IPA approach, much like Cialdini's, suffers simultaneously from being too exclusive and too inclusive. In terms of exclusion, the IPA provided a limited list of seven unwarranted devices and missed other techniques that are frequently abused, such as logical fallacies and evasive and emotional appeals. Henry Conserva provides a corrective, although his list of eighty-nine techniques is rather unwieldy to apply in practical situations.[36] In separate analyses, Garth Jowett and Victoria O'Donnell and J. Michael Sproule note that a narrow focus on content analysis of the IPA type misses the wider social reality and implications that may be of more significance in detecting good and bad propaganda.[37]

The IPA devices also identified as unwarranted some influence and propaganda that many would see as acceptable if not good. For example, Pericles's speech in honor of Athenian youth killed in the Peloponnesian War is chock full of glittering generalities, testimonials, transfer and associations, and card-stacking, all done with the goal of uniting Athens against enemies and in support of its newfound democratic ideals. In its use of IPA devices, Pericles's oration is similar to most epideictic speeches, such as Lincoln's Gettysburg Address and Dr. King's "I Have a Dream" speech, which, in contrast to the demagoguery, seek to bind together a group of people around a common set of positive values—a smuggler's altercast.

Wayne Minnick further questions the overreach of the IPA's devices by asking these rhetorical questions: "Is it wrong, for instance to call Thomas Aquinas a saint or Judas a traitor? Is it wrong to tell an audience that Albert Einstein was opposed to the use of atom bombs? Is it wrong to tell Americans that the majority of Americans are opposed to war?"[38] Consistent with Cialdini's sleuth, Minnick sees many of these cases as examples of the good use of propaganda and influence.

In 1942, William Garber raised an even more fundamental critique of the IPA approach—it led to cynicism and a confused understanding of the social world.[39] Garber's argument is that teaching the IPA devices results in an "artificial scepticism" that something "has been neatly put over on the public."[40] This cynicism does not lead to understanding—a speech by Adolf Hitler is treated the same as a fireside chat by Franklin Roosevelt in terms of the devices each employs without understanding the context and purpose of each speech. As Garber put it, "Was there not something fallacious in the Institute's definition of propaganda, in that it made no distinction between truth and falsity, between good and evil . . . ?"[41] As one answer to Graber's concerns, Ralph K. White's value-analysis empirically differentiated the underlying democratic values of FDR compared to the authoritarian naked aggression of Hitler.[42] The IPA was ultimately shut down over the issue of how to treat war propaganda of democracies and autocracies in World War II—same techniques or different values?

The demise of the IPA provides some important lessons about understanding the nature of propaganda. An emphasis on technique can create unwarranted skepticism. It is easy to arm students with a list of techniques and send them on a hunt to find these immoral devices—the craze surrounding the books of Wilson Bryan Key on subliminal seduction is a recent case in point. Such an exercise can result in cynicism and actually become a bad propaganda device in its own right. As William Schrier warned, it is very easy to find the propaganda techniques of those with opinions you disagree with; less so for your own causes.[43] As such, the cry of "false propaganda" becomes a form of name-calling to dismiss the opposition without considering the merits of their case. It might serve us well to remember to first take the propaganda plank out of our own eye, and then we will see clearly to remove the propaganda speck from another's eye (a corollary to my first Commandment). And while it is useful to have a set of devices for understanding how influence works (especially those validated by an experimental science),[44] the ethical evaluation of any given device also requires an understanding of purpose and goals. Our discussion of the IPA leads to the conclusion of Commandments 1, 2, 5, and 6.

FRANKLYN HAIMAN'S REASONED DISCOURSE: THE CULT OF RATIONALITY

Professor of speech Franklyn Haiman has perhaps the most austere proposal for what is good and ethical influence and propaganda: only reasoned discourse.[45] By reasoned discourse, he means: "the presentation of evidence and logic which induces the listener to accept the speaker's point of view."[46] Haiman also finds as acceptable devices to improve style, arrangement, and delivery to hold attention and obtain an open-minded hearing, but he rejects all means that might induce suggestibility in the audience, such as deliberate omission or minimization of counter-evidence, emotional appeals that short-circuit thinking, and any form of hidden persuader.[47] In other words, good persuasion is of the type that would appeal to Mr. Spock but not necessarily Dr. McCoy of *Star Trek* fame.

Haiman's call to exclude all persuasion except that based on reasoned discourse and facts, while extreme, is often the implicit gold standard for evaluating persuasive speech as found in texts on argumentation, critical thinking, rhetoric, decision making, science, and attitude change.[48] There are very good arguments for basing decisions on reason and facts. Imagine what would happen in a society if we ignored reason and facts and based agricultural policy on, say, Lysenko's notion that acquired traits are inherited, or attempted to make a great leap forward by adopting agricultural and industrial practices that ran opposite to expertise, or believed that global climate change was due to natural gravitational and magnetic oscillations of planets in the solar system. No doubt the consequences of such action would be disastrous.

Frank Haiman justifies his advocacy of reasoned discourse by appealing to the value of rational free choice at the core of free market capitalism and of democracy. The idea is that each individual in a capitalistic democracy must be free to make her or his own decisions in order to express self-interests, thus requiring the individual to be free of force or the threat of force (coercion), including nonrational influences. (This is similar to the desire for purity discussed and critiqued above).

Of course, there are other competing values upon which to justify a scheme for classifying propaganda as good. For example, one could value wide-open, no-holds-barred freedom of speech that many see as necessary for a democracy to thrive and prosper (see the next section on the proposal of Saul Alinsky).[49] Ironically, Haiman, a leader in the ACLU, was also an adamant supporter of First Amendment rights and argued for the protection of speech that others would classify as hate speech, sexual harassment, and obscene that would be the epitome of irrational and nonfactual discourse.[50] (Haiman believed there were different standards for evaluating what was good and moral and what should be illegal; in addition, he believed that the norm of reasoned discourse applied only to the powerful and not the powerless). Yet another possible value for justifying propaganda as good is the value of Ubuntu (see the penultimate good propaganda section on symmetrical communication), or an appeal to community, social harmony, and mutuality of influence.[51] Ubuntu recognizes that "a person is a person through other persons" and thus emphasizes generosity, caring, compassion, and respect for individuality within community—a value that many (including Adam Smith) also see as necessary to ensuring the moral fiber of democracy and capitalism.[52]

In addition to the issue of which value or values should be the basis for defining "the good," there are at least three other concerns with Haiman's cult of rationality. First, it is often both theoretically and practically difficult to identify a reasoned argument and a fact. Theoretically, Stephen Toulmin and Chaïm Perelman have both attempted to develop frameworks for understanding when it is reasonable to accept an argument, whereas Douglas Walton has investigated various logical fallacies (arguments from ignorance, appeals to popular opinion) to identify cases where it is reasonable to accept such a claim.[53] Practically, it is difficult to apply these sorts of analyses to assess the reasonableness and factuality of a persuasive appeal, especially when those appeals are in a message-dense environment of the type found in mass media, including the Internet.[54] As such, targets of propaganda often do not have the ability or motivation to systematically evaluate a communication (central route) and instead rely on simple rules, such as source credibility or packaging (peripheral route), to evaluate a claim.[55] One common simple rule that is often (mistakenly) used to evaluate the logic of an appeal is agreeableness—does the conclusion support or oppose one's attitudes? For example, Thistlethwaite among others found that attitudes toward the conclusion of a syllogism influence the ability to determine if the syllogism is logically valid or not.[56] The use of an attitude to evaluate arguments and facts turns the search for truth into Stephen Colbert's intuition of truthiness.[57]

Winston Brembeck and William Howell identified a second concern with the cult of rationality: it provides prestige to the use of pseudologic (truthiness) in persuasion.[58] Imagine the demagogue who says, "Now let's be logical and look at the record" and then presents a hodge-podge of illogical arguments, nonfacts, and selected facts designed to appeal to the audience's preexisting attitudes. Such an appeal is likely to be effective and send the audience member home thinking, "Gee, I am rational, unlike those who oppose me." Indeed, such a strategy was pioneered by big tobacco in its assault on the science of cancer and now is used to counter reason and facts about global climate change, evolution, asbestos, and vaccines, among other issues.[59] In these cases, a presumed expert presents "facts" and "arguments" that counter the legitimate facts and reasons produced via the scientific method, leaving the message recipient with the happy thought that it is okay to keep smoking or pumping carbon monoxide into the atmosphere or at the very least that science has not reached a conclusion about these issues. The appearance of rationality is not rationality.

Finally, and perhaps most importantly, emotions can help arbitrate the truth (for example, feelings of anger over racial injustice or sorrow over the hunger of a child can aid in making moral judgments). As both Richard Whately and William Schrier have argued, emotions are an important component of persuasion.[60] Reason alone does not galvanize a person to action, and the emotions are needed to convince someone to make a decision and to act on it. While the emotions can be misused and abused, the same can be said of reason (as noted above). Brembeck and Howell further argue that "the voluntary self-limitation of the persuader to the tools of facts and reason may purify his ethics but does little for his effectiveness (which is also a matter of ethics, since he may not have the moral right to be ineffective in a crisis)."[61]

The ethical tension over the use of emotions can be found in Henry Ward Beecher's discussion of effective preaching.[62] Beecher acknowledges that the rhetorical illustrations (what we would term the influence tactics of vivid appeal, storytelling, and metaphor) are not "true" arguments in the classic sense and appeal primarily to the emotions. However, these tactics work and without them souls will be lost. Beecher's compromise is to use such appeals if they can be associated with the truth. George Baker and Henry Huntington elaborate on Beecher's compromise by proposing a set of rules for how to appeal to the motives (emotions) of an audience.[63] According to Baker and Huntington, the persuader should appeal to the highest motives of the audience (for example, justice or the good of humanity) as opposed to lower motives (raw self-interest). If this is not possible, appeal to the lower motives but lead the audience to higher ground and their better angels. The rub, of course, is that with an audience motivated by truthiness and adversaries who appeal to these baser motives, it is difficult if not impossible to practice the rules of Beecher and of Baker and Huntington. As such, the influence environment is characterized by ever-decreasing reason and facts and ever-increasing cheap appeals to emotions, resulting in what Robert Entman poetically terms "a democracy without citizens."[64]

In *Age of Propaganda,* Elliot Aronson and I compare the influence tactics used by Abraham Lincoln at Gettysburg and Rush Limbaugh on his talk radio show.[65] Both employ similar emotional influence tactics, but with quite different results. Lincoln used emotions to stimulate thought and questioning, whereas Limbaugh uses emotions to stop thought and questioning. Jay Black makes a similar analysis and defines good propaganda as that which promotes an open mind versus a closed one.[66] Our discussion of Haiman's call for reasoned discourse leads to the conclusion of Commandments 1, 5, 6, 7, and 10.

SAUL ALINSKY'S INFLUENCE FREE-FOR-ALL: THE ADVERSARY MODEL

The community organizer Saul Alinksy presents an ethical perspective diametrically opposed to that of Haiman—don't worry about the ethics of influence; use any tactic that will work and accomplish desired ends.[67] Alinsky's view of ethics is rooted in his perceptions of how ethics impact social change and the ability to secure rights and benefits for his constituency of the Have-Nots. In his analysis, ethics are frequently used to prevent social change and justice for the poor by such remarks as: "We agree with the ends but not the means" or "Now is not the time." There usually isn't a means to be agreed upon, and the time never seems to come.

For Alinsky's community organizer there are only these questions: Are the ends achievable and worth the cost? Will the means (influence tactics) work? What are one's actual resources and possible courses of action? In war, the ends justify almost any means. Ethical behavior is only possible if one has a choice of influence tactics to achieve an end. Without a choice of tactics, then the only moral question is if the ends are worth it. With choices, a pragmatic calculus (which may include ethical reasons) determines the course of action. The perceived morality of a given action is determined by such factors as agreeableness of the position taken, victory, historical context, and how the action is clothed in moral terms. As such, control of the perceived morality of an action becomes an influence tactic (making the adversary live up to their own book of rules).

Alinsky is a political realist who views his book as the counterpart for the Have-Nots to Machiavelli's *The Prince* for the Haves. As Alinsky puts it, "Political realists see the world as it is: an arena of power politics moved primarily by perceived immediate self-interest, where morality is rhetorical rationale for expedient action and self-interest."[68] The world of Alinsky is a world of adversaries engaged in a political and influence free-for-all.

Alinsky's beliefs about the nature and value of influence are similar to those expressed by Sophists in fifth century B.C.E. Greece. The Sophists believed that there was no absolute truth, or at least no access to it. The

Sophist Protagoras put it this way: "there are two sides to every issue" and "humans are the measure of all things." Alinsky echoed Protagoras's view by quoting Learned Hand: "the mark of a free man is that ever-gnawing inner uncertainty as to whether or not he is right."[69] Given this state of affairs, the best way to determine the best course of action is through persuasion and influence; by argument, debate, and discussion the many facets of an issue can be laid bare and the advantages and disadvantages of a course of action more plainly seen. As with the Sophists, Alinsky's goal was to teach others how to engage in this act of influence.

The Sophist/Alinsky model of influence is at the heart of the design of the U.S. government (an irony, given the pillorying of Alinsky in the 2008 U.S. presidential campaign). For the most part, the founders of America were political realists who sought a form of government that checked power with power and pitted argument against argument with a goal of forging compromise and a search for the best course of action. In their government, a Bill of Rights guaranteed freedom of speech and of assembly, the right to petition, and the writ of habeas corpus, among other safeguards, to ensure a free discussion of issues. Their government balanced the power of smaller states against larger ones, instituted three branches to check the power of the others, two legislative houses to balance each other, and a legal system based on pitting adversaries against each other.

In an adversarial model, each participant is assigned a clear role: an advocate for a case, a judge or referee to ensure fairness, and a neutral arbiter to decide the matter (judge or voters) or a mechanism for forging compromise (as in a legislative body). An adversarial system encourages opponents to find and present their best evidence.[70] The adversarial system values dissent, and with good reason—the mere presence of a dissenting or minority opinion (even if wrong) can greatly increase the quality of decision making by the group.[71]

The problem with Alinsky's model of ethics can be seen by asking this question: What happens if the rules, roles, and referees regulating the influence free-for-all among adversaries breaks down and goes away? The American system is a set of interrelated rules (Bill of Rights, Congressional districting, rules of the Senate), social roles (lawyers are officers of the court, the press is a watchdog), and referees (courts of law) that is designed to ensure a fair proceeding. Thomas Hobbes in *Levia-*

than gave a clear answer to what happens if such a system is dismantled: "To this war of every man against every man, there also is consequent; that nothing can be unjust."[72]

The end result of dismantling adversarial rules, roles, and referees is an ever-escalating war of adversaries.[73] If an opponent uses a political attack ad, then why not counter with a false character assassination and innuendo? If an adversary attacks with a character assassination, then why not counter with a real assassination? As a result, power and influence concentrate into the hands of a few, thereby limiting dissent and undermining the value of the adversarial system to explore and evaluate alternative courses of action.

The adversarial model assumes that advocates with different perspectives will emerge and do persuasive battle. Without rules, roles, and referees to ensure fair play, there is no guarantee that such advocates will be able to take the stage to argue for a cause. (The First Amendment guarantees freedom of speech but not necessarily an audience to listen to that speech). Such is the case for special interest lobbyists who quietly advocate for special favors for their clients with little organized opposition even though the outcome may not be in the interests of society. (Alinsky attempted to counter special interests by trying to secure the proxy votes of corporate shareholders, but was unsuccessful in this venture). Censorship—whether it be direct through the exercise of concentrated power, subtle through the concentration of media channels, or, perhaps more perniciously, self-imposed (by psychologically avoiding disagreeable facts)—eliminates dissent and the positive outcomes from such dissent. Society is treated to a selective telling of the facts.

The adversarial model further breaks down if there are no mechanisms for resolving the fight—a judge to declare a winner, a means for forging a compromise or negotiating an outcome. Alinsky valued and praised compromise and saw it as the goal of the community organizer to obtain a favorable one. However, what happens in the case when an adversary refuses to compromise and is hell-bent on destroying the opponent?[74] Similarly, it is difficult to compromise when an issue involves core moral values, such as slavery or abortion.[75]

Although he is no doubt correct that ethical systems are not neutral in their consequences (he or she who makes the rules rules), Alinsky's cavalier manner toward rules, roles, and referees to regulate an adversarial system further underscores the need for them. Indeed, moral capital is essential to enacting and sustaining social change and for ensuring the legitimacy of the use of influence.[76] Alinsky's community organizer would be imprisoned or killed without a moral community to cry foul.

As such, we all have a responsibility for crafting and enforcing the rules, roles, and refereeing that governs influence. This observation was clearly understood by both Niccolò Machiavelli and Thomas Jefferson, who believed that a republic was not possible without citizen virtù—a set of behaviors exhibited by citizens in support of democracy. (I call it virtù in deference to its classical roots and to distinguish it from virtue or moral purity.) I will discuss this democratic virtù in upcoming sections. But for now, we should realize that Saul Alinsky has taught us much about the ways of power and that the discussion of his work has reinforced the value of Commandments 4, 8, and 10 specifically and all ten of the Commandments in general.

TWO-WAY SYMMETRICAL COMMUNICATION: MUTUALITY OF INFLUENCE AMONG STAKEHOLDERS

Over the last three decades or so and across disciplines, a number of models of influence have been developed that emphasize mutual influence among stakeholders. In other words, as opposed to a uni-dimensional flow of influence (for example, the influence agent induces the target to believe or do something), these models attempt to have stakeholders influence each other to reach compromises and possibly better solutions than any given stakeholder could imagine. These models emphasize a "win-win" approach.

In the field of public relations, Professor James Grunig has advanced an approach he termed the "two-way symmetrical model."[77] In this approach, PR agents take the role of adjusting and adapting the behaviors of their employers (corporate and governmental agencies) to help bring them closer together with their publics. The purpose of communication is to promote understanding among stakeholders, who are defined as equal and autonomous. The goal is to resolve conflict through negotiation and compromise, not force or manipulation. The two-way symmetrical model can be contrasted with other PR approaches that emphasize client advocacy, including the two-way asymmetrical model (in which an influence agent listens to a target to understand how to increase the effectiveness of persuasion) and the one-way models of press agentry (gaining favorable publicity for a client) and public information (disseminating information favorable to a client).[78] Grunig believes that it is impossible for one-way models of influence to be an ethical or socially responsible approach to public relations.

In the area of sales, sales trainer Stephen Schiffman has developed a similar model which defines the selling relationship as based on problem-solving.[79] The sales agent listens to the customer and then offers solutions to problems for mutual gain. In marketing, Charles Duke, Gregory Pickett, Les Carlson, and Stephen Grove have developed an interesting framework for evaluating the ethics of an influence attempt which they term the ethical effects-reasoning matrix.[80] In their approach, the perspectives of multiple stakeholders coupled with multiple ethical reasoning perspectives are used to identify conflicts that may arise when a given influence tactic is used (in their case, fear appeals) as an input to conflict resolution. In management, mutuality of influence among workers and managers has been the hallmark of participatory management rooted in Lewin's early work on democratic leadership.[81]

The most well-developed and researched mutuality of influence model is the "Getting to Yes" approach to negotiation developed at the Harvard Negotiation Project in 1981 by Roger Fisher, Bill Ury, and Bruce Patton.[82] "Getting to Yes" is an approach to negotiation and conflict resolution that emphasizes finding mutual gains (as opposed to a win-lose or zero-sum frame) by employing a set of social-psychological principles for changing the focus of the negotiation from one of arguing about positions to one of finding each stakeholder's interests and developing options capable of satisfying these sets of interests. The approach focuses on these maxims: "Don't bargain over positions; focus instead on interests," "invent options for mutual gain," "insist on using objective criteria," and "separate people from the problem." "Getting to Yes" was used by Jimmy Carter as part of the framework for negotiating the Camp David Accords—the only peace treaty to date in the Middle East.

From the perspective of "good propaganda" there is much to like about the use of mutual influence. The use of mutual influence maintains the self-determination of the target of influence and thus would be more acceptable to the purist while also appealing to the action-focused orientation of the partisan (although perhaps not enough to satisfy that partisan). The two-way symmetrical model is consistent with a pure democracy, where each stakeholder has a vote and a say in matters. Further, the use of mutual influence can provide a forum for dialogue, discussion, discourse, debate, and argument among stakeholders to create deliberative persuasion on the issues. Mutual influence invokes the universal norm of reciprocity and thereby invites a give and take that builds interpersonal relationships. Finally, and perhaps most importantly, mutual influence requires stakeholders to listen to each other and thereby increases the likelihood of realistic empathy as opposed to the naive realism that one's own worldview is the only and correct one.[83] The use of mutual influence increases the perceived legitimacy of one's own influence.

Some of the ethical limitations on the use of mutual influence can be seen by analyzing an example of the use of such influence—the Missouri Compromises of 1820. (A similar analysis can be done for the other pre–Civil War compromises.) In this case, the interests of free and slave states of the union were treated as stakeholders who argued, debated, bargained, and discussed until reaching a compromise, brokered by Henry Clay, that allowed Maine to enter as a free state, Missouri as a slave, and no restrictions on slavery south of the 36°30' parallel. The Union was preserved through the mutual respect and influence of the representatives of free and slave states. Nevertheless, it was not an effective solution for resolving America's original sin of race-based slavery that flies in the face of the American creed of equality, as evidenced by the Compromises of 1850 and 1876, the Kansas-Nebraska Act, a bloody civil war, and a long civil rights movement.

One obvious problem with the Missouri Compromise is that the negotiations did not include some obvious stakeholders—slaves and radical (now mainstream) abolitionists. An advocate for symmetrical influence would no doubt have urged their inclusion in the discussion, but this would have made for an impasse for securing a compromise. What compromise would a slave or abolitionist accept—a Slave Review Board to ensure better treatment or the right of a slave to cast his own 3/5 vote? The determination of stakeholder begins with a definition of the problem (save the union vs. human rights), and that definition is not necessarily a politically neutral process.[84] Nancy Snow's analysis of the U.S. Information Agency's relationship with corporate America adds further complexity to the issue of who is a stakeholder for whom.[85]

From the vantage point of history, the moral heroes of the slavery debate were not the compromisers but those who stood firm in their opposition to the peculiar institution. The likes of Granville Sharp, William Wilberforce, Frederick Douglass, and William Lloyd Garrison were not of the mutual influence kind, and instead they used with full-force the minority influence tactics of the confident, consistent expression of a position linked to shared norms and values of the community.[86] The same can be said for those who oppose wars, support civil rights, and whose adversarial advocacy changed history for the better or for the worse (albeit the most effective often coupled this tough advocacy with mutual influence and reconciliation at the endgame, as did Martin Luther King Jr., Nelson Mandela and Cyril Ramaphosa in South Africa, and Lincoln beginning at Gettysburg).[87]

The mutual influence model underestimates the moral value of leadership, especially leadership that leads others to make moral sacrifices or to take unattractive but necessary actions. When Abraham Lincoln weighed in on the slavery issue by suspending the writ of habeas corpus in Maryland, seeking to arrest and try Copperheads, and sending Sherman storming through Atlanta, he was not seeking to engage in a two-way symmetrical flow of influence. He sought to win a war, save a nation, and end slavery. During his presidency, Lincoln was America's most despised president in history; today he is viewed as its most eminent. Leadership is often about moving constituents to take unpopular action that the leader believes to be the right course. When Branch Rickey hired Jackie Robinson to play baseball, he did not engage in a process of mutual understanding with racists but instead used his authority, rhetoric, power, and the psychology of the inevitable to enact change.[88] As the Nazi menace spread across Europe, Franklin Roosevelt knew that he would need to move an isolationist nation made cynical by a previous war to go to war. He did this by listening to the American public and understanding their views so that he could effectively use rhetoric and take preliminary actions to move public opinion in support of the Allies. In other words, he engaged in a two-way asymmetrical communication (listen to know how to persuade) and not a two-way symmetrical discussion of the merits of letting a world genocide go unchecked. As Brace and Hinckley have shown, presidents who structure their agendas based on what the American public would approve often take actions that the American public would not support. Their analysis of polls of presidential approval ratings reveals that "presidents have to choose whether they wish to be active and 'vigorous' or popular. Making one choice hurts the other."[89]

Now, the extent to which I have persuaded you that mutual influence can sometimes result in immoral outcomes and one-way influence results in moral outcomes most likely depends on how much you approved of and accepted my examples of the Missouri Compromise and the influence of abolitionists, war dissenters, Abraham Lincoln, Branch Rickey, and FDR. And that is the point. As demonstrated with our analysis of the Institute of Propaganda Analysis, the definition of "good" propaganda requires more than just using an acceptable technique, such as mutual influence; we must also follow Commandment 2 and evaluate purposes and goals. (Don't believe me? I bet I can come up with other examples to make the point that you would find acceptable). Nevertheless, the mutual influence models underscore the significance of realistic empathy and Commandment 8 for good propaganda, as well reminding us of the importance of Commandments 2, 4, and 10.

RALPH K. WHITE'S DEMOCRATIC PERSUASION

Our final approach to the ethics of influence and propaganda is one that has been advocated by many students of persuasion: make your persuasive appeals consistent with the values and purposes of a democracy. In 1942, as a member of the Committee on Morale for the Society for the Psychological Study of Social Issues (S.P.S.S.I.) during World War II, famed psychologist Gordon Allport recommended that attempts to maintain homeland morale during a war be consistent with the values of a democracy, including voluntary participation, respect for the person, majority rule, freedom of speech, and tolerance. Similarly, Robert Merton in his analysis of the effects of the Kate Smith bond drive urged researchers not to limit their questions to the immediate results of persuasion but also to include the questions of how does a given persuasion technique impact a society and is that tactic consistent with democratic values (a specific call for Commandment 9). Karl Wallace, a professor of speech, advocated that communication be consistent with the democratic values of individual dignity and worth, equality of opportunity, freedom, and personal growth. Psychology professors James Friedrich and David Douglass make the point that teaching is often a process of persuasion and as such should be guided by a democratic ethic.[90]

The most detailed attempt at creating a morally acceptable propaganda based on democracy comes from the social psychologist and USIA researcher Ralph K. White.[91] As a graduate student, White worked with Kurt Lewin on his democratic leadership experiments. This work, along with his advocacy for America during the Cold War, serves as the basis for White's ethical analysis of propaganda. White's morally acceptable influence tactics include: (a) getting and keeping attention, (b) getting and keeping rapport, (c) building credibility, (d) appealing to strong motives and emotions, and (e) using action involvement (such as the foot-in-the-door tactic). He deems the following techniques to be morally questionable: (a) lying, (b) innuendo, (c) presenting opinion as fact, (d) deliberate omission, and (5) implied obviousness. White uses the word "questionable" as opposed to wrong or totally immoral because it may be necessary to use these tactics if the goal of persuasion is urgent enough.

I would like to discuss two general issues with the use of democracy to define good propaganda and influence. First, there is really no ultimate reason for preferring democratic ethics and persuasion over other forms. The authoritarian and autocrat most certainly would reject such a thing. Aristotle believed that ethics should be driven by a desire to live a good life.[92] But yet, what is a good life—living in Ubuntu community with others or dominating them for your own ego and enjoyment? This point is driven home by the attorney Arthur Allen Leff, who argues convincingly that without a God or ultimate decider there can be no normative system of ethics or natural law of right and wrong.[93] I would argue that even with a God, there is no normative system; what is right and wrong depends on the specific nature of the God who is worshiped. Some Christians, for example, believe that God has privileged Christians over others (especially those who differ from the Christian) and thus they are entitled to wage war and engage in a politics of domination, whereas other Christians walk humbly with God and seek to serve and respect others, including those not like themselves. (A similar point can be made about other religions as well). Although I can array the advantages of living in a democracy,[94] it ultimately remains an existential choice, hopefully made consciously, about how one is to live one's life.

Nevertheless, once a decision about the nature of the good life is made, an ethical system logically follows. For the autocrat, the Ten Commandments of Good Influence and Propaganda reduce to only one: Ulpian's principle of "*Quod principi placuit legis vigorem habet,*" or "What pleases the prince has the force of law." Obeying the Ten Commandments is for the little people or, at best, to lend a pretense of morality to the actions of the autocrat.

Second, more work needs to be done in regard to how to translate democratic values into the specific use of an influence tactic. White's list of questionable and unquestionable tactics is a good first step, but it paints with a broad brush and leaves certain questions unanswered. For example, are there cases when the use of an action involvement device, such as the foot-in-the-door tactic, is questionable? Conversely, are there cases when is it okay to lie?

To help address these questions, Marlene Turner and I looked at the nature of autocratic and democratic leadership in the Lewin democracy experiments and asked: what is the nature of influence and persuasion under autocratic and democratic leadership?[95] Our answer is ten opposing pairs of characteristics (presented in table 2.1). The opposing pairs are based on an understanding that the essence of a democracy requires self-reliant citizens engaged in deliberative persuasion, whereas autocracy is best served by propaganda designed to appeal to the uninformed.

TABLE 2.1. THE NATURE OF INFLUENCE IN AUTOCRACY AND DEMOCRACY

Autocracy	*Democracy*
Predetermined solution by ruling elite.	Co-participation of leader in discovering solution.
Authority used to induce acceptance of predetermined solution.	Leader authority used to stimulate discussion.
Leader behavior is not constrained by rules or other group members.	A system of checks and balances is placed on power.

TABLE 2.1. (CONTINUED)

Autocracy	*Democracy*
Unidirectional influence from elites; single or colluding sources of information.	Reciprocity of influence between leaders and members; multiple independent sources of information.
Centralized communication structures.	Decentralized communication structures.
Rigid group boundaries and social roles to limit discussion and options.	Flexible group boundaries and roles that allow additional resources to be obtained and problems to be solved.
Minority opinion is censored via neglect, ridicule, jeer and social pressure, or persecution; feedback is discouraged.	Minority opinion is encouraged as a means of making a better decision; feedback is encouraged.
Agenda, objectives, and work tasks set by elites.	Agenda, objectives, and work tasks set through group discussion weighed by expertise.
Rewards used to maintain group structure and leaders' status and power.	Rewards used to move group toward objectives.
Persuasion plays on prejudices and emotions to induce acceptance of a message and to truncate thought; persuasion as communication.	Persuasion based on debate, discussion, dialogue, argument, and a careful consideration of options; persuasion as discovery.

The characteristics of table 2.1 beg the question: Which forms of institutions are needed for good influence and propaganda within a democracy? For example, democracy requires a mass media with a diversity of ownership and news sources marked by a free-flowing debate of the issues and a watchdog press. Democracy also requires political campaigns to engage in deliberative persuasion on issues and to move the country toward closure on issues. The democratic characteristics of table 2.1 allow us to ask such questions as "How are we doing in our institutions?" and "What sorts of reforms are needed to promote democratic persuasion?"[96]

These characteristics of democracy also allow us to evaluate the selection and use of any given social influence tactic. For example, in a wonderful documentary Bill Moyers interviewed the head propagandists in World War II for the Nazi and American causes, Fritz Hippler and Major Frank Capra.[97] Moyers asked them: How did you persuade your nations to go to war? Hippler responded with the autocrat's formula for propaganda: "Simplify complicated issues. Repeat, repeat, repeat." Note that such a communication from a centralized source truncates thought to induce acceptance of a predetermined solution. Major Capra gave quite a different answer. He used only the footage from Nazi propaganda films, so that the viewer could see for him or herself what the Nazi regime was about and draw his or her own conclusions. In other words, Major Capra used the tactic of self-generated persuasion in a manner consistent with democracy.

To illustrate with another example, consider the granfalloon tactic—the use of a social identity such as Nazi or American in persuasion. An autocratic use of such a tactic would be based on rigid group boundaries and induce fear of out-group members and fear of being excluded from the group, as Goebbels did by playing on anti-Semitic prejudice and promoting Aryan superiority. In contrast, the democratic use of granfallooning would provide a basis for flexible group boundaries and would unite people of diverse backgrounds for common purpose and a higher cause, as did Abraham Lincoln in his Gettysburg Address and Martin Luther King in his "I Have a Dream" speech. For those interested in the moral use of influence, an important next step would be to look at each of the 107 influence tactics[98] and ask: How can each be used in and by a democracy (if indeed the tactic can be)?

The democratic approach to good propaganda unequivocally demands that we follow all ten of our Commandments. As professor of public relations John Marston states: "Democracy lives by the road it travels."[99]

INFLUENCE AS A TOOL

> What those who condemn rhetoric and rhetoricians fail frequently to realize is that speech is a tool, and that it may therefore by used and abused; it may be employed in worthy causes or toward evil ends.
>
> —WILLIAM SCHRIER, "Ethics of Persuasion"

For the most part, propaganda studies have used the metaphor of "influence as a weapon" for describing the use and abuse of persuasion and propaganda. In this metaphor, propaganda is used to conquer minds and beliefs; propagandists are the enemy engaged in military-like maneuvers using advanced munitions to take over reality; they must be disarmed and our minds fortified against attack. I used this weapon metaphor with my coauthors in writing both *Age of Propaganda* and *Weapons of Fraud*.[100] The metaphor also underlies the work of the Institute for Propaganda Analysis, the concept of brainwashing, and is used in novels such as George du Maurier's *Trilby* and Thomas Hardy's *Tess of the d'Urbervilles*. From an educational standpoint, the goal is to show students how these weapons of influence can be used, emphasizing their more nefarious uses with the purpose of teaching how to resist these attacks. The weapon metaphor is very useful for illustrating the potential autocratic use of persuasion, but it comes with a price of cynicism, as the influence process is reduced to tactics and countermoves. From an ethics standpoint, the weapon metaphor leaves us with one of two choices about the use of influence: we are either a partisan armed to the teeth with no-never-mind about ethics or a purist demanding disarmament and left with little means for achieving goals save for an occasional vague feeling of hope.

As the quote from William Schrier suggests, there is another possible metaphor for the use of influence that opens up the opportunity for a more nuanced ethics of the use and abuse of persuasion: influence as a tool. This metaphor is captured by such phrases as "laying a foundation" or "building an argument." Influence is a tool to reach a goal; ethics are based on how to use the tool of influence to reach that objective. Goals come infused with oughts.

Influence as a tool is a means to build Aristotle's good life. This metaphor conjures up images of a leader as an artist using influence as paint to form an image on a canvas or of citizens as Amish at a barn-raising, where each influences the other in pursuit of a common goal. Influence is a means of bringing people together to build positive social relationships and to form better lives by constructing a case for sounder health practices and environmental behaviors, erecting improved governments through nation building, and forging a peace out of conflict. Of course, tools can also be used to build houses that are eyesores and block a neighbor's view or factories that pollute while making dangerous products. Tools also can be used as weapons, as illustrated by Maxwell's silver hammer and the chainsaws and axes found in low-budget horror films. The tool metaphor underlies the use of influence in Jane Austen's *Persuasion,* in which the characters sometimes use persuasion as a weapon to get their way but also as a tool to shape and fashion (sometimes appropriately and sometimes not) relationships and desired outcomes.

From an ethical standpoint, the tool metaphor requires us to ask such questions as: What am I building and how am I using my tool of influence? Specifically, we need to ask: What is being built? Is it worthwhile? How is my tool of influence used? Are my means moral or at least appropriate for the goal I am building? How does the tactic promote the overall goal? Have I considered that the means (influence tactics) determines the ends (the building)? What if everyone built as I build? What if everyone did as I did? Would I want to live in a community and world that used influence in that way? Are there unintended consequences that might hurt others (such as reinforcing a harmful stereotype, demonizing someone, or teaching inappropriate behavior)? What do my choice of influence tactics and the way I use influence reveal about me and my cause? The answers to these questions are important because, ultimately, you must live with yourself: Once you use a tactic, the results are yours to keep. What you build with influence is yours to live in and with.

The tool metaphor also raises the issues of what trade-offs arise in using an influence tool to build. As any builder or engineer will tell you, there are always trade-offs. Putting in the upgraded granite counters comes at a cost; adding more features to the robot uses up battery power. The same is true when using influence as a tool.[101] The effective builder understands the trade-offs and makes wise choices.

Unlike with the Commandments of Moses, my Commandments often involve moral trade-offs. In the Ten Commandments of Moses, one rarely has to make a choice between, say, committing adultery and stealing (indeed, one may need to steal to afford the mistress). However, with the Ten Commandments of Good Influence and Propaganda, one is often required to make trade-offs—what ends are to be pursued with which means? Concretely, in 1820 would you have adopted the morally correct position of the abolitionists and their morally questionable means or the morally correct mutual influence of Henry Clay and his morally questionable outcome? Or would you have taken the course of the partisan and justified whatever you did as right or the course of the purist and pretended to be above it all?

Here are two examples of the types of trade-offs faced by influence agents. A social marketing effort can effectively promote a remedy for infant diarrhea by taking advantage of a false belief in the target that diarrhea is caused by a bag of worms in the child. The belief is untrue, but if it is ignored the campaign will fail. Spending more money to change the false belief means that other diseases cannot be addressed.[102] Peace activists sought world attention and pressure to tip the balance of power in Liberia's civil war of the 1990s. To gain attention, narratives were developed based on a false atrocity statistic: 75 percent of women in wartime Liberia were raped. The best estimate is 10–20 percent of women for all forms of sexual violence.[103] How would you resolve these trade-offs?

Furthermore, positive values underlying the use of influence can conflict. Hate speech, to take one example, is consistent with the value of freedom of speech (a necessary component for dissent in a democracy) but is equally inconsistent with the Ubuntu value of community and inconsistent with rationality and scientific facts when claims are made about the genetic differences of races. Hate speech violates many of the Ten Commandments (such as 6, 7, and 9) and thus is immoral, but should it be allowed to foster dissent?

And what is one to do when the social situation is such that mutual influence and democratic persuasion are not viable options but yet the cause may be important? When is it permissible to engage in Alinsky-style adversarial advocacy or strong leadership that employs asymmetrical influence? Suppose the leader is faced with a situation of a "democracy without citizens," where fellow citizens are not interested in understanding an issue or policy but in hearing emotionally pleasing sound bites? Certainly, Henry Ward Beecher and Baker and Huntington provide one solution,[104] but that solution may not be viable in a competitive environment such as a political campaign or on the international stage.

I would urge that when faced with the inevitable moral trade-offs that the use of influence brings, we face them honestly and recognize that we are faced with a moral trade-off. The partisan ignores them. The purist pretends to be above them. In both cases evil may occur, and the result is a rationalization trap where we dig ourselves into a deeper and deeper hole of self-justification—"my cause is even more righteous and worthy of even more extreme action"; "my inaction is even more righteous and others who enter the fray are even more evil."

It is also incumbent on those of us who study influence to provide more and better choices for those who wish to change things for the better. As Saul Alinsky argued, it is impossible to be moral without a choice. In this regard, I am heartened by such activities as the investigation of the use of social influence to promote prosocial causes of the environment and conflict resolution, the development of principles of strategic nonviolence to change autocratic regimes to democratic ones,[105] and the efforts by organizations such as Eastern Mennonite University's Center for Justice and Peacebuilding in training more peacemakers.

Ultimately, in facing the moral trade-offs inherent in the use of influence, I would recommend the approach I have used in this chapter: take a given instance of a moral trade-off and engage in deliberative persuasion of argument, debate, and discussion to understand how best to obey the Ten Commandments of Good Influence and Propaganda in reaching a course of proper action.

DEMOCRATIC VIRTÙ

> In a republican nation, whose citizens are to be led by reason and persuasion and not by force, the art of reasoning becomes of first importance.
>
> —THOMAS JEFFERSON, *The Writings of Thomas Jefferson*

> With great power comes great responsibility.
>
> —STAN LEE, *Spider-Man*

The use of influence as a tool brings with it a great responsibility—to use that tool wisely and without unwarranted harm, to build good things, and to take care that others are using and building with influence responsibly. One of the most intense uses of propaganda and influence is the propaganda of hatred and the raw flex of power found in genocides. The moral lesson of the Holocaust is expressed in the poem "First They Came" by Martin Niemöller:

> First they came for the communists,
> and I didn't speak out because I wasn't a communist.
>
> Then they came for the socialists,
> and I didn't speak out because I wasn't a socialist.
>
> Then they came for the trade unionists,
> and I didn't speak out because I wasn't a trade unionist.
>
> Then they came for me,
> and there was no one left to speak for me.

Democracy requires that each citizen stand up for the other and to stand up for the principles of democracy.

Democratic virtù is taking responsibility for how you and others use influence as a tool. It involves an understanding of the nature of influence and what is required to use it morally, the promotion of the institutions needed for fair, moral persuasion, such as the characteristics of democracy listed in table 2.1, toleration and respect for others but an intolerance of intolerance, the practice of realistic empathy, and the courage to stand up for others. Following the Ten Commandments of Propaganda and Influence is democratic virtù. The use of democratic virtù in influence is consistent with Sproule's call for a return to eloquent speechmaking drawn from great ideas, passionate commitment, and the highest values of a society.[106] The writings of Niccolò Machiavelli and Thomas Jefferson will help us develop the meaning of democratic virtù.

After writing a how-to manual on the cutthroat use of power to rule (*The Prince*), Niccolò Machiavelli turned his attention in later life (in the Orti Oricellari garden) to the task of controlling the power of a tyrant within a republic (*Discourses on Livy*).[107] The end product was a set of principles such as the separation of powers and the use of power to check power, which formed the core blueprint for the U.S. Constitution. Among these principles was the classical concept of virtù. In an autocratic regime, virtù means doing whatever is needed to maintain the power of the ruler. In a republic, virtù means doing what is needed to maintain the Republic and to place the good of the community above private interests and corruption. Leaders and citizens must be prepared to advance not their own interests but the general good. It is a leader's responsibility to inspire others to seek virtù, including the characteristics of care, prudence, courage, control of envy, and respect of others and to uphold civic values and responsibilities, including respect and promotion of the institutions of the republic. Machiavelli believed that a republic would be lost through the degeneration of virtù as some lost interest in politics and others placed individual ambitions and factional loyalties ahead of public welfare. The loss of virtù was a loss of a check and balance on intemperate and uncontrolled influence.

As a student of the classics, Thomas Jefferson also understood the role of virtù in a democracy.[108] For Jefferson, virtù was needed in a democracy as a counterbalance to unbridled liberty. Given that virtù could not be coerced through force, it needed to be established by persuasion and was obtained through virtùous rhetoric. Jefferson's own definition of virtù came from both the Bible (humble before God and toward oneself; love of thy neighbor) and the classics (wisdom, temperance, courage, and justice). The practice of virtù in rhetoric and persuasion involved these components: (a) use of conciliatory strategies; (b) "mutual sacrifice of opinion" (compromise); (c) communicating to others as a friend; (d) honest and ethical speech; (e) speaking with wisdom and courage to state what is right and not what the audience wants to hear; (f) use of consistent and coherent arguments ever-faithful to the evidence; (g) emphasis on question-asking and thus self-generated persuasion; and (h) words not given in anger nor to hurt falsely others' reputation. Jefferson was also deeply concerned about the nature of the rules and procedures that govern persuasion and influence (for example, parliamentary procedure). He believed that such rules protected the rights of the minority to be heard and to have an impact, and, as such, Jefferson believed that the rules should be impartially applied and that we each have a responsibility to see that this happens.

The implication of democratic virtù and influence as a tool for those of us who teach about persuasion and propaganda is clear: it is not enough to teach how to be critical of propaganda as a weapon. We must also teach how to use influence with democratic virtù and the importance of standing up for the institutions of democracy.[109] I think we should take as our inspiration my candidate for the best "good" propaganda of all time—a New Deal WPA propaganda poster attacking propaganda that proclaims: "Know the facts!" Perhaps we can craft additional posters for each of Mr. Jefferson's other attributes of democratic virtù.

In America today, there is a dire need to build support for the practice of democratic virtù. Even a cursory look at contemporary politics reveals that gridlock and dysfunction have come to define American government, as ideologues on both sides of the aisle engage in a partisan food fight at the expense of solving problems.[110] Partisanship reigns supreme, with few concerned with (much less promoting) the virtùous use of influence needed in a democracy. One group attempting to counter this trend is No Labels (full disclosure: I am a founding member, and you can find out more at www.nolabels.org). No Labels is advancing sets of congressional and presidential reforms for the purpose of injecting some of Mr. Jefferson's democratic virtù into our political system, including such improvements as bipartisan gatherings and seating to increase communications among friends, rule changes to encourage mutual sacrifice of opinion and compromise, guaranteed congressional question time and meetings with the president, along with citizen press conferences to stimulate debate, discussion, and deliberative persuasion, all done with the goal of making government more productive in consequence.

I had the opportunity to present for the first time the ideas in this chapter at a wonderful conference organized at the Louisiana State University in honor of Senator John Breaux. In his professional life as a member of the U.S. Congress, Senator Breaux regularly displayed democratic virtù. He took stands to protect the institutions needed for deliberative persuasion in a democracy—for example, by opposing changes in FCC rules that would allow multiple media in the same community to fall under a single owner. Everyone understood where Senator Breaux stood on the issues, and everyone equally understood that differences of opinion would be respected. Indeed, Senator Breaux's stock-in-trade as a member of Congress was to bring together bipartisan coalitions to debate, discuss, and hash out the issues to build an end result of productive consequences. The body of Senator Breaux's political work stands as testimony that the goal of this chapter to forge an ethical persuasion is not just a dreamy ideal of an academic, but represents a course of action that can withstand the test of the crucible of the American political system.

Notes

I thank Titus Bender for discussions over thirty years ago that finally led to this chapter and Nancy Snow for her continued leadership in developing a scholarly field of propaganda and public diplomacy.

1. For a discussion of the roots of American persuasion, see E. Brooks Holifield, *Era of Persuasion: American Thought and Culture, 1521–1680* (Lanham, Md.: Rowman and Littlefield, 2004).

2. Lee Ross and Andrew Ward, "Naive Realism in Everyday Life: Implications for Social Conflict and Misunderstanding," in *Values and Knowledge*, ed. S. Reed and T. Brown, 103–135 (Hillsdale, N.J.: Erlbaum, 1996).

3. Rollo May, *Power and Innocence: A Search for the Sources of Violence* (New York: Norton, 1972).

4. Kurt Lewin, Ronald Lippitt, and Ralph K. White, "Patterns of Aggressive Behavior in Experimentally Created 'Social Climates,'" *Journal of Social Psychology* 10, no. 2 (1939): 271–299; Ralph K. White and Ronald Lippitt, *Autocracy and Democracy: An Experimental Inquiry* (New York: Harper, 1960).

5. For a description of realistic empathy, see Ralph K. White, *Fearful Warriors: A Psychological Profile of U.S.-Soviet Relations* (New York: Free Press, 1984); Ralph K. White, "Enemy Images in the United Nations-Iraq and East-West Conflicts," in *The Psychology of War and Peace: The Image of the Enemy*, ed. Robert W. Rieber, 59–70 (New York: Plenum, 1991).

6. Robert P. Abelson and Philip G. Zimbardo, *Canvassing for Peace: A Manual for Volunteers* (Ann Arbor, Mich.: Society for the Psychological Study of Social Issues, 1970); Philip G. Zimbardo, "The Tactics and Ethics of Persuasion," in *Attitudes, Conflict, and Social Change*, ed. B. T. King and E. McGinnies, 81–99 (New York: Academic Press, 1972).

7. Carl R. Rogers and B. F. Skinner, "Some Issues Concerning the Control of Human Behavior," *Science* 124 (1956): 1057–1066; B. F. Skinner, *Walden Two* (New York: Macmillan, 1948).

8. William Graebner, "The Small Group and Democratic Social Engineering, 1900–1950," *Journal of Social Issues* 42 (1986): 137–154; William Graebner, "Confronting the Democratic Paradox: The Ambivalent Vision of Kurt Lewin," *Journal of Social Issues* 43 (1987): 141–146; William Graebner, *The Engineering of Consent: Democracy and Authority in Twentieth-Century America* (Madison: Univ. of Wisconsin, 1987). For a convincing rebuttal, see Miriam Lewin, "Kurt Lewin and the Invisible Bird on the Flagpole: A Reply to Graebner," *Journal of Social Issues* 43 (1987): 123–139.

9. Leo Tolstoy, *The Kingdom of God Is Within You* (Mineola, N.Y.: Dover Press, 2006); John Howard Yoder, *The Politics of Jesus*, 2nd ed. (Grand Rapids, Mich.: Eerdmans, 1994); Martin Luther King Jr., *Stride Toward Freedom: The Montgomery Story* (New York: Harper and Row, 1958); Gene Sharp, *There Are Realistic Alternatives* (Boston, Mass.: Albert Einstein Institution, 2003); Krishnalal Shridharani, *War without Violence: A Study of Gandhi's Method and Its Accomplishments* (New York: Harcourt, Brace, 1939).

10. For definitions and a discussion of the scope of propaganda, see Dan Kuehl, "Propaganda in the Digital Age," in this volume; Garth Jowett and Victoria O'Donnell, *Propaganda and Persuasion*, 5th ed. (Thousand Oaks, Calif.: Sage Publications, 2011); Randal Marlin, *Propaganda and the Ethics of Persuasion* (Peterborough, Ontario: Broadview Press, 2002).

11. Anthony R. Pratkanis and Elliot Aronson, *Age of Propaganda: The Everyday Use and Abuse of Persuasion*, 2nd ed. (New York, N.Y.: W. H. Freeman, 2001).

12. For summaries of ethical approaches, see Warren Ashby, *A Comprehensive History of Western Ethics: What Do We Believe?* (Amherst, N.Y.: Prometheus Books, 1997); Vernon Joseph Bourke, *History of Ethics: Graeco-Roman to Early Modern Ethics,* vol. 1. (Mount Jackson, Va.: Axios Press, 2008); Vernon Joseph Bourke, *History of Ethics: Modern and Contemporary Ethics,* vol. 2. (Mount Jackson, Va.: Axios Press, 2008); Christopher K. Panza and Adam Potthast, *Ethics for Dummies* (Indianapolis, Ind.: Wiley, 2010); Michael J. Sandel, *Justice: What's the Right Thing to Do?* (New York: Farrar, Straus and Giroux, 2009).

13. For an outstanding review and analysis of this question, see Marlin, *Propaganda and the Ethics of Persuasion.*

14. Anthony R. Pratkanis, "Social Influence Analysis: An Index of Tactics," in *The Science of Social Influence: Advances and Future Progress,* ed. Anthony R. Pratkanis, 17–82 (Philadelphia: Psychology Press, 2007).

15. I chose these six answers to Antigone because they seemed particularly representative and either well-known or well-developed approaches. For those who are interested in other approaches, here is a list of some of the ethical principles I have found:

social responsibility	Thomas Cooper and Tom Kelleher, "Better Mousetrap? Of Emerson, Ethics, and Postmillennium Persuasion," *Journal of Mass Media Ethics* 16 (2001): 176–192; Wilbur Schramm, *Responsibility in Mass Communication* (New York: Harper and Row, 1957).
the public interest	Alex Messina, "Public Relations, the Public Interest, and Persuasion: An Ethical Approach," *Journal of Communication Management* 11 (2007): 29–52.
unfettered and unregulated free market principles	Robert I. Wakefield and Coleman F. Barney, "Communication in the Unfettered Marketplace: Ethical Interrelationships of Business, Government, and Stakeholders," *Journal of Mass Media Ethics* 16 (2001): 213–232.
accountability to targets	Thomas Cooper and Tom Kelleher, "Better Mousetrap? Of Emerson, Ethics, and Postmillennium Persuasion," *Journal of Mass Media Ethics* 16 (2001): 176–192.
conforming to norms of role constraints	B. J. Diggs, "Persuasion and Ethics," *Quarterly Journal of Speech* 50 (1964): 359–373.
ethical principles governing therapeutic change	Gerald P. Koocher and Patricia Keith-Spiegel, *Ethics in Psychology and the Mental Health Professions: Standards and Cases,* 3rd ed. (Oxford: Oxford Univ. Press, 2008), 6–7.

Talmudic principles	Hershey H. Friedman, "Ancient Marketing Practices: The View from Talmudic Times," *Journal of Public Policy and Marketing* 3 (1984): 194–204.
social utility and the survival of the group	Winston L. Brembeck and William Smiley Howell, *Persuasion: A Means of Social Influence,* 2nd ed. (Englewood Cliffs, N.J.: Prentice-Hall, 1976).
dialogue	Eugene C. Kreider, "Religious Pluralism, Dialogue, and the Ethics of Social Influence," *Cultic Studies Journal* 2 (1986): 329–339; Ron Pearson, "Business Ethics as Communication Ethics: Public Relations Practice and the Idea of Dialogue," in *Public Relations Theory,* ed. C. H. Botan and V. Hazelton, 111–131 (Hillsdale, N.J.: Lawrence Erlbaum, 1989); Lisa Schirch and David Campt, *The Little Book of Dialogue for Difficult Subjects* (Intercourse, Pa.: Good Books, 2007).
appeal to higher altruistic motives as opposed to lower selfish motives	George Pierce Baker and Henry Barrett Huntington, *The Principles of Argumentation,* rev. ed. (Boston: Ginn, 1905); Giles Wilkeson Gray and Waldo Warder Braden, *Public Speaking: Principles and Practice* (New York: Harper, 1951).
reverence for life	Albert Schweitzer, *Albert Schweitzer's Ethical Vision: A Sourcebook* (New York: Oxford Univ. Press, 2009).
appreciative understanding of what others know and value	Henry Nelson Weiman and Otis M. Walter, "Toward an Analysis of Ethics for Rhetoric," *Quarterly Journal of Speech* 43 (1957): 266–270.
influence that respects the choices and identity of the target	Michael D. Lagone, "Cults, Evangelicals, and the Ethics of Social Influence," *Cultic Studies Journal* 2 (1986): 371–388; Michael D. Lagone, "Social Influence: Ethical Considerations," *Cultic Studies Journal* 6 (1989): 16–24.
edifying discourse as opposed to compliance	A. Duane Litfin, "The Perils of Persuasive Preaching," *Cultic Studies Journal* 2 (1986): 267–273.
elimination of hidden persuaders	Franklyn S. Haiman, "Democratic Ethics and the Hidden Persuaders," *Quarterly Journal of Speech* 44 (1958): 385–392; Vance Packard, *The Hidden Persuaders* (New York: David McKay, 1957).

influence that is freely chosen and does not limit choice	David Zarefsky, *Argumentation: The Study of Effective Reasoning,* 2nd ed. (Chantilly, Va.: Teaching Company, 2005).
the pillars of PR, including truth-telling, do no harm, do good, respect privacy, and be fair	Patricia Parsons, *Ethics in Public Relations: A Guide to Best Practice* (London: Kogan Page, 2004).
various baselines for evaluating communications, including self-interest, entitlement, enlightened self-interest, social responsibility, and kingdom ends	Sherry Baker, "Five Baselines for Justification in Persuasion," *Journal of Mass Media Ethics* 14 (1999): 68–81.
seven rules of ethical evangelism and proselytizing	Gordon Lewis, "Ethical Evangelicalism, Yes! Unethical Proselytizing, No!" *Cultic Studies Journal* 2 (1986): 306–307.
no general rules save for general ethics	William Schrier, "The Ethics of Persuasion," *Quarterly Journal of Speech* 16 (1930): 476–486.
TARES test for truthfulness of the message, authenticity of the persuader, respect for the target, equity of appeal, and social responsibility	Sherry Baker and David L. Martinson, "The TARES Test: Five Principles for Ethical Persuasion," *Journal of Mass Media Ethics* 16 (2001): 148–175.

16. Robert B. Cialdini, "Social Influence and the Triple Tumor Structure of Organizational Dishonesty," in *Codes of Conduct: Behavioral Research into Business Ethics,* ed. D. M. Messick and A. E. Tenbrunsel, 44–58 (New York: Russell Sage Foundation, 1996); Robert B. Cialdini, "Of Tricks and Tumors: Some Little-Recognized Costs of Dishonest Use of Effective Social Influence," *Psychology and Marketing* 16 (1999): 91–98.

17. J. Turner, "The Company They Keep," *Science* 134 (July 14, 1961): 75.

18. Richard Jackson Harris, ed., *Information Processing Research in Advertising* (Hillsdale, N.J.: Lawrence Erlbaum, 1983); Ivan L. Preston, "Research on Deceptive Advertising: Commentary," in *Information Processing Research in Advertising,* ed. R. J. Harris (Hillsdale, N.J.: Lawrence Erlbaum, 1983), 289–305.

19. Richard L. Miller, Philip Brickman, and Diana Bolen, "Attribution versus Persuasion as a Means of Modifying Behavior," *Journal of Personality and Social Psychology* 31 (1975): 430–441.

20. Anthony R. Pratkanis, "Altercasting as an Influence Tactic," in *Attitudes, Behavior, and Social Context,* ed. D. J. Terry and M. A. Hogg, 201–226 (Mahwah, N.J.: Lawrence Erlbaum, 2000); Robert Rosenthal and Lenore Jacobsen, *Pygmalion in the Classroom: Teacher Expectation and Pupils' Intellectual Development* (New York: Holt, Rinehart and Winston, 1968).

21. For a discussion, see Edgar H. Schein, "Learning When and How to Lie: A Neglected Aspect of Organizational and Occupational Socialization," *Human Relations* 57 (2004): 259–273.

22. Seth Godin, *All Marketers Are Liars: The Power of Telling Authentic Stories in a Low-Trust World* (New York: Portfolio, 2005).

23. Pratkanis, "Social Influence Analysis."

24. Erich Fromm, *To Have or To Be?* (New York: Harper and Row, 1976); Erich Fromm, *You Shall Be As Gods: A Radical Interpretation of the Old Testament and Its Tradition* (New York: Henry Holt, 1991).

25. Robert H. Mnookin, *Bargaining with the Devil: When to Negotiate, When to Fight* (New York: Simon and Schuster, 2010).

26. For an excellent history, see J. Michael Sproule, *Propaganda and Democracy: The American Experience of Media and Mass Persuasion* (Cambridge: Cambridge Univ. Press, 1997).

27. Alfred McClung Lee and Elizabeth Briant Lee, *The Fine Art of Propaganda: A Study of Father Coughlin's Speeches* (New York: Harcourt Brace and Company, 1939); Alfred McClung Lee, *How to Understand Propaganda* (New York: Rinehart, 1952).

28. Violet Edwards, *Group Leader's Guide to Propaganda Analysis* (New York: Institute for Propaganda Analysis, 1938); Institute for Propaganda Analysis, *Propaganda: How to Recognize It and Deal with It—Experimental Unit of Study Materials in Propaganda Analysis for Use in Junior and Senior High Schools* (New York: Institute for Propaganda Analysis, 1938).

29. For taboo tactics for debates, see Henry Lee Ewbank and J. Jeffery Auer, *Discussion and Debate: Tools of a Democracy,* 2nd ed. (New York: Appleton-Century-Crofts, 1951). For unethical advertising techniques, see Charles H. Sandage and Vernon Ray Fryburger, *Advertising Theory and Practice,* 6th ed. (Homewood, Ill.: R. D. Irwin, 1963). For hidden persuaders, see Vance Packard, *The Hidden Persuaders* (New York: David McKay, 1957). For a list of unethical deceptions, see Wayne C. Minnick, *The Art of Persuasion* (Boston, Mass.: Houghton Mifflin, 1957). For deceptive practices used in news and journalism, see Eleanor O'Donnell MacLean, *Between the Lines: How to Detect Bias and Propaganda in the News and Everyday Life* (Montreal: Black Rose Books, 1981). For expansion of the IPA taboo devices to eighty-nine techniques, see Henry T. Conserva, *Propaganda Techniques* (Bloomington, Ind.: 1stBooks Library, 2003). For proposals for dealing with hate speech, see Raphael Cohen-Almagor, ed., *Liberal Democracy and the Limits of Tolerance: Essays in Honor and Memory of Yitzhak Rabin* (Ann Arbor: Univ. of Michigan Press, 2000); Cass R. Sunstein, *Democracy and the Problem of Free Speech* (New York: Free Press, 1993).

30. Sproule, *Propaganda and Democracy.*

31. James L. Sanderson and Walter K. Gordon, *Exposition and the English Language: Introductory Studies,* 2nd ed. (Englewood Cliffs, N.J.: Prentice-Hall, 1969).

32. WIS. STAT. 100.171 and ATCP 127.08, ATCP 127.14(44), ATCP 127.36, and ATCP 127.44 (14).

33. ATCP 127.04, ATCP 127.06, ATCP 127.14(14), ATCP 127.32, ATCP 127.34, and ATCP 127.44(14).

34. ATCP 127.04, ATCP 127.06, ATCP 127.32, and ATCP 127.34.

35. ATCP 127.14 (11) and ATCP 127.44 (11).

36. Conserva, *Propaganda Techniques.*

37. Jowett and O'Donnell, *Propaganda and Persuasion*; J. Michael Sproule, *Channels of Propaganda* (Bloomington, Ind.: ERIC/EDINFO Press, 1994).

38. Minnick, *Art of Persuasion,* 281.

39. William Garber, "Propaganda Analysis—To What Ends?" *American Journal of Sociology* 48 (1942): 240–245.

40. Ibid., 242.

41. Ibid., 240.

42. Ralph K. White, "Hitler, Roosevelt, and the Nature of War Propaganda," *Journal of Abnormal and Social Psychology* 44 (1949): 157–174; Ralph K. White, *Value-Analysis: The Nature and Use of the Method* (Glen Gardner, N.J.: Libertarian Press, 1951).

43. Schrier, "Ethics of Persuasion."

44. Pratkanis, "Social Influence Analysis."

45. Franklyn S. Haiman, "A Re-Examination of the Ethics of Persuasion," *Central States Speech Journal* 3 (1952): 4–9.

46. Ibid., 4.

47. Haiman, "Democratic Ethics and the Hidden Persuaders."

48. On argumentation: Ewbank and Auer, *Discussion and Debate*; James Howard McBurney and Glen Earl Mills, *Argumentation and Debate: Techniques of a Free Society,* 2nd ed. (New York: Macmillan, 1964). On critical thinking: Nicholas Capaldi, *The Art of Deception: An Introduction to Critical Thinking,* 3rd ed. (Buffalo, N.Y.: Prometheus Books, 1987); Jonathan C. Smith, *Pseudoscience and Extraordinary Claims of the Paranormal: A Critical Thinker's Toolkit* (Malden, Mass.: Wiley-Blackwell, 2010). On rhetoric: Francis X. Connolly, *A Rhetoric Case Book,* 2nd ed. (New York: Harcourt, Brace, and World, 1959); Edward P. J. Corbett, *Classical Rhetoric for the Modern Student,* 3rd ed. (New York: Oxford Univ. Press, 1990). On decision making: Daniel Kahneman, Paul Slovic, and Amos Tversky, eds. *Judgment under Uncertainty: Heuristics and Biases* (Cambridge: Cambridge Univ. Press, 1982); Richard E. Nisbett and Lee Ross, *Human Inference: Strategies and Shortcomings of Social Judgment* (Englewood Cliffs, N.J.: Prentice-Hall, 1980). On science: Richard P. Feynman, *Surely You're Joking, Mr. Feynman! (Adventures of a Curious Character)* (New York: Norton, 1985); Richard P. Feynman, *What Do You Care What Other People Think?: Further Adventures of a Curious Character* (New York: Norton, 1988). On attitude change: Pratkanis and Aronson, *Age of Propaganda.*

49. For the argument for and against free speech, see Marlin, *Propaganda and the Ethics of Persuasion.*

50. Franklyn S. Haiman, "The Rhetoric of the Streets: Some Legal and Ethical Considerations," *Quarterly Journal of Speech* 53 (1967): 99–114; Franklyn S. Haiman, "Nonverbal Communication and the First Amendment: The Rhetoric of the Streets Revisited," *Quarterly Journal of Speech* 68 (1982): 371–83.

51. Michael Battle, *Reconciliation: The Ubuntu Theology of Desmond Tutu* (Cleveland, Ohio: Pilgrim Press, 1997); Desmond Mpilo Tutu, *No Future without Forgiveness* (New York: Doubleday, 2000).

52. Adam Smith, *The Theory of Moral Sentiments* (Indianapolis, Ind.: Liberty Fund, 1982).

53. Stephen Toulmin, *The Uses of Argument* (Cambridge: Cambridge Univ. Press, 1958); Chaïm Perelman, *The Realm of Rhetoric* (Notre Dame, Ind.: Univ. of Notre Dame Press, 1982); Chaïm Perelman and Lucie Olbrechts-Tyteca, *The New Rhetoric: A Treatise on Argumentation* (Notre Dame, Ind.: Univ. of Notre Dame Press, 1969); Douglas N. Walton, *The Place of Emotion in Argument* (University Park: Pennsylvania State Univ. Press, 1992); Douglas N. Walton, *Arguments from Ignorance* (University Park: Pennsylvania State Univ. Press, 1996); Douglas N. Walton, *Appeal to Expert Opinion: Arguments from Authority* (University Park: Pennsylvania State Univ. Press, 1997); Douglas N. Walton, *Appeal to Popular Opinion* (University Park: Pennsylvania State Univ. Press, 1999).

54. Pratkanis and Aronson, *Age of Propaganda.*

55. Richard E. Petty and John T. Cacioppo, *Communication and Persuasion: Central and Peripheral Routes to Attitude Change* (New York: Springer-Verlag, 1986).

56. Donald Thistlethwaite, "Attitude and Structure as Factors in the Distortion of Reasoning," *Journal of Abnormal and Social Psychology* 45 (1950): 442–458. For a list of ways that attitudes impact cognitive processes, see Anthony R. Pratkanis, "The Cognitive Representation of Attitudes," in *Attitude Structure and Function*, ed. Anthony R. Pratkanis, S. J. Breckler, and Anthony G. Greenwald, 71–98 (Hillsdale, N.J.: Lawrence Erlbaum, 1989); Anthony R. Pratkanis and Anthony G. Greenwald, "A Socio-Cognitive Model of Attitude Structure and Function," in *Advances in Experimental Social Psychology*, vol. 22, ed. Leonard Berkowitz, 245–285 (New York: Academic Press, 1989).

57. Farhad Manjoo, *True Enough: Learning to Live in a Post-Fact Society* (Hoboken, N.J.: Wiley, 2008).

58. Brembeck and Howell, *Persuasion.*

59. David Michaels, *Doubt Is Their Product: How Industry's Assault on Science Threatens Your Health* (Oxford: Oxford Univ. Press, 2008); Naomi Oreskes and Erik M. Conway, *Merchants of Doubt: How a Handful of Scientists Obscured the Truth on Issues from Tobacco Smoke to Global Warming* (New York: Bloomsbury Press, 2010); Eugenie Carol Scott, *Evolution vs. Creationism: An Introduction*, 2nd ed. (Berkeley, Calif.: Univ. of California Press, 2009).

60. Richard Whately, *Elements of Rhetoric*, 7th ed. (London: John W. Parker, 1846); Schrier, "Ethics of Persuasion."

61. Brembeck and Howell, *Persuasion*, 238.

62. Henry Ward Beecher, *Yale Lectures on Preaching* (New York: J. B. Ford, 1872).

63. Baker and Huntington, *The Principles of Argumentation.*

64. Robert M. Entman, *Democracy without Citizens: Media and the Decay of American Politics* (New York: Oxford Univ. Press, 1989).

65. Pratkanis and Aronson, *Age of Propaganda.*

66. Jay Black, "Semantics and Ethics of Propaganda," *Journal of Mass Media Ethics* 16 (2001): 121–137.

67. Saul D. Alinsky, *Rules for Radicals: A Practical Primer for Realistic Radicals* (New York: Vintage Books, 1972).

68. Ibid., 12–13.

69. Ibid., 11.

70. Ralph D. Barney and Jay Black, "Ethics and Professional Persuasive Communications," *Public Relations Review* 20 (1994): 233–248.

71. N.R.F. Maier and Allen R. Solem, "The Contribution of a Discussion Leader to the Quality of Group Thinking: The Effective Use of Minority Opinion," *Human Relations* 5 (1952): 277–288; Charlan J. Nemeth, "Differential Contributions of Majority and Minority Influence," *Psychological Review* 93, no. 1 (1986): 23–32.

72. Thomas Hobbes, *Leviathan, Parts I and II* (Indianapolis: Bobbs-Merrill, 1958), 108.

73. For a discussion of harm that can occur in an adversarial system, see Arthur Isak Applbaum, *Ethics for Adversaries: The Morality of Roles in Public and Professional Life* (Princeton, N.J.: Princeton Univ. Press, 1999).

74. Mnookin, *Bargaining with the Devil.*

75. A framework for resolving such conflicts has been proposed by Amy Gutmann and Dennis F. Thompson, *Democracy and Disagreement* (Cambridge, Mass.: Harvard Univ. Press, 1996).

76. John Kane, *The Politics of Moral Capital* (Cambridge: Cambridge Univ. Press, 2001).

77. James E. Grunig, "Symmetrical Presuppositions as a Framework for Public Relations Theory," in *Public Relations Theory,* ed. C. H. Botan and V. Hazleton, 17–44 (Hillsdale, N.J.: Lawrence Erlbaum, 1989).

78. For a discussion of these models and their links to classical rhetoric, see Charles W. Marsh, "Public Relations Ethics: Contrasting Models from the Rhetorics of Plato, Aristotle, and Isocrates," *Journal of Mass Media Ethics* 16 (2001): 78–98. For a discussion of ethics in client-centered models, see Barney and Black, "Ethics and Professional Persuasive Communications."

79. Stephan Schiffman, *The 25 Most Dangerous Sales Myths (and How to Avoid Them)* (Avon, Mass.: Adams Media, 2004).

80. Charles R. Duke, Gregory M. Pickett, Les Carlson, and Stephen J. Grove, "A Method for Evaluating the Ethics of Fear Appeals," *Journal of Public Policy and Marketing* 12 (1993): 120–130.

81. Douglas McGregor, *The Human Side of Enterprise,* annotated ed. (New York: McGraw-Hill, 2006).

82. Roger Fisher, William Ury, and Bruce Patton, *Getting to Yes: Negotiating Agreement without Giving In,* 2nd ed. (New York, N.Y.: Penguin Books, 1991).

83. For a discussion of the significance of listening for current U.S. public diplomacy, see Nancy Snow, *The Arrogance of American Power: What U.S. Leaders Are Doing Wrong and Why It's Our Duty to Dissent* (Lanham, Md.: Rowman and Littlefield, 2007).

84. Charles T. Salmon, "Campaigns for Social 'Improvement': An Overview of Value, Rationales, and Impacts," in *Information Campaigns: Balancing Social Values and Social Change,* ed. C. T. Salmon, 19–53 (Thousand Oaks, Calif.: Sage Publications, 1989).

85. Nancy Snow, *Propaganda, Inc.: Selling America's Culture to the World,* 1st ed. (New York: Seven Stories Press, 1998).

86. Frederick Douglass, *Life and Times of Frederick Douglass* (New York: Gramercy Books, 1993); William Hague, *William Wilberforce: The Life of the Great Anti-Slave Trade Campaigner* (Orlando, Fla.: Harcourt, 2007); Henry Mayer, *All on Fire: William Lloyd Garrison and the Abolition of Slavery* (New York: St. Martin's Press, 1998); Steven M. Wise, *Though the Heavens May Fall: The Landmark Trial That Led to the End of Human Slavery* (Cambridge, Mass.: Da Capo Press, 2005).

87. Robert Mann, *Wartime Dissent in America: A History and Anthology* (New York: Palgrave Macmillan, 2010); George Hendrick and Willene Hendrick, *Why Not Every Man?: African Americans and Civil Disobedience in the Quest for the Dream* (Chicago: Ivan R. Dee, 2005); Allister Haddon Sparks, *Tomorrow Is Another Country: The Inside Story of South Africa's Road to Change* (New York: Hill and Wang, 1995).

88. Anthony R. Pratkanis and Marlene E. Turner, "The Year Cool Papa Bell Lost the Batting Title: Mr. Branch Rickey and Mr. Jackie Robinson's Plea for Affirmative Action," *Nine: A Journal of Baseball History and Social Policy Perspectives* 2 (1994): 260–276; Anthony R. Pratkanis and Marlene E. Turner, "Nine Principles of Successful Affirmative Action: Mr. Branch Rickey, Mr. Jackie Robinson, and the Integration of Baseball," *Nine: A Journal of Baseball History and Social Policy Perspectives* 3 (1994): 36–65.

89. Paul Brace and Barbara Hinckley, *Follow the Leader: Opinion Polls and the Modern Presidents* (New York: Basic Books, 1992), 82.

90. On democratic persuasion: Gordon W. Allport, "The Nature of Democratic Morale," in *Civilian Morale,* ed. G. Watson, 3–18 (New York: Houghton-Mifflin, 1942); Robert King Merton, *Mass Persuasion: The Social Psychology of a War Bond Drive* (New York: Harper, 1946), 188; Karl R. Wallace, "An Ethical Basis of Communication," *Speech Teacher* 4 (1955): 1–9; James Friedrich and David Douglass, "Ethics and the Persuasive Enterprise of Teaching Psychology," *American Psychologist* 53 (1998): 549–562.

91. Ralph K. White, "Propaganda: Morally Questionable and Morally Unquestionable Techniques," *Annals of the American Academy of Political and Social Science* 398 (1971): 26–35.

92. Sandel, *Justice.*

93. Arthur Allen Leff, "Unspeakable Ethics, Unnatural Law," *Duke Law Journal* (1979): 1229–1249.

94. I listed some of the advantages of a democracy in Anthony R. Pratkanis, "Public Diplomacy in International Conflicts: A Social Influence Analysis," in *Routledge Handbook of Public Diplomacy,* ed. Nancy Snow and Philip M. Taylor (New York: Routledge, 2009), 111–153.

95. Anthony R. Pratkanis and Marlene E. Turner, "Persuasion and Democracy: Strategies for Increasing Deliberative Participation and Enacting Social Change," *Journal of Social Issues* 52 (1996): 187–205.

96. For my answers to these questions in regard to mass media and elections, see Anthony R. Pratkanis, "The Social Psychology of Mass Communications: An American Perspective," in *States of Mind: American and Post-Soviet Perspectives on Contemporary Issues in Psychology,* ed. D. F. Halpern and A. Voiskounsky (New York: Oxford Univ. Press, 1997), 126–159; Anthony R. Pratkanis, "Propaganda and Deliberative Persuasion: The

Implications of Americanized Mass Media for Emerging and Established Democracies," in *The Practice of Social Influence in Multiple Cultures,* ed. W. Wosinska, R. B. Cialdini, J. Reykowski, and D. W. Barrett, 59–285 (Mahwah, N.J.: Lawrence Erlbaum, 2001).

97. Bill Moyers, *WWII: The Propaganda Battle* (Washington, D.C.: PBS Video, 1984).

98. Pratkanis, "Social Influence Analysis."

99. John E. Marston, "Right and Wrong in Public Relations," in *Ethics and Persuasion,* ed. R. L. Johannesen, 173–191 (New York: Random House, 1967).

100. Epigraph: Schrier, "Ethics of Persuasion," 476. Pratkanis and Aronson, *Age of Propaganda*; Anthony R. Pratkanis and Doug Shadel, *Weapons of Fraud: A Source Book for Fraud Fighters* (Seattle: AARP, 2005).

101. For examples of trade-offs in influence, see Helmut Jungermann, "Ethical Dilemmas in Risk Communication," in *Codes of Conduct: Behavioral Research into Business Ethics,* ed. D. M. Messick and A. E. Tenbrunsel, 300–317 (New York: Russell Sage Foundation, 1996).

102. William A. Smith, "Ethics and the Social Marketer: A Framework for Practitioners," in *Ethics in Social Marketing,* ed. A. R. Andreasen, 1–16 (Washington, D.C.: Georgetown Univ. Press, 2001).

103. Dara Kay Cohen and Amelia Hoover Green, "Dueling Incentives: Sexual Violence in Liberia and the Politics of Human Rights Advocacy," *Journal of Peace Research* 49 (2012): 445–458.

104. Beecher, *Yale Lectures on Preaching*; Baker and Huntington, *The Principles of Argumentation.*

105. Sharp, *There Are Realistic Alternatives.*

106. Sproule, *Channels of Propaganda.* See also Stanley B. Cunningham, "Responding to Propaganda: An Ethical Enterprise," *Journal of Mass Media Ethics* 16 (2001): 138–147.

107. Niccolò Machiavelli, *The Prince* (Northbrook, Ill.: AHN Publishing, 1947); Niccolò. Machiavelli, *Discourses on Livy* (Chicago: Univ. of Chicago Press, 1996). For an excellent discussion of Machiavelli and his concept of virtù, see Quentin Skinner, *Machiavelli: A Very Short Introduction* (New York: Oxford Univ. Press, 2000).

108. I base the following on the brilliant analysis of James L. Golden and Alan L. Golden, *Thomas Jefferson and the Rhetoric of Virtue* (Lanham, Md.: Rowman and Littlefield, 2002).

109. For early twentieth-century examples of teaching about democratic virtù, see George Albert Coe, *Educating for Citizenship: The Sovereign State as Ruler and as Teacher* (New York: Charles Scribner's Sons, 1932); Educational Policies Commission, *Learning the Ways of Democracy: A Case Book of Civil Education* (Washington, D.C.: National Education Association of the United States and the American Association of School Administrators, 1940).

110. Ronald Brownstein, *The Second Civil War: How Extreme Partisanship Has Paralyzed Washington and Polarized America* (New York: Penguin Press, 2007); Mickey Edwards, *The Parties versus the People: How to Turn Republicans and Democrats into Americans* (New Haven, Conn.: Yale Univ. Press, 2012).

3

PROPAGANDA AND PUBLIC DISCOURSE

Seven Deadly Dangers

J. MICHAEL SPROULE

Propaganda can simply designate a normal process whereby interested parties diffuse messages in pursuit of objectives. Yet there is always the matter of that other usage of the term—a denotation highlighting hidden or disreputable elements of persuasion. In this connection, Edward L. Bernays, a founder of public relations, used to quip that social influence could be divided into two categories, "propa-ganda" and "im-propaganda."[1]

In developing my list of suspicious contemporary persuasions, I selected situations displaying one or more of four commonly recognized danger signals. These include: (1) covert activity that disguises the true source of the message; (2) massive orchestration of symbolism under the auspices of institutions, media channels, or professions; (3) tricky language in its various forms, together with distorted visual images; and (4) an overall orientation to a narrower special interest rather than a more generally public interest.[2] What follows is my report of seven dangerous communicative liaisons, having social and/or governmental tangents, given in an ascending order reflective of their relative threat to the public interest.

Deadly danger Number 7 concerns the *ideological use of the law*. One of the hallmarks of American democracy—something that we proudly invoke to distinguish ourselves from totalitarian regimes—is the rule of law. It follows that students of propaganda will be concerned about cases where politicking or self-interest may have influenced indictments brought to the court by federal, state, or local prosecutors. Under the headline of "Prosecutors Gone Wild," John Farmer, former attorney general of New Jersey, criticizes prosecutors for recent indictments thrown out or convictions overturned. Prosecutorial error included: (1) overreach, as evidenced by the dismissal of corruption charges against Senator Ted Stevens; (2) failure to disclose evidence, as when terrorism convictions were reversed in the case of two Detroit men; or (3) publicity seeking and other misconduct, as in the case of a county district attorney disbarred in the aftermath of the 2006 Duke lacrosse players rape case. Equally worrisome were allegations that the Bush administration fired nine federal prosecutors in response to complaints by local Republicans or political operatives such as Karl Rove.[3] An internal investigation by the Bush Justice Department supported charges that in at least three cases political pressures evidently had been behind the dismissals, as when David C. Iglesias of New Mexico lost his job on account of insufficient zeal in prosecuting scandals involving Democrats.[4]

Arguably propagandistic uses of the law are not restricted to excesses of government, as is discernible from suits brought for alleged misrepresentation or libel. In 2011, an Alabama attorney filed a class action suit for $5 million in damages on the basis that Jimmy Carter's book, *Palestine: Peace Not Apartheid,* was marketed as truthful despite containing many errors. Carter's publishers argued that the suit represented a simple case of undermining free speech rights on the basis of mere political disagreement, and three months later the suit was withdrawn.[5] In this connection, it is not just U.S. courts that can be used against American advocacy, because under the auspices of the Internet overseas tribunals may consider a U.S. author to be under their jurisdiction. The term "libel tourism" has been applied to the filing of libel suits against foreign authors in British courts. Prompted by suits filed against Americans, four U.S. states passed laws protecting their residents from adverse judgments originating in England.[6] One case attracting particular attention was that of Rachel Ehrenfeld, whose legal costs in England exceeded $200,000, and who, in addition, was ordered to pay damages to three Saudi businessman for alleging that they had financially supported al-Qaeda before September 11, 2001.[7]

Deadly danger Number 6 in the list of propaganda's contemporary intersection with discourse gives more direct attention to the Internet and concerns possible *limitations on Internet access.* The discursive availability of the World Wide Web is a matter of some concern in a time when the Internet shows signs of becoming the predominant public forum. Accessible through computers, smart phones, and handheld gaming devices, the web holds the promise of equalizing to an extent the attention given to society's competing voices. Where press critic A. J. Liebling famously observed that "freedom of the press is guaranteed only to those who own one,"[8] ordinary people may succeed in getting their views circulated widely through Internet blogging, tweeting, social media networking, and through commentary on message boards and chat rooms. In all cases, digital advocates leverage the web to gain a kind of public forum visibility more analogous to that of a publisher than that of a street corner orator. Illustrative was the video game community rallying online against a report broadcast on the Fox News Channel program *The Live Desk with Martha MacCallum.* In a case of individuals equalizing the clout of a major cable outlet, the group organized against criticisms broadcast on FNC that *Mass Effect,* a popular science fiction game, constituted women-exploiting pornography. One aspect of this grassroots Internet uprising was an organized effort to give low ratings on the Amazon website to a book written by a source quoted on the program, a person who later admitted to misconstruing the game based on indirect and hearsay information.[9] Although the greatest threat to the Internet as a public forum may be the phenomenon of information overload in a context where media consumption has increased threefold since the 1960s,[10] it remains the case that anything lessening relatively equal website and content access is of interest to propaganda critics.

Analysts concerned about constraints on web access frequently focus on the idea of "net neutrality," that is, the extent to which Internet carriers—cable and phone companies—afford equal treatment to websites and to varying forms of Internet content. In an example often pointed to, the Federal Communications Commission in late 2008 sanctioned Comcast for slowing down certain peer-to-peer sharing of public domain material on its lines, a regulatory action later overturned by an appeals court.[11] Questions relevant to net neutrality include whether Internet service providers charge some users higher rates for carrying their content, whether dominant websites such as Google employ so-called agent servers to place their content closer to end users, or whether broadband providers (such as Comcast or Verizon) favor their own content-streaming services over independent ones. Some commentators recommend that the Federal Communications Commission require Internet service providers to offer subscribers unfettered access to all legal web content as well as all applications, services, and devices. A persistent opposing argument is that constraints on the pricing policies of Internet providers interfere with their ability to recover costs for building net infrastructure.[12] For propaganda critics concerned with the access of ordinary citizens to the public forum, net neutrality will be an issue to watch.

Item Number 5 in a list of intersections between propaganda and discourse shifts our attention to the *use of science for institutional or partisan gain.* As with the law, science represents an arena of human endeavor ideally governed by principles higher than those of self-interest or remuneration. Given the elevated purposes of science, propaganda critics would be interested in the apparent subordination of science to institution or party. In this connection, I would point to two contemporary situations, one corporate and the other partisan, where science arguably has been leveraged to special interest advantage.

The first instance has to do with ties between the medical device and pharmaceutical industries and scientific medical research. What's the danger of propaganda here? Let us count the ways. Exhibit A relates to covert activity in academic articles assessing the effectiveness of medical devices. A Columbia University study found that in twenty-five of the thirty-two cases examined the authors failed to disclose the financial support they received from medical companies.[13] Exhibit B concerns findings that an estimated 7 percent of articles published in the *Journal of the American Medical Association,* and 11 percent in the *New England Journal of Medicine,* were ghostwritten by drug company-sponsored writers. In such cases, independent academicians later agreed to work with a preexisting draft and serve as the named authors.[14] In the case of research on hormone replacement therapy, ghostwriters for pharmaceutical companies produced twenty-six scientific papers in eighteen medical journals between 1998 and 2005 supporting the therapy and minimizing such risks as heart disease; in no case did the research reports disclose the role of Wyeth Pharmaceuticals in underwriting the work.[14]

Obviously, medical research is not necessarily invalid for the fact of its having been industry-financed or ghostwritten, although when researchers are beholden to institutions, and fail to disclose the fact, we should be doubly alert as to the possibility of fraud. In 2009, Baystate Medical Center in Springfield, Massachusetts, reported that a researcher at the hospital had fabricated data in clinical trials that had served as the basis for twenty-one journal articles. This research was largely underwritten by Pfizer and offered favorable clinical assessments of two pain-relieving drugs sold by that company.[15]

In addition to propagandistic liaisons in medical studies, we may turn to climate research as a case where partisan politics has become inextricably linked to inquiry. Here it is a matter of interest to a propaganda critic that for the Tea Party movement, rejection of global warming has become an article of faith. A poll conducted in late 2010 showed that only 14 percent of Tea Party supporters viewed global warming as an environmental problem, as contrasted to 49 percent of the rest of the public.[16] Edward L. Bernays built his public relations practice around the idea that most opinions of the kind related to climate change originate with group leaders and filter down to the general public.[17] Such a process may be observed in comments by a Tea Party founder in Corydon, Indiana, who argued that climate change was "a flat-out lie" based on what he had learned from Rush Limbaugh, and as further sanctioned by the Bible's declaration that God made the earth for the use of people.[18] Others of a similar mindset argue that climate scientists are part of a larger conspiracy to impose world government, a view reflected in a letter to the editor from my own local paper where the author alleged that recent disclosures proved that climate change was a "scam" in which Al Gore and others misrepresented natural variations so as to profit financially.[19]

Climate change, generally, and global warming, particularly, seem poised to become scientific principles that, like Darwinian evolution, will energize passionate opposition for generations. But with this difference: The results are predicted to show up decisively by the middle of this century. So, it is a matter of some concern to a propaganda critic when high-level opponents of climate change engage in what some would construe as partisan ploys. What are we to make of demands by the attorney general of Virginia for thousands of documents related to work by a leading climate researcher? The demand was based on the premise that this scientist's research was fraudulent, a claim repudiated by the University of Virginia which, in turn, alleged that the attorney general was simply taking aim at findings he disagreed with.[20] What about allegations that the White House in 2008 ordered the Environmental Protection Agency to recompute data so as to minimize the potential economic benefits of reducing carbon dioxide emissions?[21] Or that the vice president's office demanded that descriptions of health risks of global warming be deleted from EPA testimony to Congress?[22] Similarly, what are the implications of Texas oil companies having spent millions of dollars to place on the ballot and widely advertise an initiative that would suspend a California air pollution control law focused on greenhouse gas emissions?[23] Governor Arnold Schwarzenegger characterized the struggle over Proposition 23 as "a great battle between good and evil—it's like a movie. You have the villain dressed in dark black, and the good guys in white and green."[24]

And now we are on to danger Number 4 in my list of worrisome encounters of propaganda and discourse—*propaganda in the news.* News has long been regarded as crucial in the informational nourishing of the public sphere, a democratic function that greatly concerned Walter Lippmann, who noted that while small-town folks were able to encounter directly and personally the circumstances of their daily life, big-city people needed to rely on journalism as an intermediary between themselves and important doings in the metropolis.[25] The business model of so-called mainstream channels—CNN seemingly representing the paradigm case—appears to be that of audience maximization by avoiding offense to viewers on either end of the left-right continuum. Such a constructed "objectivity" chiefly is effected either by a softer (less probing) treatment of current events or by panels of commentators balanced for ideology. Yet we may question whether this endeavor ultimately offers the public a superficial and unhelpful coverage of politics.

Although cable news outlets are loath to explicitly define themselves in ideological terms, the familiar political breakdown includes MSNBC's recently skewing left, Fox's longstanding tilt even farther to the right, and CNN's "positioning itself as the objective option for viewers."[26] Here some commentators criticize CNN and other broad-spectrum outlets for an arguable overreliance on one of journalism's characteristic story frames—that of pro/con. In a parody of this approach, Paul Krugman hypothesized that "if one party declared that the earth was flat, the headlines would read 'Views Differ on Shape of Planet.'"[27] Seemingly a special provocation is required for a mainstream journalist to tiptoe into the political fray by going below the discursive surface. Just such an instance occurred when CNN's Anderson Cooper apparently became incensed by Representative Michele Bachmann's having used his program to inject into the mainstream the claim that President Obama's trip to India would cost $200 million per day. Instead of framing the story as a simple pro/con phenomenon—as in such a hypothetical headline as "Controversy Continues on Cost of Presidential Trip"—Cooper traced the story to its apparent origin, an Indian press service that allegedly quoted an unnamed provincial official. Cooper then demonstrated that the story was being circulated as fact by the Drudge Report, Rush Limbaugh, Glenn Beck, and others, and Cooper offered an inflation-adjusted estimate of about $5.2 million a day based on Bill Clinton's trip to Africa.[28] Anderson's modern muckraking episode aside, Arianna Huffington opined that the media's biggest problem was a wont "to present all sides to the story [and] wash their hands of the possibility of finding the truth."[29]

Probably it was of no great moment whether certain media outlets and commentators exaggerated the cost of President Obama's Asian trip. However, the case of 1950s McCarthyism shows that there may be a danger to democracy when journalists passively lend credibility to questionable claims. In his classic history of American newspapers, Michael Schudson reminds us of the typically serious treatment given by newspapers to Senator Joe McCarthy's always-interesting charges even though reporters were, in the main, privately dismissive of them. As a result, McCarthy benefited from a faux balance produced by mainstream journalism's self-conscious and self-protective effort to appear objective.[30]

The mainstream mania for drawing broad audiences through such talismans of neutrality as face-value or pro-con reporting takes us, inevitably, to the contrapuntal approach of catering to one end of the spectrum, famously embraced by Fox News Channel (FNC), the cable news outlet currently enjoying the largest audience. Commentary on the politics of television news typically commences with some kind of content analysis that asserts, or probes for, a rightward or leftward slant of coverage. With regard to Fox, one of the most extensive efforts in this regard emerged in the documentary film *Outfoxed,* which, in one case, compared the number of Democrats vs. Republicans who appeared in one-on-one interviews with Brit Hume on his *Special Report* program during a period of twenty-five weeks. As reported by monitors for Fairness and Accuracy in Reporting, the ratio was five Republicans for every one Democrat.[31] The same rightist favorability ratio obtains on a new Fox talk show, *The Five,* where the pattern is for a lone liberal to be opposed by four conservatives.[32] Yet the trouble with content data of these kinds is that they are never really convincing to someone who doesn't want to believe them. One can always pick apart the results both by faulting such internal criteria as labeling commentators conservative or liberal or by faulting the analyst—for example, by noting that *Outfoxed* was promoted by MoveOn.org, a left-leaning Political Action Committee. So, it is useful to take a more institutional tack in looking for indicators of political bias on Fox.

We may begin by contrasting the historical origin of network broadcasting to that of Fox News. Broadcast news began some eighty years ago largely as a way to fill radio time for which the networks were unable to secure commercial sponsorship, and was expanded when news shows began to draw a profitable audience.[33] As news broadcasting became more prevalent, networks used the balance format as a convenient way to help affiliated local stations count news programming as part of public service according to Federal Communications Commission guidelines. News broadcasting was heavily influenced by the FCC doctrines of fairness in coverage and equal time for opposing candidates.[34] In contrast, Fox News originated as the particular project of Rupert Murdoch of the News Corporation, who brought on Roger Ailes, a former media strategist for presidents Nixon, Reagan, and George H. W. Bush, to head up the operation. (Ailes has directed it ever since). In remarks given at a news conference announcing the birth of Fox News, Ailes admitted that some might question his appointment, given his career-long work in politics; nevertheless, he insisted, "I left politics a number of years ago and have run a news organization for the last two years."[35]

Given its politico-institutional origins, it's not particularly surprising that Fox draws far more attention for alleged bias than any other major news outlet (ABC, CBS, CNN, MSNBC, NBC). When a network name is combined with "news bias" and entered into a search engine—as in "Fox news bias" or "MSNBC news bias," the results for Fox in a Google search show the Murdoch-Ailes network to be thirty times more associated with the expression "news bias" than CNN and seven times more associated with this phrase in a Yahoo search. Compared to MSNBC, Fox proved to be fifty times more associated with bias via Google and thirteen times more via Yahoo.[36] Commentators have noted two recent partisan characteristics peculiar to Fox as a news outlet, one being its having employed before 2011 many of the major Republican political leaders, including Mike Huckabee, Sarah Palin, Newt Gingrich, John Bolton, and Rick Santorum.[37] In addition, Gawker, the New York-based blog, reported that Roger Ailes actively lobbied Governor Chris Christie of New Jersey to throw his hat into the Republican ring. When Gawker filed suit to obtain official records of Christie's contacts with Ailes, the governor asserted executive privilege, implying that Ailes was an adviser.[38] Another somewhat unique-to-Fox feature is the network's sometimes permitting Republican candidates—GOP Ohio senate candidate John Kasich and Nevada senate candidate Sharron Angle—to solicit for funds in the context of an interview, something that MSNBC officials cite as evidence that their network does not simply constitute an opposite-side version of Fox.[39]

Evidences that Fox News powerfully tilts to the right, and in favor of the GOP, are worrisome because of the generally accepted notion that news reporting represents an informational bulwark of democracy in a complex world. Magnifying this basic concern would be further indications that there is something identifiable as a "Fox News Effect" in American politics. A study by the National Bureau of Economic Research indicated that Fox News increased support for Republican presidential candidates by 0.4 to 0.7 percentage points—in 1996 and 2000—as reflected in a survey of 9,256 towns served by Fox News. Similar effects were reported for Republican senate candidates. The study concluded: "Our estimates imply that Fox News convinced 3 to 8 percent of its viewers to vote Republican."[40]

Perhaps an even more insidious danger to democracy than news bias is the *manipulation of copyright law* to stifle socio-political commentary—item Number 3 in my list of propagandistic threats to public deliberation. In its original form, copyright emerged not only to protect authors and other content creators but also to preserve the common culture by means of a limitation in the length of copyright. From 1790 through relatively recently, copyright protection was available for a period of fourteen years, later made renewable for another fourteen. Today, successive alterations of the law have transformed these modest original privileges into an almost permanent kind of intellectual ownership that extends for seventy years past the death of the author (who, paradoxically, as a result of work-for-hire impositions and an unequal negotiating power may have been stripped of any ownership).

With billions to be earned from the Internet distribution of music and video—and with the concomitant problem of content piracy—profit-protection looms large in present-day applications of copyright to electronic communication. Draconian penalties for music downloads, provided for under the Digital Theft Deterrent Act, have given a rather crass appearance to the media industry's content-ownership pursuits, as in the case of a woman ordered to pay $220,000 after conviction for pirating twenty-four songs, although a Federal judge granted a new trial on the basis that the award was obviously exorbitant in relation to the claimed harm.[41] Ironically, this second trial resulted in a $1.92 million penalty for the two dozen tunes shared in a noncommercial context.[42] In a 2010 case, a jury awarded $675,000 to four record companies to be paid by a graduate student who downloaded and distributed thirty songs, a penalty that an appellate judge found to be so "unprecedented and oppressive" as to violate the due process clause of the Fifth Amendment.[43] Seemingly, American copyright law has now moved past the point of parody. Arguably we have in operation a propagandistic use of law, that is, an industry employing the courts as a collection agency rather than adjudicator of justice.

The apparently manic profit-protectionist mindset of content rights holders represents a threat to public discourse particularly as regards new media. Notwithstanding a provision in the law for fair use of copyrighted material by new content creators, maladroit excesses in defending copyright on the part of the communication industry inherently narrow the field for expression in the public domain. Yet in addition to this money-motivated leveraging of copyright against new content, we may point to cases where copyright law has been used directly to restrict public communication for reasons of institutional image or ideological advantage. Under the Digital Millennium Copyright Act of 1998 websites gain a presumptive protection against suits for copyright violation if they promptly remove content objected to by a claimant. Just such an instance occurred when YouTube, bowing to CBS, removed a segment in which David Letterman discussed an alleged instance of extortion relating to his relationship with a female employee.[44]

The U.S. Congress is continuing hearings on legislation that further augments this power of copyright claimants to interfere with content posted on aggregating websites such as YouTube and Facebook. The proposed House bill, the Stop Online Piracy Act (SOPA), would empower copyright claimants to seek a court order blocking all access to an allegedly offending website. Although proponents of the law point to the existence of foreign sites where copyright piracy is rampant, critics of SOPA are concerned with the law's arguable overreach in stifling online content. More generally, this proposed legislation reflects the worrisome tendency in digital media law to grant broad prerogatives to copyright claimants and to minimize the rights of other content creators who operate under the doctrine of fair use.[45] Content amalgamators such as the *Huffington Post* invoke fair use to justify their excerpting material from other sites, an activity that they claim actually adds value to the original content by making it more widely visible. Nevertheless, the *New York Times*'s Brian Stelter reported that "copyright infringement lawsuits directed at bloggers and other online publishers seem to be on the rise."[46] Harvard Law School professor Lawrence Lessig cited one particularly egregious case of copyright law leveraged to stifle political content. Lawyers for New York assembly candidate George Amedore asserted that their client's remarks could not be displayed in an opponent's TV spot because Amedore had "exclusive copyright rights" to all parts of this video interview that had been given originally to the *Albany Business Review*.[47] Another instance of the potentially chilling effect of copyright invocation may be seen in the "Fox News Channel Statement on 'Outfoxed.'" The network's response to criticisms contained in *Outfoxed* began with these words: "The illegal copyright infringement actions. . . ."[48] If granted credence, such a copyright assertion potentially would eliminate the use of news channel material in political commentary. In the digital age, will copyright claims replace "patriotism" as the "last refuge of the scoundrel?"

Item Number 2 in the list of worrisome connections between propaganda and discursive democracy takes us a bit beyond the borders of the United States, calling our critical attention to Rupert Murdoch as a worldwide media baron. Exhibit A in this connection would not be Fox News in the United States, but rather broader evidences in England of Murdoch's using media as a political lever to advance his varied interests. Let's first examine the term "media baron," a phrase which represents an updating of the 1930s expression "press lord." As related in George Seldes's classic *Lords of the Press,* newspaper royalists imposed their personal political slant on media content as a way, simultaneously, to enhance their business prospects. Best remembered today is chain owner William Randolph Hearst, although Seldes provided revelations concerning some two dozen media owners, including Harry Chandler of the *Los Angeles Times,* who allegedly skewed coverage of labor to benefit his newspaper operation and skewed coverage of the Mexican revolution to advance his land and cattle interests south of the border.[49]

Propaganda critics would express concern about reports that Murdoch has personally influenced the content of political reporting in his *New York Post* newspaper.[50] However, it is not just academicians who object to Rupert Murdoch as a possible reincarnation of the 1930s-style press lord. Long troubled by his highly idiosyncratic style of operation, hardheaded traders routinely discount the stock price of Murdoch's News Corporation by 20 to 40 percent as compared to such comparable media companies as Walt Disney or Time Warner.[51] An illustration of Murdoch's politically activist approach would be his quickly seizing upon the opportunity presented by *Citizens United v. Federal Election Commission*—a 2010 Supreme Court decision permitting corporations to donate unlimited sums directly to political organizations—to favor the Republican Governors Association with a $1 million contribution from the News Corporation.[52] Pressed by shareholders to explain the donation, Murdoch conceded that his action was "unusual," but he defended channeling corporate dollars to Republican politics as consistent with "the interests of our shareholders and the country."[53] Yet News Corporation shareholders have for decades complained that the company, lacking a board of directors truly independent of the Murdoch family, shows a questionable track record in a business profit-focused acquisition of media properties.[54] A notable case was when Murdoch apparently overpaid substantially to acquire the politically influential *Wall Street Journal.*[55]

Further reflecting the perceived propagandistic orientation of the

Murdoch media has been the unfolding scandal centering upon allegations that the News Corporation's outlets in Britain engaged in illegal phone- and Internet-hacking, destroyed evidence, directed numerous payments to police officials, and paid lavish settlements to buy silence in connection with early lawsuits alleging misconduct. To such allegations of illegality need be added troubling questions of political influence raised, on the one hand, by Murdoch-controlled tabloids abusing politicians together with, on the other hand, arguably obsequious official and social connections existing between Murdoch and his executives and the last three British prime ministers.

Although the full facts of the Murdoch scandal in Britain are not yet known, already entered into the public record is a troubling litany of allegedly propagandistic uses of media power. Prosecutors and Scotland Yard are now taking very seriously the suspicions directed against the News Corporation, and potentially against other media outlets. Such sober appraisals of recent months stand in stark contrast to previous assurances given to parliament and the public over a period of several years by the now somewhat compromised Metropolitan Police Service that nothing in the evidence they had gathered warranted further investigation.[56] By May 2012, police had initially arrested more than forty individuals in connection with the probes, a majority of whom were current or former Murdoch employees.[57] Further relevant is that by January 2012 Murdoch's News Corporation had agreed to pay damages to thirty-seven celebrities, sports figures, and politicians whose mobile phones or e-mail accounts had been hacked by *News of the World*. Although the Murdoch media denied that the settlements constituted admissions of illegal activity, lawyers representing the victims issued a press statement asserting their having learned that high officials of Murdoch's News Group Newspapers in England "knew about the wrongdoing and sought to conceal it by deliberately deceiving investigators and destroying evidence."[58] In this connection, denials continuing to emanate from the News Corporation should be considered in reference to the company's earlier, vehement, and longstanding assertions that no more than two low-level employees had engaged in any illegal hacking.[59] This strategy of denial seems to be decreasing in effectiveness, as is evidenced by a May 2012 parliamentary report branding Murdoch as "not a fit person" to control media corporations.[60]

What could be of greater concern to a propaganda critic than the international machinations of a media baron? In answering this question, I would point to the potential for widespread socio-political mischief emanating from what I am listing as propagandistic danger Number 1, namely, the 2010 decision of the U.S. Supreme Court in *Citizens United v. Federal Election Commission.* Here the court majority, by a narrow 5–4 vote, granted free speech citizenship rights to corporations, thereby overruling laws and overturning precedents that, heretofore, had limited corporate contributions used explicitly to support or oppose political issues or candidates. The court moved away from considering corporations as artificial legal constructs specially chartered to facilitate business purposes, such as limited personal liability. Instead, the court argued for treating corporations as full political persons whose free-speech rights would be abrogated by restricting either the size or purpose of their political donations. The majority explicitly rejected the idea that unlimited corporate funding of so-called Super Political Action Committees (Super PACs) might lessen the public's political education by skewing the available communicative content. Similarly, the court's majority doubted that corporations would coordinate efforts with politicians and political groups.[61] In addition to removing limitations on the size of contributions and on explicit proselytizing with regard to issues and advocates, *Citizens United* seems likely indirectly to facilitate the skirting of disclosure requirements for political contributions. With freedom to make unlimited contributions for unlimited purposes, corporations and wealthy individuals arguably would find it desirable to bring more money to bear through nonprofit political corporations—501(c)(4) entities—that are exempt under current tax law from requirements to report donor identities. Special interest communication supported by massive, secret contributions—it's beginning to look a lot like Christmas for propagandists.

Even before *Citizens United,* corporations and well-heeled political players were easily able to generate fulsome discourse on such topics as financial regulation, energy policy, health-care initiatives, and regulations governing unionization by creating front organizations, paying signature collectors to place initiatives on the ballot, busing employees to protest sites, hiring public relations firms to send fake letters to legislators, and soliciting members of Congress with lobbying and campaign donations. These efforts have proved to be variously considerable—as in the case of the reported $2.7 billion spent for financial industry lobbying between 1999 and 2008[62]—and productive of a large discursive footprint—as in the case of contributions to Tea Party-related groups by the Americans for Prosperity Foundation (founded by industrialists Charles and David Koch).[63] All this aside, in the aftermath of *Citizens United* we have reason to center attention upon the enhanced ability of wealthy interests to reach out to the public by funding communications of Super PACs or 501(c)(4) groups.

The foregoing list of seven propagandistic danger points threatening democratic communication conjures up a dystopia of society and politics controlled by Big Money. Against such pessimism, those of more sanguine mind would point to cultural forces that in the West have long opposed the socio-political juggernaut of riches. The Aristotelian theory of politics includes important objections to governmental domination by the wealthy, a form of political control that Aristotle terms *oligarchy*. This peripatetic philosopher criticized oligarchs for furthering their own riches rather than advancing freedom or virtue. In addition, he maintained that a free state requires "the conjuncture of the rich and the poor."[64] We may further reference the religious objection to obsessive reliance upon wealth as found in the Sermon on the Mount: "But woe unto you that are rich! for ye have received your consolation."[65] Paul adds that "they that will be rich fall into temptation and a snare, and *into* many foolish and hurtful lusts, which drown men in destruction and perdition,"[66] setting the stage for his famous conclusion that "the love of money is the root of all evil."[67]

Given deep-seated cultural antipathy to oligarchy and greed, it is likely that Big Money's efforts to co-opt law, Internet, science, news, and political campaigning will meet with resistance. Propaganda's contemporary seven deadly dangers must be a cause for concern—but not for despair. Such a more optimistic view of current propaganda is consistent with the discussions at the 2012 Breaux Symposium. Panelists noted that propaganda typically has been opposed by the flow of information, by efforts in the direction of education, and by the socio-political participation of ordinary Americans. In a time when mobile phones offer constant Internet access and photographic documentation, we have ever more reason to be hopeful that individual initiative and interpersonal contact will hold in check the various propagandas of Big Money.

Notes

1. Edward L. Bernays, interview by author, Cambridge, Massachusetts, May 19, 1984.

2. J. Michael Sproule, *Channels of Propaganda* (Bloomington, Ind.: ERIC/EDINFO Press, 1994), 2–8.

3. Eric Lichtblau and Eric Lipton, "E-Mail Reveals Rove's Key Role in '06 Dismissals," *New York Times,* August 12, 2009.

4. Eric Lichtblau, "Prosecutor Is Named in Dismissal of Attorneys," *New York Times,* September 30, 2008.

5. Patricia Cohen, "Class Action Suit Filed Against Jimmy Carter Book," *New York Times,* February 2, 2011, C2; Julie Bosman, "Plaintiffs Drop Suit Over Jimmy Carter Book," *New York Times,* May 5, 2011, C3.

6 Clint Hendler, "Is the End Nigh?" *Columbia Journalism Review,* July/August 2010, 10–11.

7. Eric Pfanner, "A Fight to Protect Americans from British Libel Law," *New York Times,* May 24, 2009, B3.

8. A. J. Liebling, *The Press* (New York: Pantheon, 1975), 227.

9. Seth Schiesel, "Mass Effect," *New York Times,* January 26, 2008, A19.

10. Matt Richtel, "Attached to Technology and Paying a Price," *New York Times,* June 7, 2010, A12.

11. Andy Webster, "Yearning to Breathe Free on the Web," *New York Times,* November 10, 2011, C8.

12. Chris O'Brien, *San Jose Mercury News,* December 16, 2008; Eduardo Porter, *New York Times,* May 9, 2012.

13. Natasha Singer, "Medical Papers by Ghostwriters Pushed Therapy," *New York Times,* August 5, 2009.

14 Duff Wilson and Natasha Singer, "Ghostwriting Is Called Rife in Medical Journals," *New York Times,* September 10, 2009.

15. Gardiner Harris, "Doctor's Pain Studies Were Fabricated, Hospital Says," *New York Times,* March 10, 2009.

16. John M. Broder, "Climate Change Doubt Is Tea Party Article of Faith," *New York Times,* October 20, 2010.

17. Edward L. Bernays, "Molding Public Opinion," *Annals of the American Academy of Political and Social Science* 179 (May 1935): 83; Edward L. Bernays, *Public Relations* (Norman: Univ. of Oklahoma Press, 1952), 73, 254.

18. Broder, "Climate Change Doubt Is Tea Party Article of Faith."

19. *Monterey County Herald,* 12 December 2009, A12.

20. *Chronicle of Higher Education*, June 4, 2010, A18, A19; *Chronicle of Higher Education*, October 29, 2010, A3.

21. "Posturing and Abdication," *New York Times*, editorial, Sunday Week in Review, July 13, 2008, 11.

22. *New York Times*, July 9, 2008, A13.

23. *New York Times*, April 8, 2010, A15.

24. Suzanne Goldenberg, "Arnold Schwarzenegger Flexes Muscles to Defend Climate Change Law," *Guardian*, October 28, 2010.

25. Walter Lippmann, *Public Opinion* (New York: Macmillan, 1922), 47, 248.

26. Brian Stelter, "Seeking More Viewers, MSNBC Turns Left," *New York Times*, August 22, 2008. For additional background on cable television and political ideology, see Brian Stelter, "Fresh Face on Cable, Sharp Rise in Ratings," *New York Times*, October 20, 2008; Brian Stelter, "Candidates Running Against, and With, Cable News," *New York Times*, October 24, 2010; Brian Stelter, "The Anti-Fox Gains Ground," *New York Times*, November 11, 2012.

27. Paul Krugman, "The Centrist Cop-Out," *New York Times*, July 28, 2011.

28. Thomas L. Friedman, "Too Good to Check," *New York Times*, November 16, 2010; see also the show transcript for *Anderson Cooper 360 Degrees*, CNN, November 3, 2010, at http://transcripts.cnn.com/TRANSCRIPTS/1011/03/acd.01.html. Congresswoman Michele Bachmann: "The president of the United States will be taking a trip over to India that is expected to cost the taxpayers $200 million a day."

29. Arianna Huffington, Monterey Peninsula College lecture, in MPC *Connections* (fall 2008), 1.

30. Michael Schudson, *Discovering the News* (New York: Basic Books, 1978), 167–169, 186.

31. *Outfoxed: Rupert Murdoch's War on Journalism*, 2004, produced and directed by Robert Greenwald.

32. Brian Stelter, "The Rise of 'The Five' on Fox News," *New York Times*, December 26, 2011, B1.

33. Erik Barnouw, *Tube of Plenty*, rev. ed. (New York: Oxford Univ. Press, 1982), 76, 86, 101–102.

34. Walter B. Emery, *Broadcasting and Government*, rev. ed. (East Lansing, Mich.: Michigan State Univ. Press, 1971), 318–337; Barry Cole and Mal Oettinger, *Reluctant Regulators*, rev. ed. (Reading, Mass.: Addison-Wesley, 1978), 151–160.

35. David Brock et al., *The Fox Effect: How Roger Ailes Turned a Network into a Propaganda Machine* (New York: Anchor Books, 2012).

36. Author searches conducted on January 21, 2012. Full results: "ABC news bias"—344,000 results (Google), 163 results (Yahoo); "CBS news bias"—410,000 (Google), 108 (Yahoo); "CNN news bias"—30,100 (Google), 41 (Yahoo); "Fox news bias"—913,000 (Google), 297 (Yahoo); "MSNBC news bias"—18,000 (Google), 23 (Yahoo); "NBC news bias"—162,000 (Google), 39 (Yahoo).

37. Brian Stelter, "Fox News Takes Two Potential Candidates Off Air," *New York Times*, March 3, 2011.

38. Brian Stelter, "Gawker Will Go to Court in an Investigation of Fox," *New York Times*, July 25, 2011.

39. Julie Carr Smyth (AP statehouse correspondent),"Dems Accuse Fox News of Bolstering Ohio Candidate," *Seattle Times*, September 2, 2010.

40. Stefano DellaVigna and Ethan Kaplan, "The Fox News Effect: Media Bias and Voting," *Quarterly Journal of Economics* 122 (2007): 1187–1284.

41. Steve Karnowski (AP writer), "Judge Grants New Trial in Music Downloading Case," *USA Today*, September 24, 2008.

42. Nate Anderson, "Thomas Verdict: Willful Infringement, $1.92 Million Penalty," Arstechnica.com, June 18, 2009.

43. Kelly Truong, "Judge Reduces Student's File-Sharing Fine by 90 Percent," *Chronicle of Higher Education*, July 12, 2010.

44. Brian Stelter, "CBS Removes David Letterman's Mea Culpa from YouTube," *New York Times*, October 4, 2009.

45. David Carr, "The Danger of an Attack on Piracy Online," *New York Times*, January 1, 2012.

46. Brian Stelter, "Copyright Challenge for Sites that Excerpt," *New York Times*, March 1, 2009.

47. Lawrence Lessig, "Copyright and Politics Don't Mix," *New York Times*, October 20, 2008.

48. "Fox News Channel Statement on 'Outfoxed,'" www.foxnews.com/story/0,2933,125436,00.html.

49. George Seldes, *Lords of the Press* (New York: Julian Messner, 1938).

50. Richard Pérez-Peña, "With Obama, Murdoch Defies His Image," *New York Times*, November 16, 2008.

51. Jeffrey Goldfarb, Richard Beales, and Hugo Dixon, "A Murdoch Discount in News Corp. Stock," *New York Times*, July 13, 2011.

52. Eric Lichtblau and Brian Stelter, "News Corp. Gives Republicans $1 Million," *New York Times*, August 17, 2010.

53. Jim Rutenberg, "Murdoch Defends News Corp.'s Political Donations," *New York Times*, October 15, 2010.

54. Edmund Lee, "News Corp. Investors Should Reject 13 Directors," *Bloomberg Business Week*, October 10, 2011.

55. David Carr, "Under Murdoch, Tilting Rightward at the Journal," *New York Times*, December 13, 2009.

56. Don Van Natta Jr., "Stain from Tabloids Rubs Off on a Cozy Scotland Yard," *New York Times*, July 16, 2011.

57. Indu Chandrasekhar, Murray Wardrop, and Andy Trotman, "Phone Hacking: Timeline of the Scandal, *London Telegraph*, July 23, 2012; Associated Press, "Phone Hacking and Bribery Probe: 47th Journalist Arrested," September 15, 2012, published at Huffington Post, www.huffingtonpost.com/2012/09/15/uk-police-arrest-journali_n_1886300.html.

58. Sarah Lyall and Ravi Somaiya, "Murdoch Settles Suits by Dozens of Victims of Hacking," *New York Times*, January 19, 2012.

59. Sarah Lyall, "Murdochs Deny That They Knew of Illegal Acts," *New York Times,* July 19, 2011.

60. Amy Chozick, "News Corp.'s Board Says It Has 'Full Confidence' in Murdoch," *New York Times,* May 2, 2012.

61. Ronald Dworkin, "The Decision that Threatens Democracy," *New York Review of Books,* May 13, 2010.

62. Sewell Chan, "Financial Crisis Was Avoidable, Inquiry Finds," *New York Times,* January 25, 2011.

63. Frank Rich, "The Billionaires Bankrolling the Tea Party," *New York Times,* August 28, 2010; Jane Mayer, "Covert Operations: The Billionaire Brothers Who Are Waging a War against Obama," *New Yorker,* August 30, 2010, http://www.newyorker.com/reporting/2010/08/30/100830fa_fact_mayer.

64. Aristotle, *Politics* 8.1294a.

65. Luke 6:24, King James Version.

66. 1 Timothy 6:9.

67. 1 Timothy 6:10.

4

PROPAGANDA FOR WAR

MORDECAI LEE

DOMESTIC PROPAGANDA DURING A "REAL" WAR VS. THE OTHER KIND

From 1945 to 2012 the United States has participated in dozens of wars. Big wars like Korea, Vietnam, Iraq I, Afghanistan, the Global War on Terror, and Iraq II. Lots of little ones, including Lebanon, Dominican Republic, Granada, Lebanon (again), Panama, Somalia, Yugoslavia, and Libya. And one really, *really* long war, the Cold War. All of these American military battles occurred without Congress declaring war. Some entailed indirect congressional permission, such as the 1964 Tonkin Gulf Resolution (for Vietnam) and the 2002 Use of Force Resolution (for Iraq II). Many others involved unilateral action by a president asserting that his orders to the armed forces to enter combat were based on his Constitutional role of commander in chief. Some of these combat actions occurred before the enactment of the War Powers Act (1973), but many of them after. Since 1900, only two wars were declared by Congress, World War I and World War II, making them the only two *Constitutional* wars the United States has engaged in during the twentieth and twenty-first centuries.[1]

This is no mere pedantry, nor a quaint anachronism, nor a professorial effort at arcane distinctions. If we were to assume that all these unofficial wars "counted," then an examination of domestic war propaganda would include just about every public communication of the federal government since VJ Day that related to national defense. The emergence of the Garrison State, the National Security State, or whatever you want to call it, has dominated the public square for over half a century. The problem is that if a subject covers just about everything, then in practical terms it covers nothing.

In particular, the significance of the distinction between Constitutional and non-Constitutional wars is that after a congressional declaration of war the ends can be used to justify the means. There are few to no constraints on using any means the government deems necessary to accomplish the goal of military victory. Conversely, when war is waged without a formal declaration, the freedom of domestic action by the national government (including propaganda) is severely limited. In those cases, the ends cannot be used to justify the means. Absent a formal war declaration by Congress, the public would be intolerant of communication efforts to promote the war as a "good thing," of implications that criticism of the war is disloyal and unpatriotic, of limits on speech, of suppression of dissent, and—more generally—of substantial sacrifices in lifestyle and scarcity of consumer goods.

A declaration of war inherently authorizes an active and overt governmental propaganda effort to generate domestic public support for the war. Why? Because the Congress has declared a specific nation as a national *enemy*. An enemy is dangerous, even evil, and must be vanquished. The future of the United States is on the line. Any citizen who voices disagreement with Congress's declaration of war is subject to punishment for giving "aid and comfort" to the enemy.[2] This is not merely dissent. This is treason.

As such, domestic propaganda during a war can include the power of censorship of views that are out of harmony with the goal of military victory. A declaration of war can be used to justify actively suppressing political dissent on the grounds that it undermines the agreed-upon national war effort. Such efforts at propaganda—censorship and limits on dissent—would be beyond the pale in all of America's post–World War II non-Constitutional wars. Therefore, the federal government's domestic propaganda activities during declared wars are so qualitatively different from those during nondeclared wars that they are essentially not comparable.[3]

An analysis of federal domestic propaganda during a Constitutional war brings the focus to the *purpose* of such propaganda. (As for defining propaganda for this discussion, there is no need to split hairs or to decide in advance on an inherently negative meaning. Let's go with something relatively neutral, along the lines of: governmental domestic communications intended to be persuasive and to affect American public opinion.) Simply put, the purposes of war propaganda are to maintain a high public support for the war and, as a slightly different focus, to maintain high public morale. Why? Because during a Constitutional war, a buy-in from the public of the war is expected—virtually obligated. The citizenry is expected to accept sacrifices and hardships so that the nation can win the war. Some of these can include increased taxes, campaigns to buy war bonds, accepting scarcity of consumer goods, rationing, accepting the effect of the war effort on the economy, accepting a larger role of government in mobilizing the economy to contribute to the war effort, and so on.

Consider how different this picture of the domestic front is compared to that of some of America's post–World War II non-Constitutional wars. During the Vietnam war, President Johnson aimed for "guns and butter"—i.e., that the public-at-large would not be deleteriously affected by the war. During the war on terrorism, President Bush asked the public for no sacrifices, suggesting after 9/11 that citizens go about their normal routines, including spending on shopping.[4]

THE GIVEN NARRATIVE OF U.S. DOMESTIC WAR PROPAGANDA

History is not only written by the winners, but entails the inevitable telescoping of events that forces historians to seek a narrative arc with some consistency and forward movement. This has the unintended effect of determinism, if only unconsciously presenting what happened as relatively inevitable, that there could have been no other reasonable way for events and decisions to unfold. Also, it is human to want to forget that which is embarrassing or awkward or clashes with the given narrative. In particular, when history is transmuted into a civics lesson, the story is often about the good (and, impliedly, united) America making the right decisions in the long run. No mistakes were made to tarnish the image.

American historian Eric Foner observed that history "is what the present chooses to remember about the past."[5] That is the crux of this discussion. We choose to remember World War I's domestic war propaganda poorly and World War II's positively because supposedly the former went overboard in excessive propaganda while the latter had a lighter and more information-oriented touch. I suggest that from the perspective of a supportive and united citizenry, we've gotten both wrong, though for different reasons. This comparison of federal propaganda during World Wars I and II, the last two wars that Congress declared, seeks to provide a revisionist historical reinterpretation of the conventional telling.

The official propaganda agency in World War I was the Committee on Public Information (CPI). In World War II, it was initially the Division of Information (DOI) in the Executive Office of the President, which operated from Pearl Harbor to mid-1942. The DOI was then replaced by the Office of War Information (OWI), which functioned from mid-1942 to mid-1943, when Congress virtually defunded its *domestic* activities (while maintaining a robust informational activity abroad aimed mostly at foreign audiences). President Truman abolished the OWI by executive order in August 1945.[6]

The stories of the two wars and their domestic propaganda agencies begin almost identically. In both cases, an internationalist and Eurocentric Democratic president (Wilson, FDR) was concerned about the implications of a war already under way in Europe (1914, 1939) and spreading around the world while the United States was officially neutral. Awkwardly, the president was running for reelection (1916, 1940) and understood political realities. American public opinion was not only isolationist, but also—due to ethnic immigration patterns—had sizable populations supporting opposing sides in the war. To blunt Republican accusations of being secretly prowar and planning on involving the United States after the election, both incumbent presidents made public pledges during their successful reelection campaigns that sounded like they were against involvement in the war. Once reelected, they pursued policies that—while retaining the formal Constitutional status of not being at war—increasingly involved the country in actively supporting Great Britain (and its allies) and actively undermining Germany (and its allies). The president directed that the United States engage in a series of escalating naval actions that were so provocative they virtually guaranteed counterattacks. Like Lincoln, the president understood the importance of who fired the first shot. He wanted it to look like the innocent United States was suddenly and unjustifiably attacked. The Germans obliged. Eventually, the president got the "unprovoked" attack from Germany (or its ally) that he wanted and dramatically turned to Congress for a declaration of war, which was approved quickly and overwhelmingly.

With war declared, the federal government was now in a position to engage in domestic war propaganda. Here is where the stories part ways. The historical consensus about the CPI has generally been negative, condemning its over-the-top domestic propaganda as excessive, simplistic, manipulative, misleading, and anti-democratic. I suggest the possibility of reinterpreting the CPI's historical legacy as justifiable and successful. It accomplished what it was supposed to, even though the pursuit of that success contributed to some negative consequences at the time, and much more in the seeming "lessons" of its record. Generally, I wonder if perhaps the generations of scholars who came of age during the Vietnam and Iraq wars have been mixing apples and oranges when writing about the CPI. Our delicate contemporary sensibilities about domestic government propaganda and dissent during those two undeclared, yet major and prolonged, wars should not be the basis for historical verdicts we retrospectively impose on World War I and the CPI.

The disapproving historical image of the CPI then colored both the actual work of World War II domestic propaganda and the later historical verdict of the same. Generally, the DOI and the OWI are complimented in the literature by faint praise, noting approvingly that they were not like the CPI. Instead they were practically the anti-CPI. The DOI and OWI were indeed different from the CPI, but I suggest the possible conclusion that they were—relative to the CPI—historical failures. Notwithstanding the romanticized myth of American unity after Pearl Harbor, there was vocal, persistent, and partisan dissent about the administration's conduct of the war. Neither the DOI nor the OWI aggressively tried to change that and instead took a relatively (compared to the CPI) lowered tone and nonhysterical posture of "here are the facts and then you can decide how you feel about them." The unified mobilization of the nation during World War I did not occur in World War II, nor did the DOI and OWI make any serious effort to try to do so. The argument can be made that during the interbellum period (1918–1941) the U.S. political economy and society had changed so substantially that efforts at a CPI-like agency would have failed in World War II. Nonetheless, relative to the CPI as an historical yardstick, World War II domestic propaganda efforts would probably deserve a failing grade.

FEDERAL PROPAGANDA IN WORLD WAR I: THE COMMITTEE ON PUBLIC INFORMATION

The methods, values, orientation, and personnel of the Committee on Public Information in World War I are deeply rooted in the Progressive era of the United States. This was a time of major social, technological, economic, and political change (roughly 1890–1920). They reflected the rise of the urban and educated middle class in the United States and consequently of betterment campaigns by activist citizens, objective nonpartisan journalism, and—most importantly for this discussion—the emergence of concepts of public opinion, an informed citizenry, and publicity. For Progressive reformers, the key to accomplishing their goals was publicity to arouse the public-at-large.[7] Publicity was used to promote reform ideas, to expose transgressions of corrupt and inefficient government, and to pressure policy makers. Publicity entailed educating, arousing, mobilizing, persuading, and convincing public opinion. It reached the public through writings in newspapers and magazines, mass advertising, and "Literary Bureaus" or "Publicity Bureaus," which were intended to blanket the populous with all manner of communication. The modern-day profession of public relations had its origins in the ethos of the Progressive era. In general, reformers saw in publicity a seeming ability to create a perception that public opinion "wanted" a specific reform and woe unto the policy maker who tried to resist. Punishment was the implicit threat of the gloved fist of Progressive era publicity.[8]

Woodrow Wilson was a Progressive reformer before being elected president. So was the man he chose to head the CPI, reporter and reformer George Creel. Both believed in the power of publicity and in the rightness of their preferred policies. Whatever they happened to be pursuing as policy goals, they *knew* they were right and were righteously so. They could do no wrong.

Wilson asked Congress for a declaration of war on April 2, 1917, and got it on April 6. A week later, he signed a three-sentence executive order creating the Committee on Public Information and promptly named

Creel to head it.[9] By all accounts, Creel quickly hired and organized the CPI to be a comprehensive propaganda agency. His was a full-service propaganda agency, a propaganda department store. He tapped into all media, using a veiled threat of censorship for those who refused to cooperate (even though he did not have the legal authority to be a censor). And he got just about anything he wanted.[10] For purposes of this discussion, there is no need to summarize the details of the CPI's structure and output, as there is a modest literature on it, though quite mixed in quality.[11]

Parallel to the work of the CPI were separate congressional enactments regarding the prosecution of sedition and aggressive guidelines by the postmaster general on materials that could be excluded from the mail.[12] When viewed in toto, the mentality of this declared war regarding domestic matters was that any disagreement or dissent was perceived as giving aid and comfort to the enemy. Only unqualified support for the war effort was patriotic. It was a truly binary condition, either with us or against us, backed up by the power of the state to punish and silence. Pervasive propaganda was simply a substitute for coercion, but with the same results, a different means to the same ends.

John Barry analyzed the impact of such a "total war" approach to domestic morale on efforts to deal with the influenza pandemic. Nothing seemed to be permissible that contained even the hint of a problem, obstacle, or other public priority—not even preventative measures regarding the spread of the virulently fatal influenza. It was the hardest of hard lines, when "the government compelled conformity, controlled speech in ways, frightening ways, not known in America before or since."[13] Even "songs that might hurt morale were prohibited."[14] Separately, Creel coerced Hollywood to produce what Creel wanted or else. He threatened them with "direct government censorship of all movies" even though he did not have that power.[15] The key was "to heighten and sustain enthusiasm for the war effort and *support for America's wartime leadership*."[16] Criticism of the president was verboten.

Creel and the CPI were fabulously successful, but at a price. Brewer summarized the postwar view of the CPI as having gone "over the top."[17] A backlash set in, that the CPI had gone overboard, whipping up hysteria, suppressing First Amendment rights to protest, providing a misleading picture of the management of the war, demonizing the enemy with false information, and, generally, being anti-democratic. Steele variously described the interwar perspective on the CPI's work as promoting false perceptions, vigilantism, violations of civil liberties, and jingoism.[18] As a result, "propaganda" became a semi-dirty word.

St. John tied the domestic backlash to the CPI's excesses, especially the professionalization of journalism in the 1920s and 1930s.[19] The lesson reporters learned was never to be duped, suppressed, or manipulated again. The best antidote would be a new professional culture of independence, objectivity, and all the other standard accouterments of a profession. One of the new principles of the craft was a reliance on independent experts to provide readers with objective assessment of developments. (The concept of neutral expertise also was a central tenet for Progressive reformers.) This seeped deeply into journalistic culture, and the quoted expert continues to this day to be an ingrained staple of the news media—old or new, print or digital, legacy or social. However, St. John points out that the habitual turning to expert opinion made the newly professionalized journalism even more subject to manipulation by corporate and moneyed interests who, behind the scenes, were influencing—even funding—some of these so-called experts.

In my opinion, the CPI deserves a more positive historical verdict. Time to rebunk it. This chapter is in part an attempt at a revisionist history of the CPI. Creel and his staff did what was necessary to harness the nation in support of a Constitutional declaration of war. No more and no less. And they were wildly successful. You can't knock success. Given the context of Congress declaring a war, perhaps our hindsight needs to be more forcefully and consciously filtered through that very important detail. When the nation engages in a Constitutional war it is appropriate to use all the means to reach the end—victory. Here is a situation where the ends did justify the means. That Wilson, Creel, and the Progressives thought they had a monopoly on truth and expertise is immaterial. That they were anti-democratic and had the hubris of true believers is also immaterial. They were not going to sit around and hope that public opinion in a democracy would eventually come around on its own to supporting the war. They had no delicate sensibilities about dissent and freedom to protest. A declaration of war changed everything. The goal was to win the war, and that included coercing public support for it and suppressing dissent of Wilson's leadership of it. War isn't pretty.

However, there is one other detail missing from the given narrative of the CPI's astounding success, whether told by those who agreed with what it did or those who retrospectively criticized its legacy. The CPI may have reigned virtually unopposed throughout the country, but one place was a major exception: Capitol Hill. Despite the CPI's success—or perhaps because of it—Congress was extremely hostile to it during its entire existence. This is all a bit odd, because it was Congress which had declared war in the first place. One could wonder why Congress would be concerned about winning the war it declared. After all, should not achieving victory include mobilization of public support for it (in lieu of coercion)? Congressional negativity toward the CPI was no minor thing. It was fierce, explicit, on a hair-trigger, and hot. Historians have provided a wide variety of rationales for the hostility. These included apprehensions about an underhanded use of propaganda to advance the political and institutional interests of the president, using the CPI to advance the partisan interests of the president's party, deviation from facts, misleading information, publication of an official national newspaper, wasting money, absence of a statutory-based legal charter, and all other manner that could offend the delicate sensibilities of the political prima donnas at that end of Pennsylvania Avenue.

From the hindsight of almost a century, I suggest that the red-hot legislative hostility to the CPI has a more garden-variety explanation. *Institutionally,* Congress reflexively feels threatened when it is in danger of being displaced as each citizen's closest link to the federal government. If citizens do not need to rely on members of Congress for information, then that becomes a first step in marginalizing the legislative branch and giving preeminence to the president over Congress. This was clearly apparent in the motivation of congressional attacks on FDR's Office of Government Reports even before Pearl Harbor.[20] That the attacks increased to near-hysteria *after* the declaration of war is a further signal of the link between federal propaganda and congressional hostility.

So, in that sense, the lesson Congress learned from the existence of the CPI was a kind of "never again" resolve. The brutal cutoff in 1919 of any further funding, not even a penny to shut down the agency in an orderly way, was an indication of the intensity of the legislative aversion to the CPI's work. This attitude helps set the stage for the domestic war propaganda of the federal government in World War II and how it differed from that of the CPI.

FEDERAL PROPAGANDA IN WORLD WAR II: THE DIVISION OF INFORMATION AND THE OFFICE OF WAR INFORMATION

The myth of national unity in World War II has seeped deeply into popular memory. For example, historian H. W. Brands wrote that "Americans complained hardly at all about throwing their lives and fortunes into the breach."[21] In 2011, upon the seventieth anniversary of the Japanese attack on Pearl Harbor, the romanticized and mythologized image of World War II was on display. Nationally syndicated (conservative) columnist Cal Thomas wrote that "Americans rallied around a single patriotic cause" during World War II and that this unity "lasted a lot longer" than after the 9/11 attacks.[22] Similarly, the wave of World War II nostalgia prompted by the popularity of Tom Brokaw's book *The Greatest Generation* and Steven Spielberg's movie *Saving Private Ryan* evoked a seeming collective memory of a time of unified national purpose. The opening of the World War II memorial on the National Mall in 2004 entombed that myth.

Reading history backwards, one could then reasonably conjecture that there must have been broad domestic support for the war effort. Going further back, the explanation for broad domestic support must mean two essential components: First, that substantively the cause was authentically just and the citizenry saw it so. It was a good war (sometimes even called America's last good war). Second, that the federal government must have had a domestic propaganda agency that was at least as effective, if not more so, than the CPI.

Wrong, wrong, wrong.

The nation was not unified. The conservative coalition on Capitol Hill, consisting of minority Republicans and conservative Democrats, became the incubator of all manner of dissatisfaction in the citizenry. Always paying lip service to their support for the war (which they had voted for), these conservative legislators corrosively kept raising concerns about *how* the war was being managed and repeatedly suggested that the president was bungling the war effort. As intended, this gradually leached into the body politic and then grew ever larger, with the conservative coalition carefully nurturing it daily. Thomas Fleming has noted how much this political war against the war has been erased from the given narrative, that "lost to memory was the *ferocious antagonism* between Roosevelt and Congress" during the war.[23] A few histories of that period have noted the powerful pull of negativism that the conservative coalition was able to insert into the daily flux of public perceptions of the war.[24] Fourteen months after the declaration of war a political scientist tried to make sense of the high-pitched and ongoing criticism by legislators of FDR's wartime leadership. It seemed, he commented wryly, to be understandable only if they were "damning him for not being perfect."[25]

The coalition had a willing partner in the news media. Blum wrote that "for its part, the press was querulous."[26] The head of Lend-Lease commented in his postwar memoir that he did not understand the media's logic that honest, even minor, disagreements in the war effort were major news and should be depicted negatively, while the daily disagreements on Capitol Hill seemed to pass almost unnoticed. In his view, the press "built fires under our intramural grievances," exaggerating them, enhancing conflict, giving the public a misimpression of Washington decision-making, and generally making it harder to mobilize the economy to work in a unified way.[27]

Working symbiotically, the news media and the conservative coalition were synergistic, practically the equivalent of a formal propaganda organization that was consistently pushing a negative interpretation of the news from Washington. In the run-up to the 1942 congressional elections, the media gave prominent coverage to a (conservative-dominated) Senate subcommittee report that was extremely critical of the administration's management of the war, including its public relations activities.[28] Then the conservatives obtained Senate permission to print an extra twelve thousand copies of the report, which they mailed (for free, using the frank) to conservative activists and opinion leaders around the country to use in local campaigns against liberal and Democratic candidates who supported FDR.[29] Later in the war, conservative legislators and the news media succeeded in making the Office of Price Administration (OPA) "public enemy number one in the eyes of most

Americans" and encouraged lobbying by special interest groups to be exempted from or advantaged by wartime regulations.[30]

Any historical interpretation of broad public support for World War II *because* of the work of a successful wartime propaganda agency would also be in error. There was no strong CPI-style domestic propaganda agency during World War II. When the war began, President Roosevelt knew what he *did not* want. He did not want a CPI-style propaganda agency. Having served as assistant secretary of the navy in World War I, he was familiar with the CPI's work and the strong criticism of it. He also did not want the military or a domestic war "czar" to control domestic PR.[31] *He* wanted to be in charge. And he did not believe in neat and clean organization charts. Just the opposite. By giving vague and overlapping assignments to multiple executive branch agencies, he was engaging in a kind of political Darwinism, the public administration equivalent of survival of the fittest. If his underlings argued among themselves, then that guaranteed all disagreements would reach his desk for decision (or nondecision, another aspect of FDR's management style).

After Pearl Harbor, Roosevelt quickly expanded the mission of the Office of Government Reports, headed by former reporter Lowell Mellett. The president assigned to Mellett responsibility for liaison with Hollywood and the operation of the new U.S. Information Center building on Pennsylvania Avenue. The conservative coalition and the (then-conservative) *Washington Post* dubbed it "Mellett's Madhouse." It stuck.[32]

At the same time, the Division of Information, headed by former reporter Robert Horton, was also expanding significantly. Originally founded in spring 1940 as the PR shop for the prewar arms production buildup (which, typical of FDR's fluid style, went through several name changes), the DOI gradually expanded during 1940 and 1941. After Pearl Harbor it grew even faster. During the first half-year of the war, the DOI became the largest propaganda agency in Washington, providing PR services for almost all the wartime agencies loosely housed within the Office for Emergency Management (itself within the Executive Office of the President).

With about five hundred employees, the DOI was similar to the CPI in the sense of providing a full range of publicity services: news releases, publications, radio programs, a nationwide speakers bureau, posters, exhibits, and films. One of its goals was to lift and keep up home front morale in general and the morale of workers in arms production plants specifically.[33] It had an extensive apparatus of regional offices around the country that worked closely with local radio stations, newspapers, and the like to localize the news out of Washington.

While the DOI may have been like the CPI in its organization, mission, scope, and structure, it was very different in tone and style. Horton inculcated into the DOI an organizational culture that was the opposite of the CPI's. In 1942, a professor of public relations already felt comfortable concluding that the federal government was accomplishing its wartime PR mission better than the CPI had. Harlow stated that "citizens are far better informed about this war, in all its aspects, than they were about World War I."[34] Nearly seven decades later, historian H. W. Brands wrote:

> Compared to World War I, which had been sold to the American people as the war to end all wars and to make the world safe for democracy, and which had been followed by an angry backlash when the postwar settlement failed to yield the promised result, World War II was treated almost matter-of-factly. The American government encouraged patriotic thinking but declined to whip the public mood into the frenzy of the earlier conflict. A businesslike attitude marked the struggle against Germany and Japan.[35]

This matter-of-fact nonpropaganda approach continued after Roosevelt reorganized the wartime information services in mid-1942. He abolished the OGR, the DOI, and several other organizational units and recreated them as the Office of War Information (OWI), headed by reporter Elmer Davis.[36] Davis, too, believed that CPI-style propaganda was inappropriate and followed the tone of disseminating information and refraining from over-the-top cheerleading and control.

The OWI's domestic information activities maintained most of what its predecessor agencies did.[37] Quite overtly, it did not try to engage in CPI-style war propaganda. In the rough and tumble hothouse of Washington politics, that made it a "weak" agency from the start. Perhaps because of his views about the CPI, perhaps for other reasons, President Roosevelt did not seem to care about the OWI, had little to no contact with Davis during the war, and never defended it publicly. Still, the organization faithfully implemented Roosevelt's desire to avoid CPI-type propaganda. (Unlike World War I, there was an official censor in World War II, but that agency was unaffiliated with the OWI.[38])

The congressional antipathy to government wartime domestic propaganda was on full alert from the day the OWI was created. It was almost as if the OWI's avoidance of engaging in CPI-style propaganda was irrelevant. That it existed was enough to trigger attacks from Capitol Hill. The conservative coalition and the press pounced on the OWI with the slightest rationale and hounded it ceaselessly as pro-Roosevelt, partisan, and pro-civil rights. They were successful. Battered by attacks, Davis was helpless to stop Congress when it defunded most of the OWI's domestic activities at the end of FY 1943 (July 1, 1943), only a year after it came into being. Gone were domestic publications, movie liaisons, and regional offices. Left were an underfunded U.S. Information Center and a weak role as mere coordinator of the release of war news. Congress let it continue a major overseas role, but that was mostly oriented to foreign audiences. Only slightly exaggerating, one senior OWI official said that the remaining level of funding was "carefully not enough to let us accomplish anything much," merely saving face over total abolishment.[39]

So, it is largely accurate to describe the last two years of World War II as lacking any central government-organized domestic war propaganda. The task shifted to individual agencies which had major public relations activities closely tied to their missions, such as the Treasury Department, the OPA, and the Office of Civilian Defense. The external communications activities of these freestanding agencies should probably not be considered "war propaganda" in league with the CPI, DOI, or OWI. Rather, they were mission-specific in promoting sub-causes related to a program directly administered by that agency, such as selling war bonds,[40] cooperation with rationing, and volunteering for civil defense duties.

Given the absence of central government propaganda, it is no wonder that historians give deference to the protestations of the conservative coalition and the media about FDR "bungling" the domestic war effort (which has oddly coexisted in parallel with the image of a unified population supporting the war effort). For the last two years of the war these were largely the voices that dominated the public square, creating a self-fulfilling perception of reality. There was no propaganda agency to rebut and claim otherwise.

In summary, the extent of domestic war propaganda in World War II was relatively minor compared to that under the CPI. It engaged in much less over-the-top exaggeration and emotion, and exercised less control of news coverage. While it is hard to separate cause from effect, it is accurate to depict World War II domestic propaganda as a failure, given the weakness of the propaganda agency, the successful and overt efforts to undermine national unity by the congressional conservative coalition, the ongoing negative coverage by the news media, and a grumbling population less willing to accept shortages and sacrifices for the war. Given that the myth of national solidarity in World War II is largely false, then one can—even without historical proofs—suggest that domestic propaganda was a flop. It did not create a unified population. Indeed, based on an examination of the historical record, this was indeed the case. So, at least by comparison to the CPI in World War I, World War II domestic propaganda was botched and should probably be assigned a grade of D+.

HISTORICAL LESSONS FOR CONTEMPORARY AMERICA

It is always dangerous to assert firm historical lessons about anything. While it may be true that one who ignores the past is doomed to repeat it, it is also true that no two situations are ever identical. Certainly, the demographic, social, cultural, economic, political, and technological changes in the United States since the last declared war ended in 1945 are enormous, yielding almost a wholly different nation. Still, the past continues to be a better predictor of the future than any other criterion, and the underlying values of American political culture are quite stable.

The plain historical lesson is that a president can't have it both ways. No war declaration, no expectation of public unity or permission to promote such unity through domestic propaganda. This is as it should be.

The two most significant (hot) wars that the United States fought since World War II are Vietnam and Iraq II. In both cases, the president requested a not-quite declaration of war from Congress, the Gulf of Tonkin Resolution and the Use of Force Resolution. (In the PATRIOT

Act Congress also approved some extraordinary and war-like powers to the president in the global war against terror, but—again—did not declare war.) Significantly, each president did not seek a formal declaration of war. In both nonwars, after those congressional enactments, the wars were briefly popular but then became extremely unpopular. Presidents tried to engage in some forms of domestic propaganda, treating the situation as akin to the country being at war. For example, the Johnson administration tried to censor war developments and influence news coverage. It criticized antiwar activities as undermining the troops in the field and as misleading the enemy about the government's unwavering commitment to the war. President Nixon's administration went so far as to accuse war opponents of giving "aid and comfort to the enemy," invoking the Constitutional clause relating to loyalty when the country was at war. President George W. Bush referred to himself as a "wartime president" when he was running for reelection in 2004. The refrain of "supporting our troops" seemed omnipresent, a handy sound bite to suffocate or criticize opposition to the war.

The Catch-22 that these presidents found themselves in was that they did not want to ask Congress for declarations of war, partly because the situations did not seem to rise to that level of seriousness, partly because if Congress defeated the motions the presidents would have their hands tied and freedom of action severely limited, and because they did not want to impose wartime limits and sacrifices on the populous. They wanted war on the cheap (politically). They got their wars without formal Congressional declarations, but then had to pay the price for their choices. The lack of war declarations prevented any overt and major domestic propaganda efforts to rally public support for the wars and to suppress dissent. Certainly, America had changed since the last war declaration in 1941, but the advantages of such actions by Congress would have transformed the domestic situations. With the country formally at war, dissent could legally be equated with betraying the country, of traitors giving aid and comfort to the enemy. This is a powerful game-changer that no president since Roosevelt has sought to benefit from.

As with any counter-factual version of history, it is hard to imagine domestic propaganda had Congress declared war against North Vietnam or Iraq. But some major elements can be teased from World Wars I and II. There would have been a major effort to mobilize public support for the war, likely by a special wartime federal agency with that mission. Patriotic themes would have pervaded the public square, the airwaves, the news media, classrooms, and civil society. Citizens would generally want to be loyal to their country and would seek ways to demonstrate their patriotism. Opposition to the war would be muffled, probably with legal decisions declaring limits on free speech in wartime and prominent court cases charging peace leaders with sedition. All focus would have been on victory against the enemy. The country would give the benefit of the doubt to the president and his wartime leadership. It would not even be considered propaganda (in the sinister sense of the term) for such messages to be communicated.

Probably the best example of American domestic democracy and free speech continuing to occur (rather than be suppressed) in a declared war is the 1944 presidential election. The Republican nominee, New York governor Tom Dewey, made clear that he was a patriot and supported the war which Congress had declared. But he also made clear that he disagreed with FDR's leadership and offered himself as a constructive alternative for winning the war (and subsequent postwar peace agreements).[41] This example indicates that there can be safe grounds for disagreeing with a wartime president during a declared war. It is a vivid illustration that domestic propaganda efforts and expectations do not equate with suppression of all public speech that raises questions about how a war is being fought—as opposed to against the war itself.

CUTTING THE GORDIAN KNOT: AN IDEALISTIC PROPOSAL FOR DOMESTIC PROPAGANDA IN AN UNDECLARED WAR

Having made the case that vigorous domestic war propaganda is almost exclusively the province of a declared war, it is time for a reality check. While it is possible that Congress might declare war in the future, that is unlikely. The clear and absolute trend since VJ Day has been of presidents forgoing requests to Congress for war declarations. That has been replaced with war being unilaterally (and unconstitutionally) declared by presidents, sometimes with tepid and nonbinding actions by Congress that do not have any Constitutional status. Congress barely even enforces the 1973 War Powers Act anymore.

Assuming that this is the trend for the foreseeable future, then what of domestic war propaganda in nondeclared wars? Here is a somewhat idealistic proposal regarding government domestic communication during undeclared wars. I suggest, based on past controversies during Vietnam and Iraq, that there is a need to try to separate information from advocacy, facts from spin. This is, perhaps quixotically, a desire to split the atom of propaganda into two parts, noncontroversial and controversial, government and politics.

I start with an old-fashioned concept developed about a century ago during the professionalization of public administration as a government career and as an academic discipline. The issue for Progressive reformers was how to square the circle of mass democracy with that of professional government management. These reformers abhorred the corruption inherent in urban political machines. In particular, the reformers opposed the populating of the government workforce with unqualified patronage appointees. Not only were they unqualified but, invariably, there was high turnover in these positions when voters shifted power from one party to the other. Reformers also weren't enthusiastic about the expansion of the voting franchise to all adult males, whether to non-English-speaking immigrant whites in the North or the supposedly "uneducated" African Americans in the Jim Crow South.

Specifically, these Progressives wanted to separate election results dominated by machine politics from the professionalization of a government workforce staffed by trained "experts." So emerged what came to be called the politics-administration dichotomy. The concept envisioned a merit-based civil service system for the staffing of government. All hiring, promotion, and firing decisions would be conducted by an independent civil service commission. These public administrators would have permanent positions, unaffected by election results. Elected officials would decide on the "what" of government—that is, its goals. Then they would hand off their decisions to the professional civil servants, who would control the "how" of accomplishing these goals by the most efficient means possible. This would be a neat and clean separation of politics from administration.

Within decades, professors of public administration debunked the politics-administration dichotomy as unworkable and not reflecting the reality of governmental decision-making. Fair enough. Nonetheless, the concept presents a reasonable approximation of how Americans do think government ought to operate. Without getting bogged down in the typical academic debates over picayune details, most Americans would have a basic sense that the politicians who are accountable to the electorate should make the big decisions of government and that professional, apolitical, and permanent public administration experts should be the ones to staff and operate the agencies of the executive branch.

This approach might have some applicability to the domestic propaganda conundrum in undeclared wars. The external communications that come from civil servants would be limited to *information* and the external communications that is oriented to *persuasion* of public opinion would come from politicians or from the appointees who serve at their pleasure. I realize that, just as public administration has debunked the politics-administration dichotomy, so the academic field of communication has similarly demonstrated that facts cannot be separated from spin, neutral information from propaganda. Again, I'm seeking to finesse the fine-grained academic debates and cut through to the basic common sense and reasonable approximation that the public-at-large would likely perceive. Citizens do not want neutral and permanent civil servants engaging in propaganda. They want apolitical facts from the bureaucracy. If politicians want to take those facts to try to persuade the public to support an undeclared war, they can. But two activities can roughly be separated, even if the precise border between them will always be somewhat fuzzy.

It would be important to define clearly who would qualify as a civil servant to release information and who wouldn't. The key would be who could fire that public administrator. If only an independent personnel agency like a civil service commission could fire them for cause, then they would be bureaucrats. Sometimes this category is called the classified service. If, on the other hand, they could be fired by the president or any of the president's appointees, then they would not qualify to release neutral information. So, for example, a deputy assistant secretary, serving at the pleasure of an assistant secretary (a sub-cabinet position, appointed by the president), would not count as a civil servant.[42] Rather, she or he would be part of the political side of government, the side that is permitted to engage in propaganda.

The British practice helps create a clear distinction between bureaucrats and politicians. In most cabinet ministries (akin to departments in the U.S. government), there is a cabinet minister (or secretary of state) who is appointed by the prime minister to head the department. In the British model a department would also have a permanent under-secretary. That person is the highest ranking civil servant in the department and holds office regardless of political or electoral changes. Hence, the permanent under-secretary cannot be fired by the prime minister or the departmental secretary of state. The permanent under-secretary directs the civil servants in the department and they are all accountable to him or her for the professional performance of their duty. The intent of such a model is that the permanent under-secretary can say no to a politician and not suffer any reprisals. If something is viewed as a bad idea, a waste of money, or too politicized a request, the permanent under-secretary is the face of the professional civil service insisting on keeping government management apolitical.

Using the principle embedded in the model of a permanent under-secretary, one can envision its applicability to the federal government in my normative model of the release of information being solely the province of the civil service. All war-related facts could only be released by professional public administrators who are autonomous from the president's political desires. They would release all information (that would not be in the nature of authentic secrets or military plans) automatically and without preclearance from the president's (direct or indirect) appointees.

As the subject at hand is war (even if undeclared), the release of military information should also be the duty of these civilian public servants. Notwithstanding the professionalism of the PR officers in the military, all members of the armed forces are part of the chain of command. Constitutionally, the president is their commander in chief—wartime or not. Theoretically, a president could issue orders to uniformed service members regarding the release of information and (barring Nuremberg-type exceptions) they would be expected to follow those orders.

Once civil and military information has been released by civil servants, the administration could try to package those facts as representing good news. They would try to cherry-pick the available information to show, by "connecting the dots," that a war would be justified or, once started, that they were winning. Opponents would interpret the facts to the contrary. But the bureaucracy would be a neutral source of information, not an advocate for the administration's (or any else's) propaganda.

I realize that I am romanticizing the ability to separate administration from politics, facts from opinion, information from advocacy. But, notwithstanding all the problems with this formulation, as a common sense and normative goal, it would contribute to significant improvement in government communication during undeclared wars. Politicians would be free to engage in propaganda but could not be the source of factual news. Civil servants would be walled off from politicians and could only release factual information, *all* the information they had.

There are three existing frameworks somewhat analogous to what I am proposing. Each has normative goals, strict assignments of tasks, and inevitable implementation problems. The first is the ethos of American journalism. Professional training schools and media practitioners strive for a clear distinction between news coverage and editorializing. The former is supposed to be limited to facts and the latter to opinion. We are all aware of the weaknesses of this distinction, but most of us view it as an important normative goal that one should constantly reach for. Perfection is a chimera, but the effort and striving are worthwhile.

An even closer analogy is from the public sector. It is the normative governmental framework depicted in television's *Law & Order* franchise. The police collect documentable information and the prosecution frames these facts to persuade a jury. Police (like the bureaucracy in my proposal) are not elected, while the DA (like the president) is.[43] Note also that the prosecution and police should not suppress evidence that conflicts with their developing theory of the crime. The defense is entitled to the *same facts as are available to the prosecution.* This real-world example is so close to my proposal that it suggests some degree of viability.

The third, somewhat flawed, example in the public sector of needing to separate facts from advocacy is when a local elected school board submits an issue to the electorate for decision. In some states, this is required for major school construction bonding proposals (that affect the property tax rate) or permission to exceed state-imposed tax limits.

Similarly, sometimes municipal governments have to obtain voter approval for major policy decisions. In these situations the school board or municipality has to play two distinct and contradictory roles: providing the citizenry with neutral facts and, separately, advocating for passage of the referendum.[44] My proposed normative model should be easier to implement compared to local referenda. In those cases, the *same* government agency was the source of the neutral factual information and the advocacy efforts at persuading the voters. In my proposal, these two categories of communication would come from different entities. One would be the source of verifiable military facts, the other for propaganda advocating one side. The bureaucracy would release all relevant neutral information about a war or prewar situation and politicians would try to spin the facts into a dominant narrative arc that would successfully propagandize the voters.

With my proposal to separate prewar and war information from persuasion, one would not expect the government ever to attain perfection in implementation, but the *goal* of this suggested propaganda policy would be fixed and clear. Ongoing tweaking would routinely be needed as the bureaucracy and the president's administration seek to keep getting as close as possible to the desired goal of the normative framework.

Let's retrospectively apply my idealistic proposal to the Iraq II war. Information and spin were thoroughly intermingled, with the administration of President George W. Bush cherry-picking a set of "facts" that justified going to war.[45] It was largely successful in asserting that Iraq had weapons of mass destruction and was cooperating with the 9/11 terrorists. But what if the bureaucracy had been releasing publicly all information and facts that it had determined to be reliable? Note, again, that the focus is not on political appointees—including the CIA director—but rather on civil servants, who hold permanent positions and who are immune from political reprisals. A president could not get them fired or even exiled to a bureaucratic Siberia.

Using those facts, politicians and the administration could have tried to make the case for war and, subsequently, claimed "Mission Accomplished." However, the same set of facts would be equally available to undecided and antiwar politicians. In the political sphere they would be arguing opinions, interpretations, and ideas, but all on the basis of the same publicly available documentation.[46] *During* a war the same differentiation would operate as before the war. The facts of military and civilian operations would be released by civil servants who are public information professionals. So, in the Iraq II example, the administration's effort to promote its interpretation of war news with television network military analysts would have been limited to presidential appointees in the Pentagon.[47] All war facts would emanate from autonomous civil servants.

I realize the many problems that could arise in trying to implement this normative goal. But, notwithstanding these problems, this is a common sense approach that would improve the current situation by reducing the politicization of war information. There would surely be some problems in trying to draw lines separating information from propaganda and the bureaucracy from politics. However, the general separation of roles and expectations for each side would be relatively clear *in principle*. Gradually the government's learning curve in implementing this principle would lead to improvements in operationalizing it.

There's an old adage in politics that you can't beat something with nothing. Here's where I'd suggest starting. If there are any better ideas out there, step right up.

Notes

1. U.S. Constitution, art. 1, sec. 8.

2. U.S. Constitution, art. 3, sec. 3.

3. There are only three exceptions to the normal constraints and limitations on the practice of federal PR. A declared war is one of them. See Mordecai Lee, *Promoting the War Effort: Robert Horton and Federal Propaganda, 1938–1946* (Baton Rouge: Louisiana State Univ. Press, 2012.)

4. Not to be forgotten is Nixon's elimination of the draft, changing its impact on the citizenry-at-large and all subsequent nondeclared wars.

5. Eric Foner, *The Fiery Trial: Abraham Lincoln and American Slavery* (New York: Norton, 2010), 71.

6. Executive Order 9608, August 31, 1945.

7. Adam D. Sheingate, "'Publicity' and the Progressive-Era Origins of Modern Politics," *Critical Review* 19 (January 2007): 461–480; Michael McGerr, *A Fierce Discontent: The Rise and Fall of the Progressive Movement in America, 1870–1920* (New York: Free Press, 2003); Hindy Lauer Schachter, *Reinventing Government or Reinventing Ourselves: The Role of Citizen Owners in Making a Better Government* (Albany: State Univ. of New York Press, 1997).

8. Mordecai Lee, *Bureaus of Efficiency: Reforming Local Government in the Progressive Era* (Milwaukee, Wisc.: Marquette Univ. Press, 2008); Mordecai Lee, *Congress vs. the Bureaucracy: Muzzling Agency Public Relations* (Norman: Univ. of Oklahoma Press, 2011).

9. Executive Order 2594, April 13, 1917.

10. While the CPI also engaged in propaganda abroad, those activities are outside the scope of this inquiry.

11. Alan Axelrod, *Selling the Great War: The Making of American Propaganda* (New York: Palgrave Macmillan, 2009); Susan A. Brewer, *Why America Fights: Patriotism and War Propaganda from the Philippines to Iraq* (New York: Oxford Univ. Press, 2009), chapter 2; Stephen Ponder, *Managing the Press: Origins of the Media Presidency, 1897–1933* (New York: St. Martin's Press, 1999), chapter 7; Bruce Pinkleton, "The Campaign of the Committee on Public Information: Its Contributions to the History and Evolution of Public Relations," *Journal of Public Relations Research* 6 (1994): 229–240; Stephen Vaughn, *Holding Fast the Inner Lines: Democracy, Nationalism, and the Committee on Public Information* (Chapel Hill: Univ. of North Carolina Press, 1980); James R. Mock and Cedric Larson, *Words That Won the War: The Story of the Committee on Public Information, 1917–1919* (New York: Russell and Russell, 1968); George Creel, *How We Advertised America* (1920; reprint, New York: Arno, 1972).

12. Ponder, *Managing the Press,* 94.

13. John M. Barry, *The Great Influenza: The Story of the Deadliest Pandemic in History* (New York: Penguin, 2009), 123.

14. Ibid., 127.

15. Johanna Blakley, "Propaganda, Pop Culture and Public Diplomacy," in *Warners' War: Politics, Pop Culture and Propaganda in Wartime Hollywood,* ed. Martin Kaplan and Johanna Blakley, 74 (Los Angeles: Normal Lear Center Press, 2004).

16. Richard W. Steele, *Propaganda in an Open Society: The Roosevelt Administration and the Media, 1933–1941* (Westport, Conn.: Greenwood, 1985), 84.

17. Brewer, *Why America Fights,* 71.

18. Steele, *Propaganda in an Open Society,* 84–88.

19. Burton St. John III, *Press Professionalization and Propaganda: The Rise of Journalistic Double-Mindedness, 1917–1941* (Amherst, N.Y.: Cambria, 2010).

20. Mordecai Lee, *The First Presidential Communications Agency: FDR's Office of Government Reports* (Albany: State Univ. of New York Press, 2005), 194–203.

21. H. W. Brands, *The Devil We Knew: Americans and the Cold War* (New York: Oxford Univ. Press, 1993), 148. His observation covered World War I as well as World War II.

22. Cal Thomas, "Pearl Harbor, 70 Years Later," *Milwaukee Journal Sentinel,* December 7, 2011, 17A.

23. Thomas Fleming, *The New Dealers' War: Franklin D. Roosevelt and the War within World War II* (New York: Basic Books, 2001), 558.

24. David M. Jordan, *FDR, Dewey, and the Election of 1944* (Bloomington: Indiana Univ. Press, 2011); Robert A. Caro, *Master of the Senate: The Years of Lyndon Johnson,* vol. 3 (New York: Knopf, 2002), 74; Bruce Catton, *The War Lords of Washington* (1948; reprint, New York: Greenwood, 1969), 180–184.

25. James Hart, "National Administration," *American Political Science Review* 37 (February 1943): 31.

26. John Morton Blum, *V was for Victory: Politics and American Culture During World War II* (New York: Harcourt Brace Jovanovich, 1976), 23.

27. Donald M. Nelson, *Arsenal of Democracy: The Story of American War Production* (New York: Harcourt Brace, 1946), xv.

28. Lee, *Congress vs. the Bureaucracy*, 159–160.

29. *Congressional Record* 88, no. 5 (August 27, 1942): 6974.

30. Paul D. Casdorph, *Let the Good Times Roll: Life at Home in America During World War II* (New York: Paragon House, 1989), 126–128.

31. Lee, *The First Presidential Communications Agency*, chapters 4–5.

32. Ibid., chapters 7–8.

33. Lee, *Promoting the War Effort*.

34. Rex F. Harlow, *Public Relations in War and Peace* (New York: Harper and Brothers, 1942), 199.

35. H. W. Brands, *American Dreams: The United States Since 1945* (New York: Penguin, 2010), 22.

36. Executive Order 9182, June 13, 1942.

37. Allan M. Winkler, *The Politics of Propaganda: The Office of War Information, 1942–1945* (New Haven, Conn.: Yale Univ. Press, 1978), chapter 2.

38. Brewer, *Why America Fights*, 99–100.

39. Sydney Weinberg, "What to Tell America: The Writers' Quarrel in the Office of War Information," *Journal of American History* 55 (June 1968): 89.

40. James J. Kimble, *Mobilizing the Home Front: War Bonds and Domestic Propaganda* (College Station: Texas A&M Univ. Press, 2006).

41. Jordan, *FDR, Dewey, and the Election of 1944*.

42. Based on legislation passed in 2012, the major assistant secretary positions continued to be nominated by the president and subject to senate confirmation. The lesser ones, like an assistant secretary for public affairs, became direct presidential appointments.

43. This analogy breaks down for less common instances of law enforcement. At the federal level, the FBI chief and the local U.S. Attorney are presidential appointees. At the state level, an attorney general is usually elected and oversees both the investigative and prosecutorial roles. Even at the local level, sometimes the investigating agency is the elected sheriff rather than the (unelected) police.

44. A similar example at the federal level was when USDA conducted referenda of farmers. Its proposal policy would only go into effect if approved by the voting farmers.

45. Nancy Snow, "US Propaganda," in *American Thought and Culture in the 21st Century*, ed. Martin Halliwell and Catherine Morley (Edinburgh, UK: Edinburgh Univ. Press, 2008), 107–108; Frank Rich, *The Greatest Story Ever Sold: The Decline and Fall of Truth in Bush's America* (New York: Penguin Books, 2007).

46. This is no minor detail. At the beginning of President Nixon's second term, he tried to reorganize the executive branch by naming super-secretaries to oversee four large domestic swaths of federal activity: human resources, natural resources, community de-

velopment, and economic policy. His senior domestic aide, John Ehrlichman, insisted that before any inter-agency disagreements could get to the president for a decision, the disagreeing agencies must first "start with an agreed-upon set of facts." See Mordecai Lee, *Nixon's Super-Secretaries: The Last Grand Presidential Reorganization Effort* (College Station: Texas A&M Univ. Press, 2010), 115.

47. David Barstow, "Pentagon Finds No Fault in Ties to TV Analysts," *New York Times*, December 25, 2011, A18.

5

PERVASIVE PROPAGANDA IN AMERICA

NANCY SNOW

The public is even more fond of entertainment than of information.

—WILLIAM RANDOLPH HEARST

Publicity is the life of this culture, in so far as without publicity capitalism could not survive, and at the same time publicity is its dream.

—JOHN BERGER

The United States of America is the leading purveyor of propaganda in liberal democratic societies and one of the leading propaganda manufacturers in the world today. The two dominant strains of propaganda in American society, the commercial/cultural and the military/governmental, drive American propaganda production at home and abroad. In the United States, private commercial propaganda is as important to notions of democracy as governmental propaganda. As Jacques Ellul observes in *Propaganda*: "Historically, from the moment a democratic regime establishes itself, propaganda establishes itself alongside it under various forms. This is inevitable, as democracy depends on public opinion and competition between political parties."[1] Likewise, commercial appeals to the consumer through advertising, which plays on irrational fantasies and emotional impulses, are some of the most pervasive forms of propaganda in existence today.

COMMERCIAL/CULTURAL AMERICAN PROPAGANDA

Pervasive American propaganda had its modern origins in the early twentieth century, during World War I, when the mass media were first integrated with public relations and advertising methods to advocate and maintain a frenzied public support for war.[2] It has continued to thrive for nearly a century because all successive forms of mass communication, from commercial media to social media, have become prominent channels of propaganda.[3] Without the capitalistic concentration endemic to modern mass media, there can be no media propaganda. For propaganda to pervade, the media must remain concentrated and commercially driven, public interest news agencies and services must be limited, the press must be highly allegiant to commercial and government propaganda domination, and conglomerate radio, film, and television media must remain in place. This is the propaganda landscape today in the United States.

It is easy to fall into a false sense of media competition security with the rise of the Internet, particularly social media; most of us are able to surf the net and visit websites across the globe. On Facebook we may have "friends" from across the planet. If we speak another language we have even more access to alternative media, including media outlets that may challenge the rather homogenized nature of mass media news delivery in the United States. But the reality remains that propaganda media in America are owned by major conglomerates, and the trend, not just in the United States, but everywhere, is toward fewer and fewer companies—and fewer and fewer players—continuing to control our mind's agenda. Having a WordPress blog, as I do, or blogging on the Huffington Post, as I have, does not constitute equal footing, influence-wise, to owning a radio or TV station or selling the Huffington Post to AOL.

Forty years ago, W. Phillips Davison, professor of sociology and journalism at Columbia University, noted that the trend toward pervasive propaganda internationally was "toward a greater emphasis on public and private commercial efforts, which are increasing rapidly."[4] Davison observed that "official propaganda activities have been dwarfed by the commercial publicity of private enterprise."[5] One of the most astute American propaganda scholars of his generation, Davison died in the spring of 2012, very aware of how rapidly commercial propaganda efforts had expanded in the last twenty years with the widespread availability of the Internet for private consumer use and abuse. Australian social psychologist Alex Carey, French sociologist Jacques Ellul, and British writer Aldous Huxley observed that private propaganda (for example, public relations, commercial advertising, entertainment) more than government propaganda is more pervasive in democracies, especially in the United States.[6] Noam Chomsky and Edward Herman presented a propaganda model in *Manufacturing Consent: The Political Economy of the Mass Media.* Though not without flaws, this model was the first to view American media as a propaganda system. The authors identified five filters of American propaganda: media ownership, advertising, news media reliance on official sources, "flak" (negative strategic communications) produced by wealthy interest groups, and anti-Communism as an ideological control mechanism. Of the five, four still pervade today, with anti-Communism ideology having been replaced by a number of clashing political ideologies that divide the country: anti-Democratic/anti-liberal versus anti-Republican/anti-conservative or anti-Tea Party versus anti-Obama.

American advertising in media underscores the fact that what constitutes the press or media in America is what is in the economic interests of owners and their financial supporters, advertisers. The public's role is reduced to that of sideline spectator, not active participant. For one example, consider the U.S. Diplomatic Mission to Germany's public affairs page and its explanation of the role of the media in the United States:

> Economics plays a major role in shaping the information served up to the U.S. public in newspapers, on radio and television, and now on the Internet. While nonprofit and advocacy organizations have significant voices, most of the public's primary sources of information—major urban newspapers, the weekly news magazines, and the broadcast and cable networks—are in business to make money. Media and communications, with revenues of over $242 billion, are one of America's largest business groups. In 2000, adult consumers of media information and amusement products spent over $675 a person. Advertisers spent an additional $215 billion to bring their products to the attention of the American public. The media are a great engine in American society, providing jobs for hundreds of thousands of technicians, writers, artists, performers and intellectuals and shaping attitudes and beliefs.[7]

The United States is the largest ad market in the world, with advertising costs in the mass media exceeding $200 billion.[8] America also leads the world in online advertising growth.[9] The most celebrated people in our culture are not scientists, teachers, or social workers, who may be somewhat relatable, but sports and entertainment culture celebrities. Such people, like most television commercials, are not presented as relatable, but are rolled out to the public as an advertising dream fantasy that the average Joe and Jane can only watch in awe. The non-military "Shock and Awe" in the United States today continues to be the new heights of cult of personality worship in the form of pop culture artists and entertainers. A perfect case in point is what has been described as a "Hydra-headed pop-cultural blitzkrieg"[10] led by one Beyoncé Knowles, a 1990s lead artist with pop group Destiny's Child, who is now the wife of media mogul and Hip Hop artist Jay-Z, mother of Blue Ivy, and close personal friend to the First Family. She is one of the most bankable celebrities of the post-9/11 decade and star of the 2013 Pepsi Super Bowl XLVII halftime show on CBS. Pepsi signed her to a $50 million endorsement deal, and the überstar revealed in a *GQ* (*Gentleman's Quarterly*) profile, which proclaimed her the "hottest woman of the past thirteen years," that her entire life—every photographic image, interview, video, or diary confession—is stored in an "official Beyoncé archive," temperature-controlled and digitally archived for posterity.[11] Those who create and those who watch creation drive the propaganda landscape in America. Even the watching is often insufferable. Writer Amy Wallace described this Beyoncé archive item as being "particularly revealing": "Stop pretending that I have it all together. If I'm scared, be scared, allow it, release it, move on. I think I need to go listen to 'Make Love to Me' and make love to my husband."

Beyond the archive is the propaganda effect of the Internet. The Internet's influence on the pervasiveness of propaganda is paradoxical. On the one hand, citizen and nongovernmental and noncommercial activist websites are expanding, leading to a chaotic situation for official sources and traditional media (MSM or mainstream media). Now everyone can seemingly become a journalist or a source at the click of a mouse. This would seem to be good for building up our immunity to the worst forms of propaganda that seek to deceive and mislead, and indeed the public seems more skeptical about official sources of information in the post-Vietnam, post-Gulf War, and post-9/11 era. But to counter or overcome this public skepticism, there is an expanded commercial cottage industry of public relations and advertising firms to infiltrate the blogosphere as well as popular search engines, like Google and Yahoo, and über-popular social media sites like Facebook and Twitter. The giant international public relations firm Edelman inspired a new term called "flog," or "fake blog." Edelman worked with corporate client Walmart to hire employees to act as "grassroots bloggers" for Walmart-sponsored sites like "Working Families for Wal-Mart," an oldie but goodie propaganda technique called the front group, serving as an Astroturf (fake) grassroots movement in support of Walmart labor practices.[12] In 2006, Richard Edelman publicly apologized for not disclosing that a folksy pro-Walmart blog, "Wal-Marting across America," about a man and woman staying at Walmart parking lots in their RV, was actually underwritten by "Working Families for Wal-Mart."[13] This propaganda technique double dipped in that it not only used the front group of Jim and Laura posing as discount store enthusiasts rather than paid sponsors, but it also utilized the American tradition of democratic egalitarianism, the "just plain folks" technique of having one's fellow citizens freely share their story with no commercial strings attached. We so value genuine word-of-mouth endorsements in America that we have our own Word of Mouth Marketing Association (WOMMA), to which Edelman and other credible PR firms are ethically affiliated.[14] The truth was that Jim and Laura's RV was paid for by Walmart through Edelman, along with the compensation for their blogs. Even their journey across America was no happenstance blue highway. It too was prearranged by Walmart. Edelman isn't the only violator, just the most prominent one. In 2012, the *New York Times* exposed the practice of writing five-star positive book reviews for hire. One data mining expert from the University of Illinois estimated that up to one-third of online reviews are fakes.[15]

To explain the conglomerate media landscape that occupies our mind, we have a handful of corporate media conglomerate owners in the United States that has dwindled from about fifty in the last thirty years. The "Big Five" include the Walt Disney Company, based in Burbank, California, and Time Warner, CBS Corporation, and Viacom, all based in New York City. Rupert Murdoch's News Corporation, founded in his native Australia but also headquartered in New York, is a dominant media content provider in the United States with ownership of the *Wall Street Journal* and Fox News Channel. Of the Big Five, the Walt Disney Company is the most pervasive entertainment propaganda content provider to the world, with revenues of over $40 billion. It is the largest global media conglomerate and has an oversized friendly rodent as its corporate mascot. Mickey Mouse is as representative of the United States and U.S. foreign policy to critics as it is symbolic of the Walt Disney resort. The critical representation is as an emblem of cultural imperialism, sometimes referred to as "banal imperialism," where global audiences are subjected to American commercial values that drive a homogenized and corporatized global cultural landscape.[16]

It was Neil Postman who most famously described the American mindscape as one of amusement to the point of death, death to the conscious awareness especially.[17] As fellow contributor J. Michael Sproule states in *Channels of Propaganda*, "people let down their critical guard when they are being entertained. Like a kitten mesmerized by a dangling pocket watch, citizens are likely to miss much of what is happening to them when they are focused on commercial spectacle or political amusement. Further, when citizens are fed a steady diet of charming but empty public communication, then the nation's collective economic and political intelligence may be cumulatively weakened."[18]

Phil Spector is credited with the creation of the Wall of Sound in the 1960s, what he described as "a Wagnerian approach to rock & roll: little symphonies for the kids."[19] In America we have a Wall of Propaganda, from the domestic war machine to the overseas war zone to the domestic and foreign Tinsel Town and TMZ. This wall consists of manipulation of symbols in order to maintain the interests of the privileged and powerful while driving the masses to distraction through an infinite loop of fame and celebrity entertainment and a privately financed election system that masquerades as a choice of competing philosophies for the electorate. This wall prevents a real democracy and true freedom of choice from flourishing. Like Spector's studio musicians, we have our own hosts of propagandists contributing to this wall of influence: public relations professionals, entertainment and news media industrialists, political and campaign consultants, government and corporate lobbyists, all employed by and loyal to owner and client interests, not the pubic interest. A compliant public, men and women who gaze upon this spectacle with a combination of indifference, occasional defiance, but mostly bewilderment, supports this.

And that's the way it still is since the dawn of the modern propaganda age in America over one hundred years ago. The difference today is that our entire world is spin-driven and we don't have a progressive, reform-minded press corps devoted to ferreting out propaganda campaigns. In 1906, Ray Stannard Baker, one of the original muckraker journalists, published a scathing piece about agents of the press, propagandists, who had arisen to push the commercial, antiregulatory interests of the railroad industry to publicly accountable members of Congress.[20] He explained to the mass reading audience in *McClure's* magazine that public opinion was, as Edward Bernays and Noam Chomsky would later identify it, an "engineering of consent" process, massaged by special interests that had ruling power, and not public interest, as their goal and objective.[21] Public opinion was something to be controlled, not educated and informed. Baker worried that manipulation of the press by publicity firms and press agents would advantage those who operate in organized secret over that of the public that habitually remains disorganized and confused about how governing decisions are made. Edward Bernays, nephew to Sigmund Freud and the father of public relations, viewed such consent engineering in a positive light, arguing that without competitive propaganda in a democratic society, we are left with a less accountable committee of elders who would "choose our rulers [and] dictate our conduct, private and public."[22]

It was noted American journalist and counsel to American presidents Walter Lippmann who assessed the propaganda landscape and described it as comprised of citizen bystanders driven by media stereotypes. Lippmann, like Bernays, held no high regard for these irrational folk, whom he called the "phantom public" in his follow-up to *Public Opinion*:

> The actual governing is made up of a multitude of arrangements on specific questions by particular individuals. These rarely become visible to private citizens. Government, in the long intervals between elections, is carried on by politicians, officeholders and influential men who make settlements with other politicians, officeholders and influential men. The mass of people see these settlements, judge them, and affect them only now and then. They are altogether too numerous, too complicated, too obscure in their effects to become the subject of any continuing exercise of public opinion.[23]

What a contrasting political governing theory between the pessimistic Lippmann and more sanguine Thomas Jefferson, who, in his letter to Judge William Johnson, explained the rationale for overthrowing European rule: "We believe that man was a rational animal, endowed by nature with rights, and with an innate sense of justice, and that he could be restrained from wrong, and protected in right, by moderate powers, confided to persons of his own choice and held to their duties by dependence on his own will."[24]

It may seem crazy to identify the United States as the most propagandistic country, what with all those "Axis of Evil" nominees. But we are the nation that created Madison Avenue, TMZ, Hollywood, the Super Bowl, and the Oscars. No other country can put on a show of popular propaganda quite like America. In 2010 alone, the United States had a record thirty-five postseason college football bowl games with corporate sponsors, all to reinforce our zealous economic commitment to professional sports entertainment over higher education,[25] where just half of all National Football League players have college degrees.[26]

American presidents from George Washington to Abraham Lincoln, Woodrow Wilson to Ronald Reagan, are the ultimate celebrities in the American culture. It wasn't until the twentieth century, however, that American presidents had the greatest technological power of the media to persuade the masses through film and television and to harness the power of special interests to sponsor their campaigns. Special interest money from wealthy individuals, PACs, and Super PACs is the mother's milk of politics.[27] The Center for Responsive Politics estimated that the total cost for the 2012 federal elections reached $6 billion, with nearly $1 billion spent on television advertising alone.[28] What changed the political landscape dramatically in 2012 was the record-breaking level of outside group expenditures, a result of the U.S. Supreme Court's *Citizens United* ruling in 2010, which lifted restrictions on the levels and amounts of wealthy individual and organizational contributions to campaigns.[29]

Wilson we associate forever with George Creel and his Creel Committee, aka the Committee on Public Information. It was anything but straight "just the facts" public information. George Creel, investigative journalist by profession, described the CPI's efforts to market American entry into World War I: "In all things, from first to last, without halt or change, it was a plain publicity proposition, a vast enterprise in salesmanship, the world's greatest adventure in advertising."[30] Creel eschewed calling the publicity exercise propaganda because he accused the Germans of having corrupted public understanding of the word. To many Americans, such foreign propaganda was associated with lies and deception. "Our effort was educational and informative throughout, for we had such confidence in our case as to feel that no other argument was needed than the simple, straightforward presentation of facts."[31] And what did this "simple, straightforward presentation of facts" look like? It was total propaganda for total war. All available mass media were employed: newspapers, pamphlets, radio, the nascent motion picture industry, sign boards, and posters. "There was no part of the great war machinery that we did not touch, no medium of appeal that we did not employ."[32] Seventy-five thousand civilian men, dubbed the Four Minute Men for the length of their patriotic speeches in theaters, were called into Committee service. They were credited with delivering over 7.5 million speeches to an audience of 135 million.[33] Another seventy-five thousand regular employees of the CPI, all faithfully devoted to the messianic mission of Americanism, joined them. "All that was fine and ardent in the civilian population came at our call until more than one hundred and fifty thousand men and women were devoting highly specialized abilities to the work of the Committee, as faithful and devoted in their service as though they wore the khaki.[34]

Creel viewed American propaganda in the Roman Catholic tradition, as a propagation of faith in the myth of American superiority, be it in business or war making. It is no accident that Creel used the word advertising in his book title. Advertising is an American original, and friend and foe admire government advertising, known euphemistically as public service advertising. Adolf Hitler spoke admiringly about America in general, what he believed to be its advanced industrial superiority and industrious workforce replenished by Nordic immigrants,[35] as well as American advertising tactics,[36] but as Drew Dudley, the U.S. chief of the Media Programming Division in the Office of War Mobilization and Reconversion added, "To condemn advertising simply because Hitler made the wrong use of it would be as silly as to condemn research in radiation and nuclear physics because, in the exigencies of war, a destructive role was found for atomic energy."[37] The reality is that the United States reigns supreme in the "means of communication through which to disseminate propaganda."[38] Further, as Australian sociologist Alex Carey notes, beyond the twentieth-century mass media means (television, radio, film, comic strips) and the twenty-first-century social media (Facebook, Twitter), the United States holds a preeminent position in message propaganda that no other country has: the creation and maintenance of emotionally significant symbols in American culture.[39] These symbols predispose us to view the world in contrasts: as military villains and heroes, political conservatives/Republicans and liberals/Democrats, saints and sinners, the Sacred and the Satanic. Carey's conclusion: "A society or culture which is disposed to view the world in Manichean terms will be more vulnerable to control by propaganda."[40] Consider a 2011 Gallup poll that indicates an overwhelming majority of Americans believe in God (92 percent), a figure that has remained relatively stable since Gallup first started measuring religious belief after World War II, with some pronounced regional differences in religiosity; the South is much more religious, at 96 percent, than the East (Northeast/New England), at 86 percent.[41] The United States is among the top four wealthier advanced societies that measure as much religiosity as the poorest countries in sub-Saharan Africa and Asia.[42] (The other three are Italy, Greece, and Singapore.) Such religiosity plays well into the hands of the professional hucksters who seek to play up the messianic positives of advertising, public relations, political consultants, and Super PACs.

Hucksterism is as American as baseball, hot dogs, apple pie, and Chevrolet. Messing with the capitalist showroom is like trying to expose the awful little man behind the curtain in *The Wizard of Oz*. It didn't work for Dorothy, and it won't work for us either. We need a Toto, but we don't have one person, institution, or movement to reveal the pervasive harm of our mass communication empire.[43] To make matters worse, we are drenched in pseudo-environments that drive us deeper away from personal experience related to politics and entertainment, the twin towers of pervasive propaganda. Our foreign wars, aka overseas theaters, are all-volunteer enterprises replete with remote drones.[44] Our Facebook friends and Twitter feeds are becoming overrun with celebrity-sponsored PR machines. We've gone from real friends to pseudo-fans and Little Monsters.[45]

One of the most pervasive themes to occupy the American mind is the propaganda phrase "the American way of life." The American way consists largely of a combination of economic competition mixed with commercialism that begins and ends with consumerism. It is illustrated by far more economic consumerist competition than political and free speech competition. When I lived in New Hampshire, home to America's first-in-the-nation presidential primary, I was often asked about the lack of diversity in the state, in particular its 99 percent Caucasian population and affluent status in per capita income compared to larger states like California and New York. I was quick to retort that we had plenty of diversity. Just walk down the aisle of any grocer and you could find more brands of Ben and Jerry's ice cream and salad dressing than political candidates and points of view. For a country of over 300 million, we spend billions electing one person every four years from a dozen or so multimillionaires. How could such an unrepresentative electoral politics function without an environment that elevates human distraction and consumption to dizzying levels?

The American propaganda way of life operates under a "warts and all" philosophy. You must accept our nation and its national myths (the American dream, the American way of life, cult of youth, cult of celebrity) *as it is* and, in turn, make adjustments to the capitalist democracy that will come to rule your life. The United States is open to those who can afford it, and no other country offers as many economic channels to the pursuit of American happiness as the United States of America. This is why people are still dying, in a literal and figurative sense, to come to this country. Whether one obtains the American dream is always elusive and dependent on the rise and fall of one's fortune—in pocketbook and fate.

All American media, be it in the form of movies, books, magazines, television, or the Internet, carry a set of values that we know to be distinctly American. They are part political in the form of the most famous sentence of the U.S. Declaration of Independence:

> We hold these truths to be self-evident, that all men are created equal, that they are endowed by their Creator with certain unalienable Rights, that among these are Life, Liberty and the pursuit of Happiness.

These American ideals expressed in the Declaration of Independence carry with them a consumerist bottom line attachment. The pursuit of happiness in America is infused with purchasing power. A popular antiwar poster of the Vietnam War era was "War is good for business.

Invest your son." In the 1980s, another whimsical catchphrase emerged during the Reagan years that invoked the American lifestyle of consumerism: "He who dies with the most toys wins." Three decades after Vietnam, President George W. Bush told a nation in shock after 9/11 to commence a new normalcy that included shopping. "Now, the American people have got to go about their business. We cannot let the terrorists achieve the objective of frightening our nation to the point where we don't—where we don't conduct business, where people don't shop."[46] Don't let the terrorists get in the way of your credit card purchases! The president's words, though criticized by some, were quickly adopted by San Francisco mayor Willie Brown in a public information campaign targeting international visitors. The entire city was flooded with "America: Open for Business" posters in downtown storefronts.

Thomas Jefferson, drafter of the Declaration of Independence, warned America that an overzealous commitment to banking institutions and moneyed incorporations (a nineteenth-century phenomena) would destroy the eighteenth-century ideals expressed in the American revolutionary documents. He wisely pointed out the obvious contradictions between democracy and capitalism. Nevertheless, the American way of life remains incorporated. We are a nation infused by commercial propagandists whose job it is to keep us motivated to buy.[47] Many of our purchases are impulse buys driven by emotional storylines in advertising narratives. The buy-in is both ideological/rhetorical (the American way) and literal (advertising for consumption). Consider the ubiquity of the prescription drug and alcohol industries, not only legal for adults but also the most heavily advertised in American mass communication. Big Pharma spends twice as much hawking its drugs as it does on research and development.[48] Direct to consumer advertising (DTC) of prescription drugs is a multibillion-dollar enterprise that makes the fast food industry envious. Television is a perfect vehicle for pushing drugs, not just through the ubiquitous drug commercials, but also through the less obvious television news show appearances of celebrities hawking their sponsor drug companies. Remember what Dan Kuehl reminded us through the voice of Edward R. Murrow: television is a weapon.[49]

American morning talk shows are some of the most watched programs still capturing eyeballs on over-the-air television networks, and they are (in)famous propaganda machines. NBC's *Today Show* even serves as the model for the U.S.-government sponsored three-hour prime-time news magazine *Al Youm* (Today) that broadcasts five days a week on Alhurra (Free One) network. Though there are many examples of celebrities appearing in their own pseudo-news format infomercials, none quite "takes the cake" (pun intended) as much as that of Paula Deen, whose appearance managed to combine the toxic duo of Big Pharma with Big Media. On January 17, 2012, the fatty food enthusiast Paula Deen, who vaulted to fame and fortune for lasagna sandwiches and fried-egg bacon burgers on glazed doughnut buns, sat down for a dodgy conversation with the *Today Show*'s Al Roker. Roker, typically the jovial weather guy, was chosen as a credible counterpart to the heavyset Deen because he had suffered for years from morbid obesity before dramatically transforming his physical appearance through gastric bypass surgery. After days of network commercial teasers about a big secret that Deen would be disclosing, Paula Deen's big reveal to the millions of viewers was that she had Type 2 diabetes (not a surprise) and that she had been diagnosed with the disease over three years earlier (a big surprise). The interview was sympathetic to her plight but gave Deen ample opportunity to provide her own limited medical knowledge of diabetes. When pressed if what one eats is linked to adult-onset diabetes, she downplayed the well-documented connection. "Certainly Al, that is part of the puzzle, but there's many other things that can lead to diabetes." The medical community wisdom, not the southern aw-shucks version of Paula Deen presented on *Today,* is unanimous in its opinion that Type 2 diabetes is a high risk for those who are obese or overweight, smokers, have sedentary lifestyles, or who eat unhealthy diets.[50] She assured her followers that "I'm your cook, not your doctor."[51] The news-in-name only interview was predictably an infomercial for Deen's other big reveal, her new sponsor, Danish pharmaceutical behemoth Novo Nordisk, maker of the diabetes drug Victoza, which like many pharmaceutical drugs sounds like "victory" over lifestyle-driven bad eating habits and limited exercise. It may be a minor victory, with the cost being nearly $500 per month for the daily injection.

Novo Nordisk finds television personalities like Deen who can hawk their products to unwitting consumers who are desperate for easy fixes to lifestyle diseases. Victoza is a relatively recent FDA-approved drug. Novo Nordisk manufactures consent, like so many other drug-pushing companies, by playing up the possible good effects while downplaying the "safety" issues. In this case, a safety warning reads as follows: "In animal studies, Victoza caused thyroid tumors—including thyroid cancer—in some rats and mice. It is not known whether Victoza causes thyroid tumors or a type of thyroid cancer called medullary thyroid cancer (MTC) in people which may be fatal if not detected and treated early."[52] This is not quite the sort of safety warnings we heeded as children, like "look both ways before you cross."

The pervasive propaganda of the "American way of life" comes in the form of national images recognized the world over. Though without a state-sanctioned church, we do see ourselves as a Judeo-Christian nation that tolerates minority religions. Our national anthem is a common ritual from high school football games to the Super Bowl. You can't run for public office without displaying the Stars and Stripes behind you or on you. When presidential candidate Barack Obama was first running for office, reporters asked why he didn't wear a flag lapel pin, to which he replied, "I decided I won't wear that pin on my chest. Instead I'm going to try to tell the American people what I believe . . . and hopefully that will be a testimony to my patriotism."[53] It wasn't. Shortly after an April 2008 debate in Iowa, Obama was seen sporting a flag lapel pin, which he regularly wears as president.

After 9/11 many television news anchors wore flag pins to show their support for a nation at war. Our symbols of freedom, like the flag, the American bald eagle, or the U.S. Capitol, are quasi-religious in importance. It is also practically impossible to run for office in America as an avowed atheist. We are the most religious democracy on the planet, and even if a candidate hasn't been to church or temple in ages, mentioning that fact in his or her campaign literature is a sure way to kill off support for his or her candidacy. Naturally, American religiosity varies by region. In the Deep South and Midwest, it is far more common to wear one's religious values on one's shirt sleeve. The more secular cities of the two coasts tend to have more political candidates who don't infuse their campaigns in religious rhetoric.

The American (propaganda) way favors youthful enthusiasm over senior citizen introspection. Think Levi's, Coke, the Pepsi Generation, and MTV. When one pictures America, it is not the old couple sitting on the front porch swing, but rather the rollerblading or snowboarding extreme athlete in motion. It is also more masculine than feminine in orientation. There are infinite older male lifestyle brands that dominate our mindscape, such as the Marlboro Man, Camel cigarettes, Dockers jeans, Harley-Davidson motorcycles, Winchester rifles, and Colt .45 guns. Many of these older male lifestyle brands signify man dominating the natural world; picture Arnold Schwarzenegger in his Hummer.

While we are not unique in our enthusiasm for sports, no other country so dominates in sports consumer products, such as Nike, Reebok, Champion USA, Under Armour, and the NBA. Los Angeles Lakers' guard Kobe Bryant's jerseys sell out in China more than those of the Houston Rockets' Chinese-born Yao Ming. Bryant has an advantage over Yao: He's a super-talented American black athlete who speaks fluent English, thus possessing characteristics that inspire many Chinese youth, many of whom are pulled into believing that the American way of communicating, lifestyle, sports and recreation, higher education, and popular culture are the best the world has to offer.

The American propaganda way prevails in retail and fun and leisure. We are still the world's wealthiest nation, despite recent wars in two Islamic countries, and no other country can match our global footprint in fast food (Pizza Hut, KFC, Taco Bell, Subway, McDonald's). So what's not to like about us, we ask ourselves. We tell those who aspire to be more American that it's a great life with a lot of choices, freedom to be who you want to be, and the most diversified collection of races, religions, and ethnicities on the planet. What's wrong with that picture?

Part of it may lie in the contested concept of American exceptionalism. Deep down, Americans who grow up here are inculcated with the belief that every person outside the United States, if given the opportunity, would want to be an American or pursue the American way of life. This common viewpoint is nurtured by a faith in the American dream, a sense that if a person works hard enough, he or she can become anything. Most baby boomer Americans (those born between the end of WWII and the mid-1960s), especially boys, grew up hearing that anyone could become president of the United States. Girls like myself heard that one could become Miss America. It's said that if one dreams it, one can live it. Hard work comes from a Puritan ethic that God finds favor in those who keep themselves busy with pursuit, be it happiness, business, or service. If you fall short of your goals, then you haven't worked hard enough to obtain them. Politically, we view ourselves as the city on a hill, a beacon of light in a dark world, a national experiment of freedom and liberty that others can attain if they become more like us or at least allow us to pursue our own national interests.

The American propaganda way of life advantages the doing person over the being person, the active go-getter over the passive come-hither. The phrase "the squeaky wheel gets the grease" is a reminder that you shouldn't keep silent about what you want. Don't wait and don't deliberate. We also favor the extroverted person over the introvert. We learn early on that waiting too long to establish what you want will mean that someone else will steal your dream. Such an embedded cultural mindset predisposes our population to be more likely to act first and reflect on actions later, which doesn't bode well when nations are contemplating going to war or when individuals are thinking about those purchases when shopping in megamalls.

Whatever its flaws and finer qualities, the American way is still the most oversold dream on the planet. It is no accident that the United States invented all the persuasion industries—advertising, branding, public relations, marketing, sales promotion, consumer research, television and radio spot ads, direct mail, and Sears catalogues. The 1912 craftsman bungalow that I use as my writer's cottage became so popular in design in the early twentieth century that Sears Robuck made the architectural plans available in the form of home kits. There is no reason that your dream home can't be fabricated from a mass marketing campaign.

Commerce and commercial appeal are as much our weapons of influence as any bullet or warship. Need to make a professional presentation? It's more than likely you will use the ubiquitous Microsoft PowerPoint as your standard business presentation tool. You may favor Mac over Microsoft or Coke over Pepsi, but you'd be hard pressed to avoid one or the other.

This leads us to that special conundrum in American pervasive propaganda known as cultural imperialism. It's easy to hate the American way of cultural and consumer domination. We have no parallel. And yet Americanization of the world is here to stay. It is not without adaptation to one's wants. In the Beijing McDonald's I used to pass by when on sabbatical at Tsinghua University, I noticed that cucumber slices were a standard on every burger just as the Chinese KFC served corn and rice as side dishes. What continues to cause angst and upset to some around the world is that we remain "The Big One," to use the words about the United States from the 1997 Michael Moore film. We produce more municipal waste per capita than any other nation and we don't seem too guilty about it.[54] We have led the world in consumer innovation but we are not leading the world in conservation. Even our gripes about the rise of energy prices and the price of gas at the consumer pumps around town pale in price comparison to our European or Asian neighbors. This all goes back to our love of the individual and her consumer preference, which we are quick to back up with our Constitution. If a person wants to buy the biggest gas-guzzler in town, then he should have that right. If a person wants to drink the biggest gulp of a sugary soft drink, then she should do just that. It's the American way, we shout in our defense. The world watches and wonders if the American way is sustainable, and so far it isn't, but why think about that today when we can postpone it to next year or ten years from now?

But here is where we do not question. We call our version of truth-seeking a marketplace of ideas, the fundamental cornerstone of representative democracy. But to paraphrase New York mayor Ed Koch, "How are we doing?" A true marketplace would have ample space for public discussion and dialogue that challenges the worst aspects of spin—word and image distortions, nefarious ad campaigns that harm. We don't have anyone from Public Citizen's Commercial Alert campaign speaking regularly on commercial television. Surprised? No surprise to John Feffer of Foreign Policy in Focus, who takes us to task for our double standards in moralizing, especially on all things propaganda:

> We ridicule countries that operate cults of personality—North Korea, Uzbekistan—and pat ourselves on the back that we reserve such embarrassing displays of adulation for guys who throw balls, gals who star in reality shows, and teenagers who sing pop music. At least our American idols don't kill people. But alongside our celebration of celebrities, we also have a stealth personality cult: We insist, overwhelming evidence to the contrary, that only individuals, not institutions, make history. We are constantly on the lookout for the heroic leader who can single-handedly transform the warp and weave of their society. When a movement is leaderless like Occupy Wall Street or the leadership is dispersed as with so

> much of the Arab Spring, we're not quite sure what to make of it. We are trapped in the personality cult that our culture of individualism has created.[55]

Propaganda is here to stay, and to echo Dan Kuehl, we've got to get used to it as a growth market, but at least we can better monitor its uses and abuses, which is the major aim of this collection.

MILITARY/GOVERNMENTAL AMERICAN PROPAGANDA

Since 9/11, we are quite well versed on the information and image wars that grew out of the U.S. government's Global War on Terror response.[56] Two military invasions of Muslim majority nation-states took place despite the American president's reassurance to Muslims of the world that the United States had no ill will toward those who followed Islam. The invasion of Afghanistan was generally well received by the American people as a necessary and appropriate response to hunt down those responsible for the terror attacks. Though war is always met with some level of resistance, most public opinion polls in the fall of 2001 showed that the American people trusted the America president and U.S. military to do the right thing. Very little propaganda preparation was needed on the domestic front because most Americans had seen the television footage of the World Trade Center attacks and needed no convincing to respond.

The March 2003 invasion of Iraq required the most propaganda preparation. The White House explanation to the public for the invasion was subject to a dizzying whirl of zigzag changes—from weapons of mass destruction, to imminent destruction through atomic annihilation, and then finally to if we don't fight the terrorists there in Baghdad the enemy will bring the fight to us in New York, Washington, or Los Angeles.[57] The White House worked closely with the Pentagon establishment to manufacture consent through the mainstream media channels, as was revealed in an unusual front-page media criticism story by the *New York Times* titled "Behind TV Analysts, Pentagon's Hidden Hand."[58] The investigative piece uncovered over 150 paid military consultants—lobbyists, senior executives—all financially invested in the war policies of the Bush administration, who presented their prowar views on television without any mention of these sponsorships. The viewing public watched with a perception that these respected military analysts' views were, like Jim and Laura and their roving RV, unfettered and uncluttered by outside interference. The fact that there exists a Pentagon propaganda machine is not a particularly new reality, however. Senator J. William Fulbright, chair of the Senate Foreign Relations Committee during Vietnam, had noted the effects of the information war machine on the press almost forty years earlier:

> The military public relations campaign is directed at all of the American people ("targets," they are called in the manuals, a nice military word adopted by Madison Avenue and readopted by military PR people in its new sense). The audience ranges from school children and teachers to ranchers and farmers, from union leaders to defense contractors, from Boy Scouts to American Legionnaires. The principal target of the military PR men, however, is the media.
>
> Very few Americans, I am convinced, have much cognizance of the extent of the military sell or its effects on their lives through the molding of their opinions, the opinions (and votes on appropriations) of their representatives in the Congress, and the opinions of their presumed ombudsmen in the American press.[59]

The U.S.-led Global War on Terror was a triumph of propaganda, as the U.S. executive branch chose to use tactics that were one-way asymmetrical in their communication style; in other words, the Bush administration approach was a bit like actor Robert Young's character of Jim Anderson on *Father Knows Best.* This communication practice is the most common in a war propaganda environment because it favors utilization of manipulative influence tactics (top-down, one-way, authoritative) to change the behavior of the target audience in the service of the sponsor's goals. Companies like the Lincoln Group (formerly Iraqex) and the Rendon Group contracted with the Bush White House to "sell" the American agenda in Iraq.[60] The Lincoln Group paid select Iraqi journalists to write and publish pro-U.S. articles in Iraqi newspapers.[61] One such article carried the headline "Iraqis Insist on Living Despite Terrorism."[62] As pointed out by the *LA Times*'s staff, the propaganda operation was ironic given the purported ideals of American freedom proffered by the State Department versus what was produced by the military's Information Operations Task Force in practice:

> The military's effort to disseminate propaganda in the Iraqi media is taking place even as U.S. officials are pledging to promote democratic principles, political transparency and freedom of speech in a country emerging from decades of dictatorship and corruption.
>
> It comes as the State Department is training Iraqi reporters in basic journalism skills and Western media ethics, including one workshop titled "The Role of Press in a Democratic Society." Standards vary widely at Iraqi newspapers, many of which are shoestring operations.[63]

Fellow contributor Dan Kuehl holds no harsh judgment regarding American propaganda operations in Iraq. The goal is to use Iraqi media outlets in the service of Operation Iraqi Freedom and to drive public opinion away from the enemy insurgents and toward the U.S. military objective. He told the *Los Angeles Times* in response to the practice of planting news stories: "I don't think that there's anything evil or morally wrong with it. I just question whether it's effective."[64]

The Bush White House was also engaged in propaganda on the home front. It distributed video news releases to local network affiliates without sourcing the information and paid some journalists, such as Armstrong Williams, to tout Bush administration policies, with no attribution or acknowledgment of the pay-to-play model. The Government Accountability Office criticized such practices as "covert propaganda," which was later ruled an illegal Bush administration practice based on the U.S. federal statutory ban against the use of publicity or propaganda with appropriated funds.[65] In the first four years of the Bush presidency, before and after September 11, 2001, global public views of the United States, in and out of war zone areas, were at lows not seen since the Vietnam War and President Ronald Reagan's first term.[66] Brand America and the American dream had lost their gleam.

If American propaganda has elements of Big Brother, then public diplomacy is at times Little Sister. At its best, public diplomacy refers to open-sourced communication efforts that emphasize mutual understanding through sponsored educational and cultural exchanges and international broadcasting. It includes the highly regarded Fulbright program, the U.S. government-sponsored gold standard in sponsored international educational exchange of students and scholars. But at its worst, public diplomacy can be subsumed under military-style "strategic communication" efforts, like the habits of the Lincoln Group and the Rendon Group. After 9/11, public diplomacy efforts were closely intertwined with the vagaries of globally unpopular policies like the war in Iraq and the Bush-sponsored War on Terror. Consider the State Department lineage for Under Secretary of State for Public Diplomacy and Public Affairs: Charlotte Beers, Margaret Tutwiler, Karen Hughes, and James Glassman. All four were notable political conservatives who were awarded the State Department position for their partisan loyalties, with Karen Hughes having worked with George W. Bush since his days as Texas governor. Ideological nepotism is nothing new in American politics and cuts across Democratic and Republican lines. It isn't their conservative credentials that raise concern here as much as the fact that a position as the official face of public diplomacy at the State Department should be in the service of managing and improving America's reputation in the world, not managing and improving the image of the administration in the executive brand of government. Only one out of the four under secretaries, Margaret Tutwiler, had any overseas diplomatic experience, serving as ambassador to Morocco for two years. And yet it was Tutwiler who had the shortest appointment, staying less than two hundred days before leaving to direct communications at the New York Stock Exchange. She may have foreshadowed her departure with these prescient words about her unenviable task to win hearts and minds of local populations living in a war zone: "There is not one magic bullet, magic program or magic solution. As much as we would like to think Washington knows best, we have to be honest and admit we do not necessarily always have all the answers."[67]

The White House during the Bush years viewed global publics more as malleable targets of influence than as partners in a dialogue about foreign policies. An example of this tone-deaf practice in engaging foreign publics is illustrated in "Changing Minds Winning Peace: Report of the Advisory Group on Public Diplomacy for the Arab and Muslim World," chaired by Ambassador Edward P. Djerejian, which mentions several times how often the advisory group chose to ignore the proverbial elephant in this case, U.S. foreign policy to the Arab and Muslim World:

> We were told many times in our travels in Arab countries that "we like Americans but not what the American government is doing." This distinc-

> tion is unrealistic since Americans elect their government and broadly support its foreign policy, but the assertion that "we like you but don't like your policies" offers hope for transformed public diplomacy.
>
> Unlike powerful nations of the past, the United States does not seek to conquer but to spread universal ideals: liberty, democracy, human rights, equality for women and minorities, prosperity, and the rule of law.[68]

These disclaimers offer excellent examples of American propaganda in practice. They present American public opinion as one coherent collective whole not challenged by any internal domestic dissension but especially not by any outside perspective, in this case, Arab public opinion opposition to U.S. policies in the Middle East. The dismissive nature of the report, which fails to acknowledge American dissent in U.S. foreign policy after 9/11 and completely ignores the realities attached to Arab opposition, illustrates how much official post-9/11 U.S. public diplomacy emphasized getting out a pro-U.S. message (informing) and amplifying a pro-U.S. point of view (influencing), while limiting or neglecting the most salient directive of public diplomacy—engaging and valuing the public voice of citizens.

The election of the "Yes We Can" Democratic candidate Barack Obama in November 2008 did not stem the tide of propaganda's scope. Without any hint of irony, *Ad Age* magazine proclaimed the then junior Illinois senator "Marketer of the Year," beating out his closest competitor, Apple.[69] While Obama was heralded as a progressive political leader among Democrats and those on the moderate left, and was predictably pilloried by most on the right side of the ideological spectrum, his actions as president show that he's not above the fray but just as inclined toward manipulations of public opinion and image as his gifted predecessors, like Reagan and Clinton. Some on the more radical left, like former *New York Times* reporter Chris Hedges, were quick to designate the now two-term American president as not a person but a feel-good brand who allowed a nation to switch loyalties from the tarnished brand of his immediate predecessor:

> Brand Obama does not threaten the core of the corporate state any more than did Brand George W. Bush. The Bush brand collapsed. We became immune to its studied folksiness. We saw through its artifice. This is a common deflation in the world of advertising. So we have been given a

> new Obama brand with an exciting and faintly erotic appeal. Benetton and Calvin Klein were the precursors to the Obama brand, using ads to associate themselves with risqué art and progressive politics. It gave their products an edge. But the goal, as with all brands, was to make passive consumers mistake a brand with an experience.[70]

We generally associate American presidents in the modern telecommunications age (in other words, since Wilson) with spinning the press, and here too Obama has been hard at work, with press perks like rides aboard Air Force One, state dinner invitations, rounds of golf, and the help of his first-term chief of staff Rahm Emanuel, who operated an around-the-clock press influence campaign.[71] President Obama is as adept at wooing influential political pundits as Bill Clinton, whose media strategy playbook was "You campaign in television and you govern in print."[72] Whatever the media channel, the "propagandist uses a keyboard and composes a symphony."[73] For the 2013 presidential inauguration, the White House announced that it would accept unlimited donations from corporations to help defray the $50 million budget for what was deemed a more modest second term inaugural, though it promised to post the names of all corporate donors on the web "to ensure continued transparency."[74] VIP offerings included exclusive access packages named for previous presidents (for example, the Monroe Package) and a candlelight reception to pose for a picture with the first families at the National Museum Building, at a price tag of $100,000.[75] The fundraising was going a bit slow, perhaps due to finance fatigue among donors to Obama's reelection campaign who helped him break political fundraising records with contributions of over $1 billion.[76]

It is important with propaganda's scope not to be bogged down by which party or president is the most egregious violator of the public good or public interest. Propaganda is ideological but knows no ideological boundaries. For every Frank Luntz, author of *Words That Work: It's Not What You Say, It's What People Hear,* a script for a Republican doublespeak agenda, there is a George Lakoff, author of *Don't Think of an Elephant!,* a playbook for how progressives and Democrats can frame their messages to challenge the Republican agenda.[77] Propaganda is most effective when it reinforces what is already believed by true believers—in the American case, either Democrat or Republican true believers. Converting a Democrat to a Republican or a Republican to a Democrat is exceedingly hard, if not impossible, which is why oppositional rhetoric thrives in the American political arena. Such rhetoric is designed to hold on tight to one's own and make the oppositional base intolerable and, in some cases, subhuman. Propaganda thrives in this because all propaganda is oriented toward exclusion and silencing of any vocal dissension. This divide-and-conquer method makes it easy for political campaigns in America to come across as a cult of personality (Obama vs. Romney), while the real business of the campaigns in the form of political consultants (Politics, Inc.) continues without interruption. Voters are presented the myth of "One Person, One Vote" but really serve as mass consumers of either one corporate candidate or his opposite corporate candidate. Make your choice. Pepsi vs. Coke. There is no in-between choice or none-of-the-above option. It's one thing to make your choice between two syrupy, artificially colored waters designed to corrode your teeth; it's quite another to make a consumer choice for the designated "leader of the free world," as we have come to know our presidents. Leone Baxter, the cofounder of the first American political consulting firm, Campaigns, Inc., was once asked about her profession of "leading men's minds" and its efficacy of transferring political power from the people to the few who led. Her response was, "In this profession of leading men's minds, I feel it must be in the hands of the most ethical, principled people—people with real concern for the world around them, for people around them—or else it will erode into the hands of people who have no regard for the world around them. It could be a very, very destructive thing."[78] Her remarks were shared in a 1960s interview, when political consultants did not have the technology of today. In 2012, Nate Silver's *New York Times* blog on polling found that political consultants who conduct their own internal tracking polls for candidates tend to operate with bias and spin that manipulates the poll numbers in their candidate's favor.[79] The candidate hears what he wants to hear from consultants who serve more as spin doctors than as independent assessors.[80]

In light of that possibility for the more destructive things in propaganda, as opposed to the propaganda for good and reform propaganda we learned respectively from Anthony Pratkanis and Randal Marlin, I end with a list of some of the most common negative propaganda traits associated with our expansive American propaganda landscape. As these traits persist, you can be assured that propaganda is thriving:

1. Mass media ownership is concentrated in the hands of a few.
2. Mass media is private, commercial, and advertising-driven.
3. Advertising appeals to irrational fantasies and emotional impulses.
4. Cult of personality pervades in politics and pop culture.
5. Mass population of true believers is committed to democratic process.
6. Political leadership is committed to control and management of #5.
7. Political competition is concentrated in the hands of those who can afford it.
8. "The truth" is touted as proof of the absence of propaganda.
9. Different kinds of truth pervade: half-truths, incomplete truths, out-of-context truths.
10. There is no propaganda vaccine; we all are susceptible.

Notes

1. Jacques Ellul, *Propaganda* (New York: Knopf, 1965; reprint, New York: Vintage Books, 1973), 232.

2. George Creel, *How We Advertised America* (New York: Harper and Brothers, 1920), 3–9.

3. J. Michael Sproule, *Channels of Propaganda* (Bloomington, Ind.: ERIC/EDINFO Press, 1994), 285.

4. W. Phillips Davison, "Some Trends in International Propaganda," *Annals of the American Academy of Political and Social Science* 398 (November 1971): 1.

5. Ibid., 12.

6. Alex Carey, *Taking the Risk Out of Democracy: Corporate Propaganda versus Freedom and Liberty* (Urbana: Univ. of Illinois Press), 1997; Ellul, *Propaganda,* 232; Aldous Huxley, *Brave New World Revisited,* reprint ed. (1958; reprint, New York: Harper Perennial Modern Classic, 2006).

7. U.S. Diplomatic Mission to Germany, "About the USA—The Media in the United States," http://usa.usembassy.de/media.htm, updated March 2010.

8. U.S. Census Bureau, *Statistical Abstract of the United States: 2011* (Washington, D.C.: GPO, 2011).

9. See McKinsey Global Institute, "Internet Matters: The Net's Sweeping Impact on Growth, Jobs, and Prosperity," May 2011, New York: McKinsey and Company, http://www.mckinsey.com/insights/mgi/research/technology_and_innovation/internet_matters.

10. Amy Wallace, "Miss Millennium: Beyoncé," *GQ,* February 2013, http://www.gq.com/women/photos/201301/beyonce-cover-story-interview-gq-february-2013.

11. Ibid.

12. "PR Firm Admits It's Behind Wal-Mart Blogs," CNNMoney.com, October 20, 2006.

13. Marc Gunther, "Corporate Blogging: Wal-Mart's Fumbles," *Fortune*, October 18, 2006. See also Pallavi Gogoi, "Wal-Mart's Jim and Laura: The Real Story," *Business Week*, October 9, 2006.

14. WOMAA authenticity guidelines, http://www.womma.org; Ethical Guidance for Today's Public Relations Practitioners from PRSA, http://www.prsa.org/AboutPRSA/Ethics/; see also Richard Edelman's comments on what his firm does not subscribe to, namely front groups and "duplicitous communications campaigns," http://www.odwyerpr.com/editorial/1122edelman-deadly-spin-distorts-pr-field.html.

15. David Streitfeld, "The Best Book Reviews Money Can Buy," *New York Times*, August 25, 2012.

16. Thomas McPhail, *Global Communication*, 3rd ed. (London: Wiley-Blackwell, 2010).

17. Neil Postman, *Amusing Ourselves to Death: Public Discourse in the Age of Show Business* (New York: Viking, 1985).

18. Sproule, *Channels of Propaganda*, 235.

19. Richard Williams, *Phil Spector: Out of His Head* (London: Omnibus Press, 2003).

20. Ray Stannard Baker, "Railroads on Trial: How Railroads Make Public Opinion," *McClure's*, March 1906, 535–548.

21. Edward L. Bernays, "The Engineering of Consent," *Annals of the American Academy of Political and Social Science* 250 (1947): 113.

22. J. Michael Sproule, *Propaganda and Democracy: The American Experience of Media and Mass Persuasion* (Cambridge: Cambridge Univ. Press, 1997), 58.

23. Walter Lippmann, *The Phantom Public* (New York: Macmillan), 1927.

24. Thomas Jefferson, letter to Judge William Johnson, Monticello, June 12, 1823.

25. Brent Schrotenboer, "NCAA Approves a Record 35 Bowl Games," *San Diego Union-Tribune*, April 23, 2010.

26. Jonathan Abrams, "N.B.A. Players Make Their Way Back to College," *New York Times*, October 5, 2009.

27. George Skelton, "Special-Interest Money and Politics: The American Way," *Los Angeles Times*, April 26, 2012.

28. Matea Gold, "2012 Campaign Set to Cost a Record $6 Billion," *Los Angeles Times*, October 31, 2012.

29. Date Desk, "Outside Spending Shapes 2012 Election," *Los Angeles Times*, http://graphics.latimes.com/2012-election-outside-spending/.

30. Creel, *How We Advertised America*, 4.

31. Ibid., 4–5.

32. Ibid.

33. Ibid., 85.

34. Ibid.

35. Klaus P. Fischer, *Hitler and America* (Philadelphia: Univ. of Pennsylvania Press, 2011), 9–10.

36. Ibid., 271.

37. Drew Dudley, "Molding Public Opinion Through Advertising," *Annals of the American Academy of Political and Social Science* 250 (1947): 105–112.

38. Carey, *Taking the Risk Out of Democracy,* 14.

39. Ibid.

40. Ibid., 15.

41. "More than 9 in 10 Americans Continue to Believe in God," Gallup Poll, June 3, 2011, http://www.gallup.com/poll/147887/americans-continue-believe-god.aspx; see also "How Religious Is Your State: Pew Forum on Religion and Public Life," http://www.pewforum.org/How-Religious-Is-Your-State-.aspx.

42. "Religiosity Highest in World's Poorest Nations: United States Is among the Rich Countries That Buck the Trend," Gallup Global Report, August 31, 2010, http://www.gallup.com/poll/142727/religiosity-highest-world-poorest-nations.aspx.

43. William Garber, "Propaganda Analysis—To What End?," *American Journal of Sociology* 48, no. 2 (1942): 240–245.

44. Peter Finn, "U.S. Drones Began with Garage Tinkering," *Washington Post,* December 24, 2011.

45. "Little Monsters," Gagapedia, http://ladygaga.wikia.com/wiki/Little_Monsters.

46. President George W. Bush, Primetime News Conference, October 11, 2001, http://georgewbush-whitehouse.archives.gov/news/releases/2001/10/20011011-7.html.

47. James E. Combs and Dan Nimmo, *The New Propaganda: The Dictatorship of Palaver in Contemporary Politics* (White Plains, N.Y.: Longman, 1993), 137–160.

48. Marc-André Gagnon and Joel Lexchin, "The Cost of Pushing Pills: A New Estimate of Pharmaceutical Promotion Expenditures in the United States," *PLoS Med* 5, no. 1 (2008): 29–33.

49. Edward R. Murrow, speech before the Radio-Television News Directors Association (RTNDA), Chicago, Illinois, October 15, 1958, http://www.turnoffyourtv.com/commentary/hiddenagenda/murrow.html.

50. "Type 2 Diabetes," *New York Times* Health Guide, http://health.nytimes.com/health/guides/disease/type-2-diabetes/overview.html#Causes.

51. Daniel D. Snyder, "The Evil Marketing Genius of Paula Deen, the New Face of Diabetes," *Atlantic,* January 18, 2012.

52. http://www.victoza.com.

53. Gilbert Cruz, "A Brief History of the Flag Lapel Pin," *Time,* July 3, 2008.

54. See my Tokyo-based blog post, "No Guilt about Green," at http://tokyonancysnow.wordpress.com/2012/07/13/america-no-guilt-about-green-7-2/.

55. John Feffer, "Cult of Personality," *Foreign Policy in Focus* 7, no. 3 (January 17, 2012), http://www.fpif.org/articles/cult_of_personality.

56. Nancy Snow, *Information War: American Propaganda, Free Speech and Opinion Control Since 9/11* (New York: Seven Stories Press, 2003); and Nancy Snow, *Propaganda, Inc.: Selling America's Culture to the World,* 3rd ed. (New York: Seven Stories Press, 2010).

57. See *Frontline*'s brilliant show on this topic, "Truth, War and Consequences," at http://www.pbs.org/wgbh/pages/frontline/shows/truth/.

58. David Barstow, "Message Machine: Behind TV Analysts, Pentagon's Hidden Hand," *New York Times*, April 20, 2008.

59. J. William Fulbright, *The Pentagon Propaganda Machine* (New York: Viking, 1971), 28–29.

60. James Banford, "The Man Who Sold the War," *Rolling Stone*, December 1, 2005.

61. Jason Vest, "The Hazy Story of the Lincoln Group," *Government Executive*, November 30, 2005.

62. Mark Mazzetti and Borzou Daragahi, "U.S. Military Covertly Pays to Run Stories in Iraqi Press," *Los Angeles Times*, November 30, 2005.

63. Ibid.

64. Ibid.

65. Robert Pear, "Buying of News by Bush's Aides Is Ruled Illegal," *New York Times*, October 1, 2005.

66. Stuart Oskamp and P. Wesley Schultz, *Attitudes and Opinions* (Mahwah, N.J.: Lawrence Erlbaum Associates, 2004), 351. See also Pew Research Global Attitudes Project, "Global Public Opinion in the Bush Years (2001–2008)," December 18, 2008, http://www.pewglobal.org/2008/12/18/global-public-opinion-in-the-bush-years-2001-2008/.

67. Nancy Snow, "U.S. Public Diplomacy: A Tale of Two Who Jumped Ship at State," *Foreign Policy in Focus*, May 27, 2004, www.fpif.org/articles/us_public_diplomacy_a_tale_of_two_who_jumped_ship_at_state.

68. "Changing Minds Winning Peace: A New Strategic Direction for U.S. Public Diplomacy in the Arab and Muslim World. Report of the Advisory Group on Public Diplomacy for the Arab and Muslim World," Edward P. Djerejian, Chairman, Submitted to the Committee on Appropriations, U.S. House of Representatives, October 1, 2003.

69. Matthew Creamer, "Obama Wins . . . Ad Age's Marketer of the Year," *Ad Age*, October 17, 2008.

70. Chris Hedges, "Buying Brand Obama," Truthdig.com, May 3, 2009.

71. Paul Starobin, "All the President's Pundits," *Columbia Journalism Review* (September/October 2011), cjr.org/feature/all_the_presidents_pundits.php.

72. Ibid.

73. Jacques Ellul, *Propaganda* (New York: Vintage Books, 1973), 10.

74. Sheryl Gay Stolberg, "Obama Will Accept Corporate Money to Finance Inauguration," *New York Times*, December 7, 2012.

75. Nicholas Confessore, "Fund-Raising Is Lagging, So Far, for Inaugural Plans," *New York Times*, January 11, 2013.

76. Ibid.

77. Frank Luntz, *Words That Work: It's Not What You Say, It's What People Hear* (New York: Hyperion, 2007); George Lakoff, *Don't Think of an Elephant!: Know Your Values and Frame the Debate* (White River Junction, Vt.: Chelsea Green, 2004).

78. Jill Lepore, "The Lie Factory," *New Yorker*, September 24, 2012.

79. Nate Silver, "Spin and Bias Are the Norm in Campaigns' Internal Polling," *New York Times*, December 3, 2012, A17.

80. Ibid.

6

JOURNALISTS AS PROPAGANDISTS

ASRA Q. NOMANI

After the first World Trade Center bombing in 1993, which killed six people and injured thousands more, FBI Special Agent Frank Pellegrino pursued clues that would lead him to Khalid Sheikh Mohammed, or KSM, as the uncle of the 1993 bombing mastermind, Ramzi Yousef, has come to be known. The trail took Pellegrino from Qatar to the Philippines, but he couldn't nab KSM in time to stop the infamous September 11, 2001, attacks or the brutal murder of *Wall Street Journal* reporter Daniel Pearl in February 2002. KSM is on trial in a military court for his alleged role as mastermind of the 9/11 attacks. And he has admitted to killing Danny[1] with his "blessed right hand."

In the spring of 2007, Pellegrino sat in front of KSM for the first time ever in an interview room in the Guantanamo Bay detention facility, where the U.S. military was holding him. It was Pellegrino's first opportunity to interview this man whose mission over the past two decades had been death, mayhem, and destruction of America and the West.

Pellegrino wanted to know the answer to one question: "Why did you kill Pearl?"

KSM cocked his head, twirling the ends of his long, flowing beard, and answered very succinctly: "Propaganda."

Indeed, five years earlier KSM had deliberately set off to kill Danny with a special weapon in his bag: a video camera. It lay beside a butcher knife and plastic bags in which he would later hide the parts of Danny's dismembered body.

What KSM knew was something that global media outlets and journalists have been slow to acknowledge: He was certain to find media outlets willing to splash his propaganda video onto television screens and on the pages of newspapers and magazines all over the world. Indeed, less than six months later, snippets of the murder video, headlined "The Slaughter of the Spy-Journalist, the Jew Daniel Pearl," landed on the *CBS Evening News* as well as alternative media outlets like the *Boston Phoenix,* which was the first to post the Pearl murder video online.[2]

While KSM is being tried by a U.S. military tribunal in Guantanamo Bay, Cuba, for being the operational chief of the 9/11 attacks on the United States, there is a less apparent but very important role that he has played for al-Qaeda: chief propagandist. I consider the images from the 9/11 attacks to be one of the most successful propaganda campaigns in history for their scope and potency. Even to describe them as horrific, tragic, and dramatic is to reveal just how powerful a victory the 9/11 attacks were from a propaganda perspective. The images circulated on media outlets around the world, and, as a memory, they are seared in perhaps the most powerful medium of all: the mind.

Underscoring KSM's obsession with images, the first question he asked Special Agent Pellegrino when they were face to face was whether the United States was still distributing the unflattering photo of him shot after he was captured in Pakistan. In it, he appears disheveled—beardless, but unshaven, with rumpled hair, wearing the type of white tank top called a "bunyine" in Urdu in Pakistan and known disparagingly as a "wife beater" in the United States, the kind of shirt worn by men on television police shows who are arrested for domestic violence.

"You're not using the beater wife picture are you?" asked KSM, who got a mechanical engineering degree from North Carolina A&T State University. KSM is an educated man. Yet, according to a source familiar with the interview, that's the way he phrased it: "beater wife."[3]

This is where I face the truth about myself and my profession. In pursuit of "the story," I have allowed people like KSM to manipulate me into serving as their propagandist. I look back on my twenty-five-year career, a decade and a half of those years as a staff reporter at the *Wall Street Journal,* in disbelief. I know I'm not alone. If you had asked us as young reporters whether we would act as a propaganda mouthpiece for one side of the story, we would have been highly offended. However,

I believe we as reporters and editors have spent much of our careers failing to recognize how much we are used—either wittingly or unwittingly—as mediums for propaganda. There is a new reality we need to acknowledge: Journalists do act as propagandists.

I began my professional career in 1988 as a twenty-three-year-old cub reporter at the *Journal,* and I was manipulated, deceived, and lied to, but I never once thought consciously about how I had been used or allowed myself to be used. Perhaps as a self-protective defense mechanism we fancy ourselves so sophisticated, accomplished, and just plain "right" that we believe no one—or at least very few people—will be able to pull the wool over our eyes or use us without our knowing it. Public relations professionals virtually train us to be skeptical gatekeepers by pitching stories to us constantly. We are always on guard for the story that isn't really a story.

I have thought long and hard about how it is that propagandists—on all sides of the information war—deliberately plan their strategies. Whether we call these campaigns "information operations" or "psychological operations," as the the military tends to do, or "propaganda," as we tend to call the campaigns of "adversaries," they have one component in common: using the media. In the parlance of public relations, to place a story in the media is to get a "hit," and, whether we admit it or not, many a "hit" in the media is a propaganda victory.

In graduate school, as an international communications major at the American University in Washington, D.C., I learned about propaganda and its intersection with the media. But after I joined the *Wall Street Journal* at the end of my courses, I considered myself immune from propaganda campaigns. Looking back, however, I can see how media outlets are facilitators for propaganda.

I and other reporters were susceptible to propaganda campaigns. We broke stories, pushing propaganda. In many ways, too, we created propaganda, and, with new media technologies, including social media, the media are creating a lot more propaganda opportunities. Indeed, the opportunities for propaganda messaging have expanded dramatically from what I experienced in the 1980s and 1990s with the advent of YouTube, Facebook, and Twitter, where there are few "gatekeepers," as editors, producers, and other filters in the media process are known.

CORPORATE PROPAGANDA

My recognition of media outlets as creators and enablers of propaganda has been a long journey in the making. When I joined the *Wall Street Journal* in the summer of 1988, I had never read the newspaper. My first beat was the agriculture industry. Every afternoon I called analysts and commodity traders at the Chicago Board of Trade, writing a daily commodity column affectionately called the "commode column" in the newsroom. My "sources" would wax on about porkbelly futures, soybean futures, and orange juice futures. I never challenged their analysis, and I fed the myth created by their forecasts. I switched to the airline industry after a year, at a time of financial stress for the carriers. One day, the spokesman of Northwest Airlines called me for a secret meeting. I agreed and stood at a street corner in Chicago where we had agreed to meet. A driver pulled a black Lincoln Town Car to the curb. The door opened, and the Northwest Airlines spokesman stepped out. He had big news to tell me, but only if I agreed not to attribute it to him or the airline. I agreed. It could be a big "scoop." He shared his news with me: Northwest was about to make a bid for a flailing Chicago-based airline, Midway Airlines. I dutifully took notes. I wasn't a sap, but it seemed like a good, straightforward business story. I rushed back to the office and filed a story that ran in the front of the next day's newspaper.

Northwest never bought Midway Airlines. It was a fishing expedition. I got played. We could dismiss it as a well-calcuated public relations coup by the Northwest spokesman, landing a "hit" in the country's leading business newspaper. But we have to look at the corporate machinery as something much more akin to propaganda, in light of the clear collapse of the economy spawned by the mythmaking of so much in our economy—from luxury goods to mergers, acquisitions, mortgage lending, and other aspects of the financial markets that have just lost their magic. We could think of it as economic propaganda, or "corporate propaganda," as Noam Chomsky, a scholar and writer with his own distinguished career as a propagandist, calls it.[4]

My mea culpa as a financial journalist is that I wasn't vigilant enough. I think a lot of us weren't, and I believe our industry wasn't. I hadn't heard of Chomsky when I was starting off as a reporter, but I wish I had—and, in fact, I wish every journalist would. We're not naive about the corporate agendas. But I also think we aren't as transparent as we could be about how placement in our articles can make—or break—the image of companies in the public eye. We like to delude ourselves into thinking we're fighting for the underdog, exposing injustices, evils, and corruption, but we're also very often being played.

After Chicago, I worked in the Washington bureau of the *Wall Street Journal* and then in New York City, as part of the launch of the *Weekend Journal*, a Friday section dedicated to the coverage of luxury items. We reported on the best suites to be had for $300 a night, the finest wines, and the most extravagant bath towels. I spent days chasing the most outlandish backyard pools, creations from $10,000 to $100,000 with tropical rain forests, waterfalls, and swim park slides. Another time, I almost got deported while reporting on the feud between two Caribbean resorts. All the while, the agendas were simple: to get "hits" in the *Wall Street Journal* that would promulgate the "corporate propaganda."

FRONTLINE PROPAGANDA

In the United States I had absorbed a sense of "exceptionalism" as a journalist, believing that we were beyond influence and manipulation. In Karachi I got an education on how propaganda works when I became part of the story.

After the September 11, 2001, attacks I jetted to Pakistan, where I saw that many Pakistanis viewed 9/11 as a propaganda opportunity to smear Islam and Muslims. "The Jews did it," a young girl told me.

The day the first detainees were brought to Guantanamo Bay in early 2002, *Miami Herald* reporter Carol Rosenberg, the dean of the Guantanamo press corps, watched a Defense Department photographer shoot a photo of the prisoners, hooded and in orange jumpsuits. A veteran Middle East correspondent, she warned the Defense Department's public affairs officer that, if released, the photo would be used as propaganda against the United States. It was released. Little could I have predicted how those images would be used in propaganda against America.

That same month, my friend Daniel Pearl came to visit me at a home I had rented in Karachi. On January 23, 2002, Danny set off for an interview from which he didn't return. His wife, Mariane, and I scoured the house for clues, my home becoming a virtual command center for the Pakistani police and the FBI. Three days later we got a ransom note with photos of Danny in captivity. Interestingly, the photos and ransom note weren't sent to the governments of the United States or Pakistan. They were sent to media outlets, from the *Washington Post* to the Pakistani English daily, *Dawn*. The kidnappers knew something that we as journalists don't acknowledge. We are used for propaganda. When Danny had first gone missing, Mariane and I had hunted his Toshiba laptop looking for clues. I found a photo on his computer of him and me at the Karachi Sheraton. He had a particularly befuddled look on his face, and had created an appropriate caption for the photo: "Clueless in Karachi." In many ways, I would argue, we are clueless. Indeed, every major newspaper in the world published the photos and the details of the ransom note.

Other expressions of propaganda emerged. Inside Pakistani media circles, journalists refer to "agency reporters," who loosely work for two bosses: their editors and Pakistani intelligence agencies. On January 30, 2002, I stood in my kitchen and glanced at the front page of the English-language newspaper the *News*. The headline on Danny's kidnapping caught my eye: "Indian Connection in US Newsman Case."

I was stunned by what I read: ". . . some Pakistani security officials—not familiar with the worth of solid investigative reporting in the international media—are privately searching for answers as to why a Jewish American reporter was exceeding 'his limits' to investigate [a] Pakistani religious group. These officials are also guessing, rather loudly, as to why Pearl decided to bring in an Indian journalist as his full time assistant in Pakistan. Ansa Nomani, an American passport holder Indian-Muslim lady who had come from Mumbai to Karachi with Pearl, was working as his full time assistant in the country."

Born out of the freedom of India from British rule in 1947, Pakistan is a country defined by a siege mentality. Naively, I thought brown was brown in Pakistan. I learned that day that my brown—born in India—was not the same as someone with ancestral heritage in the land known today as Pakistan. A Pakistani police officer confided that the article was part of a whispering campaign that I worked for India's external intelligence agency, the Research and Analysis Wing (RAW). I was stunned. I had never even heard of RAW, and the speculation leading to the misinformation campaign in the newspaper was that I worked for it. Unbeknownst to me, also, RAW had a cozy relationship with the Mossad, Israel's intelligence agency, and the conspiracy theory was that Danny was an Israeli intelligence officer. Later, I learned the rest of the conspiracy theory: As a RAW agent, I had been working with Danny, a Mossad agent. We had had a falling out, and I had lured him to Pakistan to be kidnapped and murdered in a wider scheme to shame Pakistan. All of this was beyond my comprehension, but in the minds of many in Pakistan it was plausible.

I studied the byline. Kamran Khan. "Who is he?" I asked.

He was a reporter for the *News*, but he was also a stringer for the *Washington Post*. By defining me, first, as an "Indian journalist" and then as "an American passport holder Indian-Muslim lady," he played into the cross-border tactics of propaganda that demonized those across the border, exploiting my birthplace in India to further conspiracy theories. By describing Danny as a "a Jewish American reporter," Khan played into the anti-Semitism of many Pakistanis. He reported falsely that Danny had "decided to bring" me "in" as a "full time assistant in Pakistan." Anyone familiar with the fractured relations between Pakistan and India can understand how this sort of characterization could tarnish Danny's reputation in Pakistan and weaken public outrage about his brutal killing, a goal some officials in Pakistan's Inter-Services Intelligence (ISI) community might have wanted.

Not long after, we got the last ransom note from Danny's kidnappers, via email from the address "strangepeoples@hotmail.com":

> We have interogated mr.D.Parl and we have come to the conclusion that contrary to what we thought earlier he is not working for the cia. in fact he is working for mossaad. therefore we will execute him within 24 hours unless amreeka flfils our demands.

Four days later, on February 3, 2002, I saw the propaganda machinery get another hit in a major media outlet. I opened the *News* again and saw an article by a reporter, Tariq Butt. The headline again framed me as Indian: "Baffling Questions about Indian Lady in Pearl Case."

Invoking the parlance of a former British colony, the journalist hardly offered me conciliatory status by calling me a "lady." He continued to push the propaganda of the intelligence apparatus, describing me as "an

American passport holder Indian Muslim lady" about whom "security agencies" had "several baffling questions" to answer: "Security agencies are probing several baffling questions pertaining to the unauthorized stay of an American passport holder Indian Muslim lady, Asra Q Nomani, with whom the kidnapped Wall Street Journal reporter Daniel Pearl had been living in Karachi." In this article, the journalist erroneously reported my stay as "unauthorized," trying to raise questions about not just my morality, Danny "living" with me, his wife's presence erased, but also the legality of my being in the country.

It was just after the article ran describing Danny as "a Jewish American reporter," police believe, that KSM arrived with his nephews at the compound where Danny was being held. He started filming Danny within minutes. The older nephew, a trusted leader in KSM's operations, started asking Danny questions in English, according to one version pieced together by Pakistani police. "The Arabs interviewed Daniel and gave no impression that he was going to be killed," a diplomatic cable later said, relaying what a Pakistani police official had told U.S. government officials.

The men gave Danny a script to read while the younger nephew filmed the scene. A guard who understood English told another guard, Fazal Karim, that the script had Danny telling the United States, "Stop the cruelty and violence against the Muslims."

Subdued, Danny followed the script. He had a flat affect, not revealing any real emotion. He wasn't wearing his glasses. He looked like he had just a few days of stubble on his face, a sign that this taping may have happened early in his detention—before the arrest of Omar Sheikh, the mastermind. "Daniel felt confident that he might be released," the diplomatic cable reported. "One of the Arabs spoke with Daniel in a language other than English or Arabic." A guard thought it might have been Hebrew. "Daniel seemed very comfortable with the person who spoke in that language," the cable said.

The group read the early afternoon prayer together. Attaur Rehman, a logistical chief for the operation, moved to leave, but first told the guards, "They have come to do something. Let them do it." Between the late afternoon prayer and the sunset prayer, Karim would tell a Pakistani police officer, Fayyaz Khan, the men told him, "We have to slaughter him."

The men tied Danny's hands behind his back and wrapped a blindfold around his eyes so he couldn't see what was about to happen, guards later told police. They made Danny lie on the floor on his left side. Khalid Sheikh Mohammed pulled two knives and a cleaver from the bundle of cloth that he'd carried into the room. He grabbed Danny by his hair. Karim, the guard, and another guard held Danny in place at his hips and legs. According to the scenario U.S. and Pakistani officials are considering, the younger nephew turned on the video camera while the older nephew helped hold Danny down. "Daniel was caught off guard from the relaxing interview and was held as they killed him and he could offer no resistance," the U.S. diplomatic cable said.

Without hesitation, KSM took a knife and slashed Danny's neck. Muhammad Muzzamil, the guard, said the "Arabs did *ziba*," the Muslim ritual of slaughter. Muzzamil started to retch. KSM yelled at him angrily and threw him out of the room. Another guard was told to go. He later described the strangers as "Arab" to police. Only Karim and the spindly guard, Siraj ul-Haq, remained. KSM then returned his attention to Danny. Ul-Haq was later quoted in his interrogation report as saying, "Sheikh Khalid slaughtered him."

But then there was a problem. It's not clear if the camera actually jammed, but the cameraman, who U.S. and Pakistani officials believe may have been the younger nephew, exclaimed that he hadn't been able to videotape the killing. KSM yelled at him. Chastened, he hurriedly fixed his camera. "The camera guy was startled," KSM later told the FBI. "He didn't put the video in." KSM reenacted the scene, "this time separating Danny's head from his body," the guard Karim said later. To prove that Danny was alive just before the beheading, KSM pressed on Danny's chest to show blood still pumping through his throat. It was a scene that would later turn the stomachs of even the most hardened Pakistani and U.S. investigators.

KSM then took Danny's decapitated head by the hair and held it in the air for the camera. "Khalid Sheikh picked up his head and said something in Arabic" before cutting the body into pieces, Siraj ul-Haq later told cops. Dispassionately, KSM later told FBI agents that, indeed, he had chopped up Danny's body. "We did it to get rid of the body," he said.

As the *Wall Street Journal* moved forward on its campaign to humanize Danny, the alleged murderers dehumanized him.

Afterward, the guards took the pieces of Danny's body and stuffed them into the shopping bags. Danny's murderers walked around the plot, debating where to bury him, and ordered the guards to dig a hole in a corner of the courtyard. Siraj ul-Haq took the pieces of Danny's body out of the shopping bags to bury them. He also buried the bags.

Then it was time to pray. The guards washed the bloody floor where Danny had been killed, and the men touched the same ground with their foreheads in prostration. KSM and the other two men packed their weapons: the murder knife and other weapons, especially the camera with its new film.

The next phase of their operation would soon begin: the propaganda. KSM had an extensive editing studio in Karachi that had been churning out propaganda films. It's not clear who edited Danny's murder video, but it was spliced with images important to the cause of al-Qaeda. One was the image of detainees in Guantanamo in orange prison suits.

Through a delicate operation, the murderers got their video to a courier. On February 21, 2002, FBI Special Agent John Mulligan fielded an unexpected phone call at the U.S. Consulate in Karachi. It was an agent-friend from the FBI's New York office. He had a lead, Mulligan recalled. A "source" had a "source" who said that he had a video that documented Danny's murder. "We had about twenty minutes from when I got the call that he was willing to make the deal," Mulligan said. "All I knew was, 'Hey, I gotta get this.' If he says he's only going to give it to somebody from NBC News, then that's who I'm gonna be."

That evening, Khalid Choudhary, a man standing a shade over six feet tall, crossed the lobby of the Karachi Sheraton to meet Mulligan. Ironically, both introduced themselves as journalists. Choudhary called himself "Abdul Khalique" from Online International News Network, Mulligan recalled. Mulligan and a second FBI agent posed as reporters for NBC News. In the man's hand: a compact digital video camera. Choudhary had gotten the video from a young man, Fazal Karim, who had been a guard during Danny's captivity. Karim later told police his militant boss had told him to publish Danny's murder video, and he had asked a friend, Shaikh Shahid, a militant raising funds for the Taliban in Karachi, for help selling the tape. Shaikh introduced Karim to Choudhary, who told him he had a buyer. He didn't tell him it was the FBI.

"Probably the most nervous I've ever been in my career was when we got the tape," Mulligan recalled. He stood face to face with the man for the exchange. The price to be paid to Online International News Network if the tape proved to be authentic: $200,000.

At 9:40 P.M. Karachi time, Mulligan got custody of the tape.

Choudhary walked away from the meeting at the Sheraton, supposedly under surveillance by Pakistani police. It was the same hotel where Danny and I had taken the photo he had called "Clueless in Karachi." According to one FBI official, the plan was for Choudhary to return later to collect his payment when the tape's authenticity had been verified; the plan was to give him a bag packed with money and a secret tracking device that would lead investigators to other participants in the plot. However, after word of the tape leaked out, the kidnappers didn't answer their phones. U.S. documents identified Choudhary as a U.S. citizen with an extensive drug-related criminal record in New York City going back to 1992.

It was on that night of February 21, 2002, a quiet Thursday night in Karachi on the eve of the holy festival of Eid-ul-Adha, marking the symbolic sacrifice that Abraham was ready to make of his son (Ishmael in Islam, Isaac in Christianity), that I really started rethinking the delicate relationship between journalists and propaganda. That night, Pakistani police officers, U.S. State Department officials, and U.S. FBI agents came to the door of my rented house. They stood shoulder-to-shoulder, filling the door frame. Danny's wife, Mariane, and I stood before them, and we heard news we hadn't even considered. The senior Pakistani counterterrorism officer in charge of the investigation stood at the door and told Mariane: "I'm sorry I couldn't bring your Danny home." He explained that they had gotten a tipoff about a video documenting Danny's murder. FBI Special Agent Mulligan stood beside him, stoic but clearly shaken.

Standing beside Mariane, I heard the words, but I couldn't register their truth. I believe that many of us live within that space, knowing that there are horrors that exist in the world but refusing—in large part for the preservation of our own humanity and innocence—to *see* the truths of the horrors of this world.

It is that space of unbelievability, for lack of a better word, that I believe propaganda has the incredible—and dangerous—capacity and power to fill. The propaganda of war, conflict, and crime has particular potency. It is gruesome. It is brutal. It is so unimaginably horrible. It shocks. It titillates. It pierces our sensibilities.

I know that space well because I lived inside of it. Worldly, educated, and successful, by external markers, I was naive to the realities of genocide, war, and strife. I had gone to Pakistan to cover the war in Afghanistan. After falling in love in Karachi, I had rented my comfortable three-bedroom home in a posh neighborhood of the city, mostly immune to the bombs dropping across the border in Afghanistan. Danny's kidnapping and murder shook me out of that space. The night we learned of his murder, I, too, got an education in how propaganda works to shake our realities.

Mariane screamed and bolted for the room she had shared with Danny just weeks earlier. She slammed the door shut, her blood-curdling scream filling the air. I followed her and sat on the stairs outside her door, saying the Muslim prayer for protection I had learned as a girl. Mariane emerged and asked, "How do we know it's true?"

I went to the U.S. Consul General in Karachi at the time, John Bauman. "How do we know it's real?" I asked him.

He said, "Are you sure you want to know?"

"Yes," I told him.

He said the murderers had filmed blood spurting out of Danny's carotid artery to prove the film was authentic and not a digitally produced fake. The detail was shocking. I apologized to Mariane for sharing the information with her before I told her. I wanted to watch the video, but I didn't. I buried the details of the video. But that wasn't long lasting.

In May 2002, Mariane and I received a phone call at her home in Paris. "It's bad news. The video is on the Internet," said the voice on the other end.

The video had been posted on Lycos, a search engine and web portal started in 1994. For two days, I maneuvered between officials from Lycos U.K. to Scotland Yard to get the video pulled and to track the source of the video's posting. Finally, Jay Kanetkar, the agent on Danny's case, told Mariane and me where the IP trail led: "An office building in Riyadh." We couldn't get any more information, and the investigation seemed to reach a dead end. For the moment, though, I had stopped the distribution of the video.

Soon after, we got another phone call: CBS News planned to air a portion of the video that night. As a journalist and citizen of the world,

I believe in freedom of the press, but I have increasingly come to understand that we have to evaluate carefully whether we are simply being used for propaganda purposes.

To no avail, Danny's parent's protested. His wife protested, as did the *Wall Street Journal.* CBS News aired images from the video of Danny, in captivity, eyes downcast and defeated, avoiding the most gruesome pictures from his murder, but showing, nonetheless, images from KSM's propaganda video. KSM and the creators of the video had scored a victory: they had gotten a prime-time "hit" on a national American television news program. After that, there was no stopping the publication of the video on YouTube, and it was published on numerous websites, underscoring the role of this medium as an agent of propaganda.

The next year, the U.S. government got its opportunity for a propaganda payback, of sorts. Shortly after midnight on March 1, 2003, CIA and Pakistani intelligence officers launched a secret nighttime raid of a house in a military cantonment in the city of Rawalpindi, outside the Pakistani capital of Islamabad. After a short gunfight, they caught their target: KSM. In his book, *Hard Measures: How Aggressive CIA Actions after 9/11 Saved American Lives,* Jose Rodriguez, former chief of the CIA's Counterterrorism Center, chronicled how—and why—a photo became part of its propaganda campaign against the alleged 9/11 mastermind: "A CIA officer snapped the now-famous image of a disheveled KSM moments after the capture. As is so often the case, word of the operation leaked almost immediately. In the aftermath of the capture, several media outlets romanticized KSM's role in al-Qa'ida, some even referring to him as the 'James Bond' of al-Qa'ida. To counter that impression, the CIA released the iconic photo of KSM looking much more like John Belushi than Agent 007."[5]

This image of the alleged 9/11 mastermind resembling the portly, rumpled American actor John Belushi zipped around the globe, landing on television screens, websites, and newspapers worldwide.

OPERATION PINK

After Danny's murder I was disheartened. What I saw in the world was an extremist interpretation of Islam defining Islam in the world today. Even calling it "extremist" is one perspective. To those who believe, they consider it "true." I saw a very dark image of Islam in the world after 9/11. To its proponents, it was a noble and brave image. But I wasn't patient about perspectives, and I realized that I wanted to challenge the prevailing image of Islam. I knew there was only one way to do it: through the media. When we think of propaganda in a pejorative context, it may seem a thing of shame to admit to being a propagandist. But if we think of reformists from Martin Luther to Mahatma Gandhi, the abolitionists, Martin Luther King Jr., and Gloria Steinem as masterful propagandists, then, I believe, it is a strategy for which there doesn't have to be shame. Much of the propaganda pushing strict interpretations of Islam put women in black robes and coverings. Thus, I chose to make pink the color of Islamic feminism, as I came to know the school of thought that I chose to propagate.

PROPAGANDA WARS

On other battlefronts, the question over the possible role of journalists as propagandists continues to rage. The U.S. military got criticism for turning journalists into agents of its propaganda with its embedded journalists program, introduced during the Bush administration by Defense Department public affairs official Victoria Clarke.[6] One of the stories that was later revealed to be largely orchestrated for propaganda purposes: the toppling of a statue of Saddam Hussein.[7]

Another Defense Department effort, putting retired military officers on television as impartial analysts, also garnered criticism, framing the television hosts, for example, as propagandists for allowing the officers to speak unchallenged. Later, former CNN executive Eason Jordan got into trouble over a Defense Department program in which journalists were hired in Afghanistan and Pakistan to write media stories for a media project, but critics suspected their information would be used for targeting strikes. A Justice Department filing revealed how former Pakistani prime minister Benazir Bhutto calculated on using television journalists such as CNN's Wolf Blitzer to put forward her propaganda for new elections in Pakistan. She succeeded in her effort and was assassinated when she returned to Pakistan to campaign.

Even in captivity, KSM wasn't going to roll over that easily in the propaganda wars. In 2007, he went before the military tribunal with a completely different look than that in the image put forward when he was captured. This time, the agent for his makeover effort was the courtroom sketch artist, Janet Hamlin. The daughter of a U.S. military officer, she lived in Brooklyn and papers from Cantor Fitzgerald fell in her yard after the 9/11 attack. In the courtroom, she had a job to do, drawing images of the defendants and the trial. In that way, I would argue that, as media, we are often unwitting agents of propaganda. In fact, when the courtroom security officer showed KSM the images Hamlin had drawn, the prisoner critiqued the drawing, saying, "She didn't get my nose right," and sent the drawing back for correction. Hamlin said, "He was right." She fixed the sketch. KSM's hand in editing his own image became notorious when *Miami Herald* reporter Carol Rosenberg broke the story: "'I did give him quite the beak,' Hamlin conceded, as she headed back to the top security courtroom to fix the nose. In her hand was a copy of the widely circulated photo of his capture in Pakistan—showing the captive known as KSM in a rumpled T-shirt, in need of a shave and with tussled hair."

When Red Cross officials met KSM in July 2009, he was fixated on replacing the "beater wife" photo of him in custody, according to accounts. He took new photos of himself, draped in a white scarf with a long beard, looking almost messianic and, interestingly, resembling Osama bin Laden, the posterboy for the 9/11 attacks.

Ali Abdul Aziz Ali, the young nephew of KSM and the alleged cameraman who got flustered videotaping Danny's murder, also had an image makeover. In a photo previously released by the Defense Department, he looked the part of al-Qaeda geek: bespectacled and wiry. He resembled the stereotypical Microsoft-certified techie and took pride in being at a military tribunal in Guantanamo. But in his new image he had beefed up and he played the part of a pious Muslim, sitting in front of a velvet prayer rug, wearing an Afghan hat, and holding a *tazbi,* or Muslim prayer beads.

By September 2009 the photos had found their way onto an Arabic-language website, www.muslm.net, affiliated with the Arabic television channel al Jazeera and websites linked to al-Qaeda. From there, the new KSM photo spread like wildfire. A counterterrorism expert in Australia, Leah Farrell, spotted the photos, alerted Jarret Brachman, former director of research at West Point's Center for Combating Terrorism, and he posted the photos on his website. Britain's *Guardian* newspaper published an Associated Press story framing the new photo as a propaganda recruitment effort, with the headline, "New Photos of Khalid Sheikh Mohammed Released: Experts Say Images Released by Khalid Sheikh Mohammed's Parents Are Being Used by Terrorist Groups to Inspire Attacks."[8] In the propaganda wars, KSM scored a point when the *New York Times* even corrected a blog about the photo, saying: "An earlier version of this post contained a slightly smaller version of the image of Mr. Mohammed at Guantánamo. The image was replaced after a reader pointed out that a slight cropping to the bottom of it had obscured the prayer beads in his hand."[9]

What I have come to see is that so often as media professionals we publish images that we consider news and others frame as propaganda. In October 3, 1993, when eighteen American soldiers died in the infamous "Black Hawk Down" battle in Mogadishu, Somalia, images of bloodied U.S. soldiers were splashed on magazine covers. To many in the U.S. Army, this was a propaganda coup for the Somali fighters. Images of a captured U.S. pilot and American bodies being dragged through the streets were all over the networks. "Trapped in Somalia," read the *Newsweek* cover. "What in the World Are We Doing?" screamed a *Time* headline, with the "subhed," as we describe secondary headlines in the print business, "Anatomy of the Disaster in Somalia." The photo on the cover was a bloodied image of U.S. Army Chief Warrant Officer Michael Durant, an American pilot who was held prisoner for eleven days in 1993. It is important to note who helped care for him during part of his time in captivity: Somali general Mohamed Farrah Aidid's propaganda minister, Abdullah "Firimbi" Hassan. He was the one who ordered that Durant be taken alive. He understood the power of Durant as a weapon of propaganda. When he was captured, Durant recalled in his memoir, *In the Company of Men,* Hassan asked him: "Tell me, Mr. Durant. Do you remember the prisoners of war in Iraq during your Operation Desert Storm? Do you remember that they appeared on television?" Durant wrote that he thought, "*Uh-oh.*" He couldn't remember "how to handle video exploitation by the enemy."[10] (When the movie *Black Hawk Down* aired in Somalia, many locals criticized it as "propaganda" that focused on the eighteen dead Americans, ignoring the estimated 315 to 2,000 Somalis who died.)

In 2005, the image of the killing of Blackwater guards in Iraq, their bodies hanging from bridge railings, became a propaganda success for the insurgency in Iraq, carried in national magazines and newspapers. Through the years, media outlets have been facilitators for numerous propaganda images, of various intentions. They include the image of an Afghan woman whose nose was allegedly cut off for leaving her husband. Later an image of Marines urinating on the dead bodies of Afghans became a token of propaganda for the Taliban, published widely by U.S. media outlets and, importantly, first published by celebrity website TMZ.

Through simple phone video technology and social media networks such as Facebook, Pakistani, Iranian, and Afghan activists have successfully promulgated their images of propaganda in several campaigns that ended up getting international media attention: the killing of a young Iranian woman, "Neda," in protests against the Iranian regime; the flogging of a young woman in the Swat region of Pakistan; and the 2012 public execution of an Afghan woman for alleged adultery, Afghan men cheering her killing.

In India, a men's magazine, *FHM,* published a photo of Pakistani actress Veena Malik in 2011 wearing a tattoo, "ISI," for the Pakistani intelligence agency, leading to the joke, "The tattoo said 'ISI,' but the photo said 'RAW,'" for the Indian intelligence agency.

And meanwhile, the 2011 operation that killed Osama bin Laden in Pakistan led to images carried in major media outlets worldwide, diminishing the al-Qaeda leader.

The Defense Department revealed that porn had been found in bin Laden's compound, leading to a mocking of the man. To some, this was a successful propaganda campaign, carried by most major media outlets. I also wrote about it for the *Daily Beast.*

Finally, I was witness again to the power of KSM as a propagandist. In a May 2012 hearing, he remained silent, but court sketches by artist Janet Hamlin spoke volumes about the alleged mastermind, casting him as a devout Muslim leading the other co-defendants in prayer.

In Guantanamo Bay, Khalid Sheikh Mohammed and his co-defendants recognize the power of images. In a motion filed by his attorney, KSM asked to be allowed to wear a camouflage vest and camouflage turban. A co-defendant, Mustafa al-Hasawi, asked to be allowed to wear the orange prison suit that the first Guantanamo detainees wore.

"The detainee's attire should not transform this commission into a vehicle for propaganda and undermine the atmosphere that is conducive to calm and detached deliberation and determination of the issues presented and that reflects the seriousness of the proceedings," the prosecutors wrote in response.

From the world of criminality and war to swimming, there is no doubt in my mind that the media serve as propagandists. Coverage of the 2012 Summer Olympics underscores how it is that journalists can act as propagandists. In their book, *Propaganda and Persuasion,* communications scholars Garth Jowett and Victoria O'Donnell note: "National celebrations, with their overt patriotism and regional chauvinism, can usually be classified as white propaganda. International sports competitions also inspire white propaganda from journalists."[11]

From KSM to the Summer Olympics, what we have is a clear pattern: the media as agents of propaganda.

RECOMMENDATIONS

My recommendation to my colleagues in journalism is that we recognize that a "news" story could be part of a propaganda campaign. Like detectives chronicling chain of possession when they produce evidence, we should include the chain of transmission. We need to spell out who gave us the information that we're reporting on, and we need to reflect on what their intentions might have been in disseminating the information. In our business, we use "TK" as shorthand for "to come," though the acronym doesn't make sense. In that spirit, we need sentences such as this: TK distributed TK as part of a larger media campaign to influence TK to believe TK.

In this way, we're not unwitting distributors of propaganda.

As journalists, we should also be better filters, evaluating agendas and refusing to be part of propaganda campaigns. In March 2012, Qatar-based Al Jazeera decided not to air the murder video of Mohamed Merah, the twenty-three-year-old Algerian native who killed three children, three soldiers, and a rabbi in southern France. Merah had allegedly filmed, edited, and sent the video to Al Jazeera for airing. Witnesses told police that he appeared to be wearing a video camera in a chest harness. Al Jazeera's Paris bureau chief, Zied Tarrouche, said the video "had clearly been manipulated after the fact, with religious songs and recitations of Quranic verses laid over the footage."[12]

We should be more discerning about falling for demonization campaigns. If we perpetuate them, we should recognize what we're doing. If we engage in ideological persuasion, we should recognize that we are, in fact, engaging in propaganda, just as much as the other side may be doing. We should stop trying to pull the wool over the eyes of our readers, listeners, and viewers, and acknowledge either our agenda or the agenda of the people about whom we are reporting. We need to bring transparency to our work. We need to put symbols in context. We need to explicate the intention behind ideas, news, and campaigns.

We can't eliminate propaganda images. In the war of ideas, they are a critical component of which I am also a purveyor. Danny's video is all over the Internet. But we can be explicit and analytical in the dynamics of propaganda and persuasion. For my part, I am emboldened in that intention with one lasting image of Danny Pearl taken by his captors in captivity. Danny twisted his fingers, a look of defiance in his face, his middle finger seemingly lifted at the camera in a figurative "F You" to the photographer. He knew he was being used as a symbol of propaganda, but he was going to have his say.

Notes

1. I refer to Daniel Pearl as "Danny" throughout the chapter. Daniel and I were longtime friends and colleagues at the *Wall Street Journal.*

2. Dan Kennedy, "Witnesses to an Execution: Reflections on the Meaning of the Daniel Pearl Video—and the *Phoenix*'s Decision to Make it Available," http://www.bostonphoenix.com/boston/news_features/dont_quote_me/multi-page/documents/02309509.htm.

3. Author interview with anonymous source, March 3, 2010.

4. Letter from Noam Chomsky to *Covert Action Quarterly,* quoting Alex Carey, Australian social scientist, http://mediafilter.org/caq/CAQ54chmky.html.

5. Jose A. Rodriguez Jr. and Bill Harlow, *Hard Measures: How CIA Actions After 9/11 Saved American Lives* (New York: Simon and Schuster, 2012), 88–89.

6. Lee Artz, "War as Promotional 'Photo Op': The *New York Times*'s Visual Coverage of the U.S. Invasion of Iraq," in *War, Media and Propaganda: A Global Perspective,* ed. Yahya Kamalipour and Nancy Snow, 82–83 (Lanham, Md.: Rowman and Littlefield, 2004).

7. Peter Maass, "The Toppling: How the Media Inflated a Minor Moment in a Long War," *New Yorker,* January 10, 2011, www.newyorker.com/reporting/2011/01/10/110110fa_fact_maass.

8. Associated Press, "New Photos of Khalid Sheikh Mohammed Released: Experts Say Images Released by Khalid Sheikh Mohammed's Parents Are Being Used by Terrorist Groups to Inspire Attacks," Guardian.co.uk, September 9, 2009, http://www.guardian.co.uk/world/2009/sep/09/khalid-sheikh-mohammed-photos.

9. Robert Mackey, "Photographs of Khalid Shaikh Mohammed at Guantánamo Appear Online," *New York Times*, September 9, 2009.

10. Michael Durrant and Steven Hartov, *In the Company of Heroes* (New York: Putnam, 2003), 98.

11. Garth S. Jowett and Victoria O'Donnell, *Propaganda and Persuasion*, 3rd ed. (Thousand Oaks, Calif.: Sage Publications, 2011), 17.

12. "Al Jazeera Not to Air French Killings Video," Al Jazeera, March 20, 2012, www.aljazeera.com/news/europe/2012/03/20123271265948416.html.

7

PROPAGANDA AS ENTERTAINMENT

GARTH S. JOWETT

There has always been an element of propaganda in entertainment forms. The key question, of course, is how do we define propaganda? This question of definition has perplexed many a scholar, politician, or anyone trying to decide if the content has a deliberate intent to inculcate a specific message or meaning to the receiving audience. For purposes of this essay, the definition of propaganda that will be used is that developed by myself and Victoria O'Donnell:

> Propaganda is the deliberate, systematic attempt to shape perceptions, manipulate cognitions, and direct behavior to achieve a response that furthers the desired intent of the propagandist.[1]

This definition emphasizes that propaganda is not conducted on some arbitrary whim, but is the result of a conscious decision to formulate a message that has the desired intent of influencing the recipient toward a certain way of thinking. There is, however, an inherent problem with using this definition of propaganda when dealing with entertainment, because it is often extremely difficult to discern with any certainty whether there is in fact a "deliberate, systematic attempt" to insert specific messages intended to "achieve a response" other than to entertain. If one takes seriously the theoretical concept which forms the underpinning of critical analysis, that there is no such thing as value-free content in entertainment, and that all content has meaning for the audience, then literally every form of entertainment can be considered to fall under this definition of propaganda. Nonetheless, there are certain historical cases where the intersection between entertainment and propaganda is more obvious, and which therefore present an opportunity for closer examination of this issue.

Of all the mass media that have developed since the first penny press in the 1830s, no medium has been more thoroughly examined and excoriated as a vehicle for potential propaganda than the commercial motion picture. In dealing with the subject matter at hand, I exclude the use of film for official instructional or propaganda purposes, with such varying content as *How to Clean Your Teeth* to *Fighting the Communist Menace.* I also exclude documentaries, such as the Nazi government film *Triumph of the Will,* which was deliberately created in order to demonstrate the increasing power of the reunified Germany under Adolf Hitler, or the series of *Why We Fight* films created by famed Hollywood director Frank Capra for the U.S. Army Signal Corps in World War II.

There is a significant irony with commercial film, in that, despite its enormous audiences and the inherent emotional and aesthetic appeal that moving pictures provide, throughout its long history the commercial cinema has never been systematically utilized for propaganda purposes. Certainly there have been specific situations where movies have proven to be extremely successful in conveying deliberately planned propaganda messages, and these are to a large extent associated with some type of conflict situation, either in the support of a real war or the proverbial "battle for the hearts and minds" of individuals associated with ideological or religious differences. In either case, the movies have been used as just one of the media in an extensive array of propaganda vehicles. Nonetheless, the popular appeal of movies, the glamour associated with movie stars, and the central part that movies have played in the growing world of international entertainment have made them a prime target for those wishing to investigate the medium's potentially insidious propaganda role.

There have always been complaints that movies have played a role in swaying public opinion, such as in the case of the 1909 film *The Great Thaw Trial,* which critics claimed influenced public attitudes in favor of the man who had shot architect Stanford White while in a jealous rage.[2] Harry K. Thaw was found not guilty for White's murder by reason of insanity, and released after only a few months in a hospital. The sympathetic treatment accorded him in this film was thought to have influenced his light treatment. Throughout history, and especially in the era of Progressive social movements, the movies have been a constant source of complaint regarding their supposed influence on audiences. In areas such as language, fashion, even romantic behavior, the movies have always had a profound influence on aspects of the culture. But can we call this propaganda?

There are specific case studies where the motion picture industry has been accused of deliberate propaganda activities. As a prime example of such an investigation we can look to the U.S. Senate's Interstate Commerce Committee's 1941 hearings on propaganda in motion pictures.[3] In the autumn of 1941, two years after World War II had begun and when the outcome was still in some doubt, a group of isolationist senators decided to make the motion picture industry own up to deliberately trying to make the American moviegoing public pro-interventionist on behalf of the Allied forces. Their basic claim was that, at the behest of President Franklin D. Roosevelt's administration, the motion picture studios were deliberately releasing a significant number of propagandistic films designed to induce the United States into a war with Germany.

On August 1st, 1941, Senator Gerald P. Nye from North Dakota, a leading isolationist, delivered a nationwide radio speech titled "War Propaganda: Our Madness Increases as Our Emergency Shrinks."[4] Nye attempted to make the case that America was once again being pushed into an unwanted foreign war. He noted:

> Who has brought us to the verge of war? Let us ask and demand the answer to this question now. Who is pushing and hauling at America to plunge us into this war? Who are the men? Who is putting up the money for all this propaganda? Who are they? We want to know. And we want to know now. Now, before we plow a million American boys under the dust and mud of Africa, Indo-China, France, and far away Russia, to make the world safe for Empire and Communism. . . .
>
> You know that this, as in the last war, has been a propaganda job. To carry on propaganda you must have money. But you also must have the instruments of propaganda. And one of the most powerful, if not the most powerful, instrument of propaganda is the movies. In Germany, Italy, and in Russia—the dictator countries—the government either owns or completely controls and directs the movies. And they are used as instruments of government propaganda. In this country the movies are owned

> by private individuals. But, it so happens that these movie companies have been operating as war propaganda machines almost as if they were being directed from a single central bureau.

Nye attacked the heads of the studios, all of whom he claimed were from Europe, as being "naturally susceptible" to the emotions elicited by the current conflict. He demanded to know what part the American government was playing in assisting the studios in the making of these "preparedness films." It was at this point in the speech that Nye then explained why he was so concerned specifically with the movies as a form of propaganda:

> But when you go to the movies, you go there to be entertained. You are not figuring on listening to a debate about the war. You settle yourself in your seat with your mind wide open. And then the picture starts—goes to work on you, all done by trained actors, full of drama, cunningly devised, and soft passionate music underscoring it. Before you know where you are you have actually listened to a speech designed to make you believe that Hitler is going to get you if you don't watch out. And, of course, it's a very much better speech than just an ordinary speech at a mass meeting. And you pay for it. The truth is that in 20,000 theatres in the United States tonight they are holding war mass meetings, and the people lay down the money at the box office before they get in.

There was little doubt that Nye's speech was a thinly disguised anti-Semitic attack on the movie moguls, and their desire to see the United States enter the war against Germany. In some respects Senator Nye was correct in his naming of specific films that he thought were deliberately designed to foster a sympathetic attitude toward America's entry into the European conflict, an opinion bolstered by the fact that Hollywood gave very little attention to the increasing tension between Japan and the United States at this time. The reality was that throughout most of the 1930s, no doubt influenced by international marketing considerations, and the important German market for American films, the Hollywood studios had been very reluctant to make films about the growing conflict in Europe and specifically about Adolf Hitler's rise to power. However, as the mood of the country began to swing slowly toward a sympathetic view of those nations opposing Hitler, the studios started making films with an anti-Nazi bias. Once Hitler banned all American films from the German market in 1940, and a war-ravaged Europe provided no substitution, there was no reason to hold back. There were no other viable markets but the unoccupied Allied countries, especially Great Britain. Starting with the release of *Confessions of a Nazi Spy* in 1939, Hollywood studios increasingly began to produce films dealing with Nazi Germany and the European war. These films—including (among others) *The Mortal Storm* (1940), *Foreign Correspondent* (1940), *The Great Dictator* (1940), and *A Yank in the RAF* (1941)—were overtly anti-German and pro-British in tone and substance.[5]

As demonstrated by Nye's radio speech, such a partisan interventionist posture emanating from an enormously popular entertainment medium alarmed those in Congress who opposed U.S. involvement in European affairs, and in September 1941 Senator Burton K. Wheeler (D-Montana), another arch isolationist and chair of the Interstate Commerce Committee, appointed a five-person subcommittee to investigate alleged war propaganda in Hollywood films. According to Wheeler and his allies, the eight largest motion picture companies were taking advantage of their access to the American people to promote involvement in a war that was none of America's concern. Over the course of several weeks the subcommittee heard the testimony of such film giants as Darryl F. Zanuck and Harry Warner before reaching an inconclusive end in late September.

Senator Nye, answering the charges that this committee was essentially fueled by anti-Semitic sentiments, said:

> I bitterly resist, Mr. Chairman, this effort to misrepresent our purpose and to prejudice the public mind and your mind by dragging this racial issue to the front. I will not consent to its being used to cover the tracks of those who have been pushing our country on the way to war with their propaganda intended to inflame the American mind with hatred for one foreign cause and magnified respect and glorification for another foreign cause, until we shall come to feel that wars elsewhere in the world are really after all our wars. . . .
>
> Those primarily responsible for the propaganda pictures are born abroad. They came to our land and took citizenship here entertaining violent animosities toward certain causes abroad. Quite natural is their feeling and desire to aid those who are at war against the causes which so naturally antagonize them. . . .

> If the anti-Semitic issue is now raised for the moment, it is raised by those of the Jewish faith . . . not by me, not by this committee. . . .[6]

The motion picture industry was initially confused as to how to handle this situation, and Will Hays, as the head of the Motion Picture Producers and Distributors Association, took his usual cautious route when dealing with Congress, suggesting that the industry merely stress that 92.7 percent of the feature-length films released since the outbreak of the war were totally unrelated to the conflict. He suggested further that the industry stress that movies were nothing more than "mere entertainment."[7] It is interesting that the only non-Jewish member of the studio heads, Darryl F. Zanuck of Twentieth Century-Fox, took the lead in attacking the subcommittee. He consulted with Ulric Bell, the executive director of the pro-interventionist organization Fight for Freedom, on how best to proceed. Bell suggested that the industry "blast the committee from the very start as a pack of Nazi smear artists." Bell also pointed out that it was the motion picture industry's patriotic duty to help forge national unity during this time of uncertainty. Zanuck took Bell's advice to heart, and he subsequently suggested that it was time that Hollywood producers "proclaim [that] they are doing everything they know how to make America conscious of the national peril."[8]

The industry then hired Wendell Willkie, the 1940 Republican Party nominee for president, to represent them before the committee. Given a fee of $100,000, Willkie proved to be an able advocate and immediately submitted a detailed memorandum suggesting that there was no need for the investigation to proceed because the motion picture industry was "proud to admit that we have done everything possible to inform the public of the progress of our national defense program." He made the telling point that: "From the motion picture and radio industry, it is just a small step to the newspapers, magazines and other periodicals. And from the freedom of the press, it is just a small step to the freedom of the individual to say what he believes."[9]

On the 9th of September, the subcommittee commenced it hearings in a highly charged atmosphere. After several weeks of evidence from both sides, the committee failed to make its case. In fact, due to the relentlessly unfavorable press coverage that these hearings received, the committee members found themselves under personal attack. The liberal *New York Herald Tribune* called the hearings an "inquisition . . . to intimidate public expression on the screen," and the *Washington Post* dismissed them as "a springboard for the expression of isolationist views."[10] The most damaging accusation, which had haunted the establishment of the committee from the first broadcast of Nye's infamous speech, was that it was motivated by anti-Semitism. The subcommittee's credibility was further undermined by another infamous speech, made by Charles Lindbergh on September 15th, in which he accused Jews of plotting with the British and the Roosevelt administration to draw the United States into war. Lindbergh was not associated with the official investigation, but speaking of the Jews he claimed, "Their greatest danger to this country lies in their large ownership and influence in our motion pictures, our press, our radio, and our Government."[11] Lindbergh's speech was widely condemned and served to focus the anti-Semitic atmosphere surrounding the investigations of the subcommittee. On September 26 the subcommittee went into recess, and by October 9 it was reported that the work of the subcommittee was being suspended until a future time. That future time never came, and soon after the December 7 attack on Pearl Harbor the subcommittee was permanently abandoned because their investigation had become moot. No final report from the subcommittee was ever issued.

This detailed case study serves to illustrate several key points about the potential of the movies as propaganda vehicles. It is accepted that the inherent attractiveness and emotional appeal of the image on the large screen, combined with a compelling narrative, and displayed in a darkened theater welcomes a level of audience involvement participation that is still unequaled by almost all other media. (Some very sophisticated technologies, such as virtual reality devices, may someday prove to be more effective.) This level of audience involvement naturally leads to a fear that, given the proper set of circumstances—such as political or civil upheaval, or individual emotional crises—the motion picture does indeed have the potential to become a powerful tool in the propagandist's arsenal. However, in the case of the commercial motion picture there are several factors, especially economic and psychological, that mitigate against such a possibility. Generally audiences pay their money at the box office expecting to be entertained, and naturally resist obvious and deliberate attempts to be propagandized. Of course the subject matter of the film may be viewed by some as being, in fact, propaganda. As an example, the release of Dr. Seuss's *The Lorax* (2012) evoked a great deal of controversy regarding its "liberal eco-friendly" agenda. (In this particular case there is partial reality to this charge, and Theodore Geisel [Dr. Seuss], himself a major contributor to the U.S. propaganda effort in World War II, once called *The Lorax* propaganda.) Other recent mainstream films, such as *The Hurt Locker* (2008) and *Dear John* (2010), have been called pro-Iraq War propaganda, while *Green Zone* (2010) is considered anti-Iraq War propaganda. Elements of propagandistic intent can be detected in almost every film if one looks hard enough. In an age of intense ideological division, even a very successful animated film like *Wall-E* (2008) suffers from criticism. Talk radio host Lars Larson, appearing on the MSNBC cable news network show *Verdict,* said of the film: "It's propaganda! We're talking about a movie that foists off on little kids the idea that human beings are bad for planet earth. And that's not true. Why are human beings bad for planet earth? . . . If you take your kids to this, understand they're going to come away with the idea that mommy and daddy are bad for the planet and the planet would be better off without them."[12]

The key question is how much of this contentious content is recognized and internalized by the paying audience? Do children who have seen *The Lorax* come away from the film with a renewed sense of ecological responsibility? Do adults accept the version of the Iraqi conflict as interpreted by *Green Zone,* or are they more likely to buy into the heroics of the Navy Seals as depicted in *Act of Valor* (2012)? Clearly, every film has a message, some more obvious than others, but only a detailed examination of the specifics surrounding the production of a film will reveal the extent to which propagandistic elements were deliberately worked into the narrative.

In the end we are left with exactly what the best propagandistic role is for the commercial motion picture, and here we do have a very clear answer. In 1939, the American film producer Walter Wanger wrote an influential article for the political journal *Foreign Affairs* titled "120,000 American Ambassadors" in which he cogently explained the true propaganda value of commercial films. He noted that at that time there were approximately 120,000 prints of American films in worldwide circulation, and they represented for their vast audience a view of American life like no other medium could:

> These pictures do not present the American as a perfect being. Yet, though they show gangsters, they also show the gangsters' punishment. They show frivolity, over-luxury; but they also show the triumph of the poor boy. Everything is jumbled, like life. There is no preachment: "We are a godlike race. Look on us. Be like us." And because of this very unpremeditated approach, 150,000,000 theatergoers accept American pictures with the instinctive, subconscious comment: "These people are merely trying to entertain us, not proselytize us." Here is a fact worth pondering. No one forces these pictures on any public. Weary feet carry patrons to the box offices. Millions of hands of every hue extend clutched earnings. Every tongue—outdoing Babel—says for American pictures, "Two tickets, please." . . . for millions upon millions . . . there still exists a way of life in which the individual counts, in which hatred and regimentation do not comprise the sole motive and method of existence. This reminder is the American motion picture.[13]

Besides film there is also American television. Because television has largely been a domestically consumed medium, it has not been extensively used as a means of direct international propaganda (with the exception of the U.S. government's TV Martí or Alhurra TV, which are not within the scope of this essay). This may change with the introduction of more sophisticated and accessible direct broadcast satellite technology, but it is unlikely that many countries would allow the cultural disruptions caused by such daily doses of foreign propaganda. Of far greater current danger is the immense amount of indirect propaganda presented under the guise of entertainment that forms the basis of the worldwide trade in television programming. As is true with the motion picture industry, the giant television industries of the United States and Great Britain, as well as India and Germany, have dominated the international market for television programs. Most Third World countries are unable to produce sufficient programming to meet their own needs, and the voracious appetite for television entertainment is met by importing programs from elsewhere. The United States alone sells more than 150,000 hours of television programs annually.[14]

The contents of these programs clearly carry ideological messages, and often they create what is called "the frustration of rising expectations" in viewers from less developed countries by presenting an attractive lifestyle that is beyond their economic means. Ultimately, it is theorized, constant exposure to such a divergence in living conditions will bring about hostility toward the originating country. Critical communications scholar Herbert Schiller noted, "To foster consumerism in the poor world sets the stage for frustration on a massive scale, to say nothing of the fact that there is a powerful body of opinion there which questions sharply the desirability of pursuing the Western pattern of development."[15]

As an example, during the years when Germany was divided into the Communist East and the Capitalist West, a major contributing factor in the collapse of the wall between West and East Germany was the daily dose of television images of "conspicuous consumption" that the East Germans could view in the context of their own relatively drab lifestyles.[16]

In more sanguine times, it was often thought that the worldwide exchange of television programs would lead to greater international understanding and tolerance, but this has not proved to be the case. Today we have the anomalous situation in which American television programs that tend to glamorize the lifestyles of the rich or beautiful, even ones that are decades old, such as *Dallas* or *Baywatch,* are followed with almost religious devotion in many countries, while at the same time those same audiences express intense political hostility toward the United States as a symbol of capitalist oppression.

Television does have a major propaganda function in the area of news reporting.[17] Complaints have always been voiced about misrepresentation in the reporting of international (as well as domestic) news. Ultimately, the concept of developing a New World Information Order that would provide more balanced coverage of news from developing countries has not had wide acceptance in the West, and images of famine, corruption, and conflicts still predominate on our nightly news broadcasts. In this way, the powerful visual images are presented to television viewers in broadcasts that seldom have enough time to develop the stories to provide adequate explanations. The shorthand nature of television news lends itself to such distortion, thus creating a form of indirect propaganda that affects our perceptions and shapes our attitudes toward a wide variety of issues. We learn to rely on the news media for information, and repeated frequently enough, these images become fixed beliefs, shaping our understanding of the world around us.

No solution to this problem of distortion is clear-cut; it is an inherent part of a free media system in which market forces dictate the content of the media. The difficulties in reconciling this free market media system—in which the commercial mass media allow audience preferences to shape content—with the understandable desire by countries and individuals to present their "best" images are almost insurmountable. Clearly all parties would like to use the media to propagandize favorably on their behalf, but if news agencies and television networks in the West think their audiences are more interested in learning about political coups, wars, and corruption in Third World countries than about increases in food production, educational advances, and stable political regimes, then that is what will be featured on the news. This type of indirect and unconscious propaganda is a major product of modern media systems.

The most blatant example of television propaganda is the introduction of TV Martí, with which the U.S. government began beaming programs into Cuba in August 1990. TV Martí broadcasts twenty-four hours per day, seven days a week on the Hispasat satellite; two and a half hours per day, five days a week from a modified aircraft, Aero Martí, on VHF and UHF frequencies; and three hours per day, five days a week on DirecTV satellite. Approximately ten hours of original, contemporary, fast-paced television programs are produced in-house weekly. In addition, Radio and TV Martí are streamed live at Martinoticias.com. Both Radio and TV Martí provided extensive news of changes in U.S. policy towards Cuba announced by President Obama in April 2009, including reactions from inside Cuba and from dissidents, members of Congress, and Cuban affairs experts.[18]

Both of these stations are bombarding the Cuban people with propaganda in the guise of entertainment, as well as deliberate political messages.[19] The use of these two broadcasting units by the U.S. government is as much a form of psychological warfare as it is a threat to Cuba's economy. The Cuban government is forced to spend a great deal of its already depleted cash reserves on a very expensive jamming operation and has declared that the watching of TV Martí or listening to Radio Martí is "an act of civil disobedience."[20]

Because of its inherent attractiveness, television offers an opportunity to propagandize in the guise of entertainment. Some countries, such as India and Mexico, have actively used soap operas on television to deliver pro-social messages on issues such as breastfeeding, birth control, and consumer fraud. These programs, designed to be as involving to viewers as any regular soap opera, have been carefully crafted by scriptwriters working with social scientists to ensure that these positive propagandistic messages are smoothly integrated into the plot.

Nothing can quite match the entertainment value of propaganda in wartime, especially when the war is playing out before the viewing audience like a popular video game. During the Gulf War (1990–1991), the emergence of Cable News Network (CNN) and the invaluable role it played as the major disseminator of news throughout the world took many people by surprise. The Gulf War was the first major conflict of a global nature since the introduction of worldwide television satellite services, and the potential of these systems was dramatically illustrated by the instantaneous broadcasts of events from the embattled area. When CNN reporters remained in Baghdad after the war had actually begun, the world was witness to an unprecedented series of live broadcasts from within the enemy's capital city while it was actually under bombardment. Some politicians and members of the public criticized CNN for playing into the hands of enemy propaganda by agreeing to broadcast Iraqi-censored reports, but on the whole these broadcasts were well received and widely viewed. The question of CNN's unwitting role in "giving aid and comfort to the enemy" by showing the damage to civilian life within Iraq was widely debated at the time, with no clear public consensus emerging except that viewers found the service almost indispensable.[21]

The reporting of the Gulf War raised new questions about the relationship between the media and the military. It was obvious that the instantaneous technologies available for disseminating news from the battlefields had clashed with the military's need and desire to control what images would actually be seen. The result was that the military denied access to all but a few reporters whom it could control through the use of official "pool" coverage with military escorts. Although this system was introduced in the name of safety and security for troops and reporters, the end result was a great deal of dissatisfaction on the part of the media and a large segment of the public, with the appearance of deliberately manipulated coverage. Some journalists were conflicted about news media censorship for a nation at war. Jonathan Alter of *Newsweek* magazine wrote: "Contrary to popular impression, most reporters actually support certain wartime restrictions. . . . Obviously, there are some legitimate concerns about the role of the news media during combat. If Vietnam was the first TV war, this could be the first live one, thanks to satellite technology. Live means no editing, a careless kind of journalism. And the presence of global networks like CNN is dicey in wartime."[22]

In contrast, the venerable American broadcast journalist Walter Cronkite was unequivocal: "The military . . . has the responsibility of giving all the information it possibly can to the press and the press has every right, to the point of insolence, to demand this."[23]

By the time of the post-9/11 conflicts, this time involving the invasion of Afghanistan in October 2001 and Iraq in March 2003, CNN had a very lively rival with the emergence of the cable news network Fox News Channel (FNC) as an alternative to the "mainstream" media and sporting the rather audacious slogan of "Fair and Balanced." FNC was blatantly in support of the Bush administration's actions and provided a largely uncritical evaluation of the events as they unfolded. Reporters for all of the television networks were embedded with the troops, and this brought about similar complaints about the lack of objective reporting. However, the constraints of the battlefield do present real problems. And realistically, reporters cannot safely be allowed to run around in the middle of a firefight trying to get dramatic footage for the audience watching its television sets that evening. Nonetheless, the use of new, more mobile technologies made coverage much more dramatic and personal, far outstripping the ability of the military to control what kinds of images were being sent out to what was now a worldwide audience.

The world of international satellite television, so long dominated by CNN, was also dramatically changed by the emergence of another entity, this time from the Arab world. Launched in 1996, the same year as Fox News Channel, but based in Doha, Qatar, Al Jazeera today has more than thirty bureaus and dozens of correspondents covering the entire globe, bringing an entirely new perspective to international news coverage. Its mission early on was as follows: "Free from the shackles of censorship and government control Aljazeera has offered its audiences in the Arab world much needed freedom of thought, independence, and room for debate. In the rest of the world, often dominated by the stereotypical thinking of news 'heavyweights,' Aljazeera offers a different and a new perspective."[24]

The station has not hesitated to broadcast programming, especially images, which are quite opposite to those distributed in the Western media, and this has given Al Jazeera the reputation of being deliberately inflammatory and propagandistic. With programming focusing primarily on news coverage and analysis, the station has earned the loyalty of an enormous, mostly Arab-speaking audience and the enmity of various critics, who argue that Al Jazeera is deliberately sensational by showing bloody footage from various war zones as well as giving disproportionate coverage to various fundamentalist and extremist groups. Criticism from various Western (and sometimes Arab) governments has only served to increase its credibility with an audience that is used to censorship and biased coverage from official government outlets. There is little doubt that Al Jazeera has opened up the world of cable television news to a much wider audience and has served to heat up the propaganda wars now being fought through satellite television.[25]

It is difficult to predict exactly how much of a role television will play in direct international propaganda in the future. It is doubtful that the use of direct broadcast satellite technology will be allowed in the same fashion as international radio broadcasting, and the methods of technological control (going so far as to destroy offending satellites) are much easier. It is very likely that we will see a continuation of the argument surrounding the misrepresentation of countries and groups in those countries in which the media are not too tightly controlled by the government. Where governments do have control of the media systems, however, television will continue to play a major role in propagandizing activities, as much through the ideological perspectives of so-called entertainment as through the management of images presented in the news. The potential use of the minicam, and more recently the smart phone, for the online circulation of recorded material in a closed network has just begun to be explored for propaganda purposes.

It was widely acknowledged that the circulation of illicit underground tapes in Eastern Europe, even though the number of privately owned VCRs was small, was a significant factor in coalescing opposition groups during the Cold War. In more recent times, the succession of videotapes purportedly coming from Osama bin Laden, in which he made personal addresses to Western political leaders or to his own followers and other terrorist leaders being sought in the "war on terrorism," served to act as quite potent propaganda vehicles. More recently we have witnessed the use of the ubiquitous cell phone recording technology to capture dramatic images, from the killing of Muammar Gaddafi in Libya to the devastating tsunami that ravaged the coast of Japan to more local events, such as police using pepper spray on students protesting on a California campus. These images can now be broadcast instantaneously throughout the world, creating a fascinating potential as a propaganda medium.

There is little doubt that we live in a world surrounded by propaganda messages, from consumer advertising to politics, and the development of new communication technologies increases the prospects that we will be bombarded with an even greater variety and number of such messages in the immediate future. Increasingly, as propagandists attempt to find unique ways of getting their message through the information clutter that now permeates our society, they will turn to more subtle methods, particularly methods that are less obvious, and more entertaining. The use of entertainment as propaganda is only now entering its Golden Age.

Notes

1. Garth Jowett and Victoria O'Donnell, *Propaganda and Persuasion*, 5th ed. (Thousand Oaks, Calif.: Sage Publications, 2011), 7.

2. For further information about this movie, see www.starpulse.com/Actresses/Nesbit,_Evelyn/Biography/.

3. "Propaganda in Motion Pictures: Hearings Before a Subcommittee of the Committee on Interstate Commerce, United States Senate, Seventy-Seventh Congress, First Session, on S. Res. 152, a Resolution Authorizing an Investigation of War Propaganda Disseminated by the Motion-picture Industry and of Any Monopoly in the Production, Distribution, Or Exhibition of Motion Pictures, Sept. 9 to 26, 1941." For more details of these hearings, see John E. Moser, "'Gigantic Engines of Propaganda': The 1941 Senate Investigation of Hollywood," *Historian* 63 (June 2001): 732–752.

4. Gerald P. Nye, "War Propaganda: Our Madness Increases as Our Emergency Shrinks," *Vital Speeches of the Day*, vol. 7 (1941): 720–723.

5. Jowett and O'Donnell, *Propaganda and Persuasion.*

6. U.S. Senate Subcommittee Hearings on Motion Picture and Radio Propaganda, 1941, http://www.digitalhistory.uh.edu/historyonline/senate_subcommittees.cfm.

7. Moser, "'Gigantic Engines of Propaganda.'"

8. Ibid.

9. Ibid.

10. See *New York Herald Tribune,* September 10, 1941, A26; *Washington Post,* September 28, 1941, B6.

11. Charles Lindbergh is quoted in A. Scott Berg, *Lindbergh* (New York: Putnam, 1998), 450–455.

12. "Lars Larson Rips Wall-E as 'Propaganda,'" http://thinkprogress.org/politics/2008/07/02/25582/larson-robot-marriage/?mobile=nc.

13. Walter Wanger, "120,000 American Ambassadors," *Foreign Affairs* 18 (1939): 45.

14. This problem is analyzed in some detail in C. C. Lee, *Media Imperialism Reconsidered: The Homogenization of American Television* (Thousand Oaks, Calif.: Sage Publications, 1980).

15. Herbert I. Schiller, *Mass Communication and American Empire* (New York: Augustus M. Kelly, 1970), 114.

16. Helmut Hanke, "Media Culture in the GDR: Characteristics, Processes and Problems," *Media Culture and Society* 12 (1990): 175–193.

17. The examination of television news here is predicated on the increasingly accepted view that news is now considered to be entertainment. See D. Kishan Thussu, *News as Entertainment: The Rise of Global Infotainment* (London: Routledge, 2009).

18. "Fact Sheet: Reaching Out to the Cuba People," White House, April 13, 2009, http://www.whitehouse.gov/the_press_office/Fact-Sheet-Reaching-out-to-the-Cuban-people/.

19. Radio and TV Martí do not only report on news and politics in Cuba, but also feature a variety of programming. TV Martí, for instance, features a show called *Let's Talk,* which focuses on issues of interest to women. The show *High Voltage* provides music videos, sports summaries, and news programs from Voice of America.

20. *Special report by the Advisory Board for Cuba Broadcasting on TV Martí,* presented to President George Bush, January 1991, 10.

21. For more detailed information on the role that CNN played in revolutionizing the coverage of such conflicts, see Barbie Zelizer, "CNN, the Gulf War, and the Journalistic Practice," *Journal of Communication* 42, no. 1 (March 1992): 66–81.

22. John R. MacArthur, *Second Front: Censorship and Propaganda in the Gulf War* (Berkeley, Calif.: Univ. of California Press, 1993), 209.

23. Walter Cronkite, "What Is There to Hide?" *Newsweek,* February 25, 1991, 43.

24. Philip Seib, ed., *New Media and the New Middle East* (New York: Palgrave Macmillan), 2009, 83.

25. On January 2, 2013, Al Jazeera announced that it had acquired Current TV, a U.S. network cofounded by former Vice President Al Gore, thereby gaining access to a much larger American audience. The new channel, Al Jazeera America, will potentially reach tens of millions of homes, although Time Warner Cable immediately cancelled its Current TV contract in the wake of the announcement.

8

REFORMING THE WORST PROPAGANDA

RANDAL MARLIN

The title of this chapter suggests the need for a preliminary settling of two questions, one about propaganda and the other about its worst forms. Two senses of the word "propaganda" can be found in common usage. The first, as used by propaganda scholars Nancy Snow and Philip M. Taylor, among others, is more morally neutral (it merely is) and is tied to the etymology of the word, from the Latin *propagare*: "to propagate."[1] In this sense, propaganda refers to the dissemination of different messages, communication of ideas, feelings, and attitudes, and so forth in the service of the propaganda institution.[2] It includes mass appeals based on both reasoned and emotion-based attempts to communicate what the disseminators believe to be their version of the truth.

In the second sense, propaganda has a negative connotation, derived from the association with deception of some kind, or the use of emotive or other means, such as repetition, for bypassing a target audience's ability to reason well and to assess properly a range of relevant factual material. It has been said that "all propaganda is lies,"[3] and in this second sense that is largely true, so long as one takes into account deceptions that don't meet the customary criteria for literal lying. It is most important to recognize that one very effective form of deception consists in telling truths so selected as to give a wrong impression. G. K. Chesterton called the selective presentation of factual material so as to give a wrong impression "the blackest of all lies."[4]

The term "propaganda" is also usually limited, in both of the above senses, to communications deliberately employed by an identifiable body of persons seeking to affect the behavior of a mass audience with a view to achieving certain aims. But that limitation becomes eroded when we think of propagandized individuals who sincerely pass on, as their own beliefs, those ideas they have accepted through a manipulative process. They may not themselves be seeking to manipulate or deceive, so if we call their relaying of a propagandist's message "propaganda" in the negative sense, we have to go behind the sincere communicator to the manipulating communicator in order to make the messages sent by the former fit the definition. But if we do this we may be led to ask about the initiators whether they have not themselves been propagandized in some way. Jacques Ellul's category of "sociological propaganda" is designed to cover the case where there is no definite source for the underlying myths, such as that of progress, the nation ("whatever is 'American' must be good, whatever is 'un-American' must be bad"), the leader, etc., that serve as "pre-propaganda" useful for the purpose of manipulating audiences.

If we now ask what are the "worst forms" of propaganda, we have the problem of deciding whether to focus (1) on the kinds of communications used to impart messages and ideas or to affect emotions (through music, for example) or (2) on the content of the communications together with the objectives sought by the propagandists. In the first instance we might think of straightforward lies, or deliberately misleading statements, seductive imagery, bandwagon appeals, racist metaphors, and the panoply of different propaganda devices one can enumerate. In the second instance, we think of what it is the propagandists want to accomplish. As an example, consider broadcasts from the Rwandan radio station RTLM in 1993–1994 where there was deliberate encouragement to commit genocide through use of the metaphor of "cockroaches" to designate Tutsis. Likewise, Hitler used metaphors of "lice" and "disease" to prepare the ground for genocide against Jews.

Deceptive or seductive kinds of communication can be paired either with worthy or unworthy content and objectives. Consider the use of images of women or men as sex objects to sell products, used in one case a decade or two ago to convince television viewers to switch to natural gas, a less polluting fuel than oil. The imagery was not conducive to rational assessment, but the end sought was a good one considering the price differential at the time, the impact on the environment, etc. Contrast that case with similar sexual imagery used by the tobacco industry to sell cigarettes, encouraging people to take up a deadly and addictive habit.

In another kind of pairing, consider the moral ambiguity where gruesome pictures are shown of victims of violence of some kind. These can be used by pacifists to show the horrors of war, or by warmongers who seek to fuel outrage and a desire for revenge against terrorists. The repulsiveness of the imagery, which we assume to be very upsetting, has attackers and defenders. Among the latter, the argument is that such means are necessary to galvanize the public to take military action, or in the case of the pacifists to stop all war-like activity. Analogous arguments arise in the case of pictures used to support one side or the other on the abortion issue.

In some cases, such as propaganda for genocide, the aim and object of the propagandist will dominate in our reckoning about the badness of the propaganda enterprise. But in other cases we may find ourselves balancing the goals of propaganda against the means used. Raising money aimed at supporting a hospital may be a worthy objective, but flat-out lies about, say, the likelihood of patients dying if the hospital support is not forthcoming would seem, to this writer at least, to merit disapproval.

The above has provided a sketch of some of the different parameters for evaluating propaganda from a moral standpoint. Enough has been said to indicate that deciding on what forms of propaganda are "worst" can take us into highly controversial territory, particularly when we reflect on the different values different people are likely to place on the various goals that different propaganda initiatives are designed to achieve. Fortunately, there are also areas where there is a large measure of agreement about ends and means alike, so that we can usefully explore the range of options for combating propaganda in such cases, before returning to controversial areas in the third main section below.

To reduce the reach and power of propaganda, it is necessary to understand its workings. By definition, propaganda does not have as its primary aim enlightening people by giving them the information on which to base their autonomous judgment. The worst propagandist, as distinct from the best educator, seeks to lead a target audience along a predetermined path by affecting their beliefs and feelings in a way appropriate to their choosing that path. This can be a very simple matter, such as making promises to people in order to get elected when one has no intention of carrying them out. It can involve use of misleading statistics, perversion of language, shouting instead of debating, silencing dissenting voices through censorship—whether directly by government or indirectly through the power of the purse exercised by corporations.

The situation of modern propaganda involves more than rhetorical devices, misleading imagery, and the like. It also involves control over the mass media. In a democratic society, where people are free to speak out, the various deceptions could in theory be exposed. Democracy should resemble the Miltonian free and equal encounter between true and false ideas. But in practice, filters operate, not always consciously, to ensure that the "free and open encounter" is less than ideal. As Nancy Snow pointed out earlier in this volume, Edward S. Herman and Noam Chomsky's classic "propaganda model" presented five different filters operating in the mass media.[5] The model has had enough confirmation to shift reasonable discussion from the question of "whether" such filters exist to that of "to what extent?" For propaganda to be successful, a targeted audience must not recognize what is communicated as propaganda. Exposure of the propagandist's deceptions is likely to make them ineffective. One way of reducing the reach and scope of propaganda is therefore to point to instances where these filters appear to be operating in and on the media to deprive the public of access to vital information relevant to important political or economic decision-making.

From these observations, it follows that efforts to reduce the reach, scope, and power of propaganda will require a multipronged approach. Exposing the various devices of the propagandist is one prong, but finding appropriate means of communicating such exposures to the public is another prong. It is no easy matter to change the minds of a public already under the influence of stereotypes and myths already perpetrated by the propagandist or through what Jacques Ellul called "sociological propaganda," which, as he defines it, does not have a definite, identifiable source.[6] Academics may even be afraid to speak out against misinformation that has become so deeply entrenched in the public mind that to question it leads to attacks on one's academic competence, patriotic spirit, or both.[7]

Those who have had a big impact on pubic opinion, such as Lord Northcliffe in Great Britain in the early 1900s and the contemporary Rupert Murdoch, have made use simultaneously of two broad media types. The first type is a respectable newspaper, such as the London *Times,* that reaches well-educated audiences who can be expected to challenge careless claims and inferences. Such a newspaper has to work hard to maintain its credibility, but the payoff is that its news and factual content is more likely to be believed by knowledgeable and critically minded readers. The second type of media is aimed at the masses and has a highly emotive content, in some cases with a lot of scandal mongering. Lord Northcliffe had the *Daily Mail* as a widely circulating newspaper and could motivate readers by exploiting hot-button issues and appealing to patriotic sentiments. Political power grows from both types of appeal, neither of which would be nearly as effective without the other. In the case of Rupert Murdoch, a third power vehicle existed in the form of the *News of the World,* essentially a widely circulating scandal sheet that attracted two sets of readers. The first set were lovers of *Schadenfreude,* who enjoy being titillated and who like to pass judgment on others. The second were those who were politically aware and realized the damage to reputations that might result from revelations read by the first set and wanted to know what was being said, not least about things affecting their own reputations. Murdoch has repeated the formula in the United States with his ownership of Fox News Channel (largely not respectable)[8] and the *Wall Street Journal* (respectable for its news stories). From this it follows that just as the newspaper barons use a multipronged approach, countering their influence will also have to be multipronged.

At this point it is worth noting the very valuable work of organizations like the Madison, Wisconsin-based Center for Media and Democracy, publishers of PR Watch and SourceWatch, and other Internet-accessible sources like Truthout, Common Dreams, AlterNet, Consortiumnews, TomDispatch, FactCheck, and many other sites that challenge the mainstream media version of news. Long before the *New York Times* thoroughly exposed in April 2008 the conflicts of interest by retired military experts called upon to defend U.S. policies in the media, PR Watch had done the same, but with less impact. The problem with these alternative media sites is that the reach of the mass media is much greater, and large parts of the public may never encounter their dissident voices. However, with the arrival of YouTube videos recommended on Facebook and Twitter, the possibility exists for very fast, widespread dissemination of particularly gripping materials from these alternate sources.

There are also excellent books by whistleblowers, such as Wendell Potter's exposé of insurance industry propaganda,[9] and movies such as *The Insider* (1999), which publicized tobacco industry propaganda as revealed by former insider Jeffrey Wigand. The list of exposés is in fact quite extensive. Every year Mickey Huff and Project Censored produce a book on the top censored stories of the previous year.[10] Noam Chomsky has been unearthing government propaganda for decades, as did I. F. Stone in the 1940s through the 1960s. Joel Bakan's book, *The Corporation,*[11] along with the movie of the same name, has done a lot to enlighten people about deceptive corporate practices. Of the dozens of important books exposing propaganda of various sorts, special mention should be made of Naomi Oreskes and Erik M. Conway's *Merchants of Doubt* (New York: Bloomsbury Press, 2010), which draws parallels between skeptical arguments made by the tobacco industry against linking smoking to disease, arguments that have since been thoroughly discredited, and similar attempts by industry to foster disbelief in scientific findings relating to acid rain, the ozone hole, and global warming. Another book worthy of special mention is Anthony DiMaggio's *When Media Goes to War: Hegemonic Discourse, Public Opinion, and the Limits of Dissent* (New York: Monthly Review Press, 2009). The educational work done by participants in the 2012 Breaux Symposium is also an important aspect of combating propaganda in all its forms. Robert Greenwald's 2004 classic documentary film *Outfoxed: Rupert Murdoch's War on Journalism* effectively exposes how unfair and imbalanced the Fox News Channel is, contrary to its bold "fair and balanced" proclamation. The scene where Fox News host Bill O'Reilly verbally bullies Jeremy Glick, whose father was killed in the 9/11 attack but who opposed U.S. military action in Afghanistan, should be seen by everyone. Glick gets the better of the exchange until O'Reilly orders his microphone to be cut. Later O'Reilly misrepresents what Glick said. Another good film exposing propaganda is Australian filmmaker Taki Oldham's *(Astro) Turf Wars.* It does a fine job of exposing the hidden funding by corporate interests of supposedly spontaneous grassroots protests from ordinary people, protests that are in fact guided and channeled to benefit those corporate interests.

All of the above-mentioned efforts to enlighten people about the forms of manipulation that beset them, though worthy, still are dwarfed by the reach of the mass media. The proportion of time people will devote to watching Fox News greatly outweighs the time they will (on average) spend watching *Outfoxed,* if indeed they watch it at all. Even the much-watched and much-discussed films by Michael Moore still seem to lack the sustained power possessed by corporate PR to affect the thinking of U.S. citizens.

The problem of combating propaganda arises partly through the existence of media oligopolies, such as the aforementioned Rupert Murdoch's ownership of key media in the United States and around the world. With the *Wall Street Journal* and the London *Times,* he has newspapers that the public views as credible sources. With Fox News Channel he can make constant theater with the news, in ways that promote the fortunes of the wealthy. Politics becomes infotainment as it degenerates into personality contests and mudslinging. This shift of focus makes it hard for the public to see how the super-rich are rewarding themselves through bailouts, tax dodges, and deregulation.

Other newspapers were also delinquent, but the phenomenon of "indexing" helps to explain how the Murdoch newspapers could also have influenced other newspapers, tilting them in a rightward direction. By "indexing" I mean the self-imposed limitations of mainstream newspapers that wish not to appear to be crusading for a cause. So, if public officials or other newspapers refrain from using the word "torture" in connection with U.S. operations in Abu Ghraib, then every media outlet that strives to be mainstream will feel pressured to drop the term, whether or not the term is in fact warranted. The Murdoch newspapers could rely on validation by (Republican) government officials, and thereby count on help to set the "index" for what could be said or not said, given the self-limiting practice mentioned.[12]

One important route therefore to reduce the reach and power of propaganda is to work to counter the consolidation of different media in the hands of very few people. Regulation is one route to pursue, with principles of free speech as enunciated by Judge Learned Hand and U.S. Supreme Court Justice Hugo Black in the case involving Associated Press's effective monopoly in the mid-1940s. One of Black's most important statements was: "Freedom of the press from governmental interference under the First Amendment does not sanction repression of that freedom by private interests."[13]

Further arguments are found in *A Free and Responsible Press,* the study of lasting value published in 1947 by the Commission on Freedom of the Press, headed by Robert Hutchins. Even if the power balance at a given time does not favor such regulation, in the process of agitating for it the biases in the media can be brought into focus. It may be true, though, that mainstream media will ignore these efforts, thus reducing or eliminating their impact. A paradox makes its appearance at this point. If the media are fair enough to allow these arguments to be carefully and thoroughly reported, thus increasing their impact, then maybe the need for such regulation is not all that urgent. If on the other hand the media refuse to give a hearing to these arguments, the unfairness and need will be demonstrated, but the power to effect the proposed changes will be lacking.

The experience in Canada with proposed regulation has not been a total failure. Even though the government of Pierre Trudeau did very little to implement recommendations of the 1981 report of the Royal Commission on Newspapers, the spotlight on the workings of the media did encourage membership in press councils and the rules of membership discourage high-handedness on the part of media owners, editors, or reporters. However, in the current political climate there is little threat of any such controls and papers of the Sun chain of newspapers in Ontario withdrew from the Ontario Press Council in 2011, a move that will likely affect the council's income adversely.[14]

Other legal mechanisms that can be used to discourage some bad forms of propaganda in the United States include reports by the Government Accountability Office that have determined some video news releases to be government propaganda illegally directed at U.S. citizens. As an example, the GAO reported in 2005 that the Bush administration violated antipropaganda rules when it paid a PR firm to produce a news video promoting the administration's education policies and also contracted with commentator Armstrong Williams to discuss the material. In neither case were viewers informed of the government's role in the production and commentary. One problem with using the law for this purpose is that the government of the day may have ideological differences with the GAO and may be reluctant to take action to prosecute infringements of antipropaganda legislation. Without adequate funding for expenses connected with investigating and prosecuting such infringements, the prosecutions may not take place, making the law ineffective. Nevertheless, the GAO reports have garnered a good share of publicity and can help to discourage the kind of propagandistic practices described.

A third legal route for combating a very bad kind of propaganda lies in potential legislation to deal with hate propaganda. The issue is a very thorny one, not just because of well-entrenched First Amendment rights against any abridgement of freedom of speech or infringement on freedom of the press, but because such rights have a sound philosophical basis in a free and democratic society. Still, there are circumstances where other considerations can override free speech considerations. The hate propaganda broadcast against the Tutsis with murderous impact ought not to have been legally permissible, and for such situations Justice Oliver Wendell Holmes's dictum against falsely shouting "fire" in a crowded theater is pertinent.[15] In Canada, the hate propaganda legislation came into being only following a thorough discussion of the free speech issues by the Special Committee on Hate Propaganda in Canada, a committee that included staunch civil libertarians. The legislation has a number of safeguards and the Supreme Court of Canada has determined that only a most extreme kind of hatred, one associated with extreme detestation and vilification of a targeted identifiable group (the specific kinds of groups are named), would qualify as prohibited under the legislation. Further limitations on the kind of hatred subject to legal prohibition is that the hatred must be emotional to a point that belies reason, and implies that targeted individuals "are to be despised, scorned, denied respect and made subject to ill-treatment on the basis of group affiliation."[16]

A fourth legal route for combating what may be the most damage-producing kind of propaganda would be to agitate for adhering to international law, such as that embodied in the United Nations International Covenant on Civil and Political Rights. Section 20 of that covenant states, "Any propaganda for war shall be prohibited by law." False or misleading information used to gain the support of a people for war would qualify as propaganda, in which case it should be prohibited. Raising a hue and cry about such deceptions before war is declared could have a big impact on a population that otherwise might be duped into supporting the war. It would also be useful to force officials who do start a war to be accountable before a judge for their actions. This might serve as a useful deterrent to subsequent leaders who might otherwise be tempted to repeat the scenario of dragging a people into a war they don't want. Practical politics may stand in the way of accomplishing such an objective, and the United States of America has refused to subject itself to the International Criminal Court. In fairness, it needs to be said that nations hostile to U.S. interests should also be subject to the same standards if the United States is to abide by them.

The more people learn about the catastrophic effects of war on populations such as Iraq, the more they may be willing to remind themselves and others about the existence of Section 20 of the ICCPR. Early advocates of sanctions to be taken against those communicators who violate ethical standards such as warmongering were John B. Whitton and Arthur Larson. Their *Propaganda: Towards Disarmament in the War of Words*[17] contains a good Code of Ethics for International Communicators and suggestions for dealing with serious violations of the code. More recently Richard Kearney has argued in *The Prohibition of Propaganda for War in International Law* that the norms prohibiting propaganda for war are not inadequate, and that the challenge for those seeking to avoid war is to find a way of enforcing those norms. Here the difficulty of changing attitudes in a society prone to ignore the norms may be lessened by the active concern of other countries that take them seriously. As Kearney states: "It would be unwise for states, particularly in an age of global media and communications, to assume that even if propaganda for war is not an issue of concern within these societies, such will always remain the case."[18]

It should always be borne in mind that courts of law are prime sources of news stories and that even if a legal objective is not attained in law, the struggle to attain it may bear fruit in the realm of public opinion. University of California linguistics professor George Lakoff has tirelessly insisted on the need to present arguments for proposed policies or actions within a framework that will resonate favorably with audiences, in a way favoring the persuader's cause. All too often logically sound arguments fail to persuade because they are embedded in a framework that triggers opposing sentiments and thought processes.[19] Pursuing a legal case may provide exactly the right kind of opportunity to present a cause within a winning framework that receives wide and sustained publicity.

The importance of frameworks was recognized in the titanic struggle in Canada to pass a law prohibiting tobacco advertising. Those who fought to pass Bill C-36 in the 1980s came to realize that if the public discussion of the issue were framed as a free speech issue their cause was doomed, but they would win if the issue could be framed in health terms. Realizing that, they did their best to steer the discussion away from being one of free speech to one of health. Their efforts paid off, and the law was passed. After initial setbacks in the courts, a revised law eventually survived the free speech challenges, leaving Canada with strong prohibitions against tobacco advertising.[20]

Just as the law is an important vehicle for countering the worst forms of propaganda, it can also be a means for facilitating those forms. Lobbyists are constantly working to shape legislation in ways suitable to their clients' or employers' interests. Countering lobbyists' efforts would require keeping an informed eye on the details of legislation. This can be expected to often require a lot of time, effort, and relevant background knowledge. The scientific, legal, or other expertise needed may be very costly.

From my experience as a community activist I see many people with the appropriate talent being willing to volunteer their time and expertise to support causes they strongly believe in. I have seen this work effectively to bring about community betterment. Whether this success was attributable to having a favorable socioeconomic culture I cannot say. But I see no good reason to believe it is impossible in the current state of western nominally democratic society to harness such talent to counteract misleading propaganda and legislation based on misinformation. Good organization is required. This does not necessarily entail a single, centralized body, but rather individual groups pooling their resources with other groups with similar aims. Research centers without strings-attached funding would be part of an effective organization. A university community as a whole can work to free scientific research from interference. Members of university boards of governors can be encouraged to address the problem of ensuring honest research uncompromised by corporate funding.[21] The public can try to ensure that universities funded by their government should preserve the appearance of integrity in scientific research by refusing corporate funding that would compromise that integrity.

An important source for countering propaganda originating in university, government, or corporate research is the whistleblower. This refers to people who work within a given system, who witness unethical activity detrimentally affecting the public interest, who ideally first try to rectify the situation within the system but when unsuccessful in these efforts then go to the media or some outspoken personage or group, such as a political party, to alert the public to the problem. All too frequently such a move terminates the whistleblower's professional career, so protection needs to be provided to prevent this from happening. Finding adequate means to protect the well-motivated whistleblower while not giving encouragement to badly motivated individuals acting out of spite or glory-seeking might be a problem. The need is great enough, however, that solving that particular problem would be worth the effort.

One potential solution to the problem has already been tried, with the arrival of WikiLeaks, the organization founded by Julian Assange and dedicated to protecting whistleblowers from being discovered. His organization lets potential whistleblowers know that their names will be thoroughly protected from discovery. Unfortunately for the success of this organization, perhaps the most famous of all WikiLeaks releases was connected to the name of U.S. Army private Bradley Manning, who was accused of leaking a half million documents, including military and diplomatic correspondence, through WikiLeaks. This happened not because his name was traced through WikiLeaks, but because he sent an incriminating e-mail to a confidante who informed on him. The effect of the disclosure may well have been to undermine confidence among the public that those who leak via WikiLeaks will have their identities safely protected from public knowledge.[22]

It is time now to address the problem of perspective. Earlier, I stressed that propaganda can consist of entirely true statements, but so selected as to present a false picture. This immediately raises the question as to what is a true picture of events or states of affairs, in relation to which defective accounts may be viewed as propaganda. The problem is not conspicuous when questions of propaganda are posed by and in a community where values are shared. But it does become prominent when it becomes apparent that there is a rift in background values and assumptions.

Dan Kuehl's chapter is very useful for providing a perspective very different from my own, and I want to articulate some of the differences with a view to sorting out truth from propaganda. The aim here is not so much to resolve differences—this would require more space than is available—but to show where the differences lie and the kinds of evidence that would be needed to settle the differences. The evidence Kuehl refers to in his notes on the WikiLeaks question, namely the article by

Larisa Breton and Adam Pearson,[23] does indeed provide a strong challenge to the editorial interpretation provided on the "Collateral Murder" video, and I have had to revise my thinking of the matter in that light. On certain matters I have come to suspend judgment where previously I had accepted the editorial commentary.

Where there is disagreement, it is always good to start with areas of agreement. I share with Kuehl the belief that Edward R. Murrow made an important and perceptive observation about propaganda when he said, "truth is the best propaganda," or in the full quotation: "American traditions and the American ethic require us to be truthful, but the most important reason is that truth is the best propaganda and lies are the worst. To be persuasive we must be believable; to be believable we must be credible; to be credible we must be truthful. It is as simple as that."[24]

I also agree with Kuehl that there is a good case for viewing WikiLeaks's commentary as propaganda. Where I think we probably differ is about the amount of deliberateness in misrepresentations casting the U.S. military in a negative light. For example, the editorial commentary spoke of a camera and tripod being carried among the group of men filmed and later killed by fire from the Apache helicopter. On an alternative military version one was carrying a rocket-propelled grenade (RPG) and another an AK-47. We do know that two of the men killed were working for Reuters, so that would make it more likely, to me, that a camera and tripod were involved. But I'm not qualified to judge from the picture alone. I'm willing to allow that those who made the editorial commentary were doing so in good faith even if they were mistaken.

A second point on which I disagree is Kuehl's judgment that WikiLeaks's "political agenda seems to be focused on 'damage the United States' instead of 'search for truth.'" That presumes that in cases where I think there could be mistaken judgment he sees deliberate distortion. Kuehl states that the "integrated use of [technologies of content and connectivity] to achieve maximum propaganda effect has become a trademark of insurgent operations over the past decade," and that "they" are better at telling and disseminating visually persuasive material than "we" are. If I shared what I think are Kuehl's background assumptions, I would be discussing how the U.S. military might compete more effectively with this kind of propaganda. But I'm not willing to start from the premise that the war in Iraq by the U.S.-organized coalition of the willing was a just and justifiable war. I tend to believe the account by "X" in the Downing Street memo of July 2002 that the U.S. intelligence was being fixed to support a preexisting policy to go to war. It is also hard not to believe the testimony of former National Coordinator for Security Infrastructure Protection and Counterterrorism Richard Clarke, who had served in the administrations of President Bill Clinton and President George W. Bush. In *Against All Enemies*,[25] Clarke states that President George W. Bush tried to pressure intelligence officials, like himself, into finding a link between Saddam Hussein and the events of 9/11. The evidence that was adduced to justify the war, the supposed possession by Saddam Hussein of weapons of mass destruction with the capacity to deliver them soon to the United States, turned out to be false.

A great many deceptions were foisted on the people of the United States and the world, with the cooperation of U.S. media such as Fox News Channel, but also sources more generally relied on, such as the *New York Times* and the *Washington Post*. When former U.S. Ambassador to Gabon Joseph C. Wilson discredited official government accounts about Niger's possession of nuclear material allegedly sought by Saddam Hussein,[26] a member or members of the Bush administration leaked information to the press revealing that Wilson's wife, Valerie Plame, was an undercover CIA official, thus serving notice that those speaking out against administration deceptions might anticipate penalties in some form.

The degree to which the Pentagon has in the past expressed willingness to deceive the public is nowhere more manifest than in the "Operations Northwoods" document presented to U.S. Secretary of Defense Robert McNamara in March 13, 1962, and signed by L. L. Lemnitzer, chairman of the Joint Chiefs of Staff. False flag operations are spelled out there in detail, aimed at provoking war with Cuba. One might discount the memorandum as a very supposititious statement of a wholly hypothetical question, but there is an eerie similarity to the Gulf of Tonkin events leading to the ill-fated war against Vietnam. If we consider further the elaborate deceptions that could only have come from U.S. military sources at the ground level or further up the Pentagon chain in the cases of Jessica Lynch or Pat Tillman, we really have no reason to automatically take on faith what Pentagon sources tell us.

Certain parts of WikiLeaks's "Collateral Murder" are clear. The people killed by fire from the Apache were not obviously involved in any fighting. Whatever the black car may have been doing earlier, what we see is someone helping a wounded person into it. We do hear a gunner communicating with others, making it clear he is itching to make a strike, even though the assembled group shows no obvious and unambiguous military involvement.

In light of all this, I return to Edward R. Murrow, but to employ the logic of *modus tollens* and say that by not telling the truth on so many things, the U.S. administration and the Pentagon in particular have not shown themselves to be credible and have therefore not been persuasive. WikiLeaks may be viewed as "anti-American" and as propagandistic, but so much has been concealed from the general public on matters affecting sound policy that I see its operations as worthy of comparison to Daniel Ellsberg's leaking of the Pentagon Papers regarding the war in Vietnam.

As a final remark on Kuehl's perspective, I want to point to a danger that lies in his emphasis on how U.S. military interests are greatly affected not so much by misbehavior of military personnel but in the capturing of this misbehavior on video and distributing it widely through the Internet. The danger is that locating the major part of wrongdoing in the dissemination rather than in the initial wrongdoing sends a terrible message both to military recruits and to the world. The so-called enemy targets may be acting in ways that collide with our interests, but they are still human beings who deserve respect as such. With a bit of empathy it is possible to understand how they would see us as invaders and how they would want to resist, in order to protect their religion, their families, and their way of life. Urinating on corpses of the vanquished enemy sends the wrong message in a war that needs to win over the hearts and minds of the people among whom insurgents find support. But as long as the concern is on keeping a lid on the news rather than on rectifying the wrong attitudes of military personnel, the problems will not be solved. The change must be made to take place in soldiers' attitudes and not in more and more draconian punishments for those who do the filming and distributing. The latter may have a legitimate motivation that has inspired many brave and decent individuals in the past, namely to call public attention to wrongdoing, with a view to rectification. Maybe some lessons about Hector, Achilles, and hubris would be worth employing in military education. The big stumbling block to U.S. success is maintenance of the *oderint dum metuant* philosophy when it is so much at odds with success in occupied territories.[27] I recognize that Dan Kuehl has provided a useful service by pointing to reasons why the WikiLeaks account may itself be deceptive, and for suspending judgment on some key matters. If we are to reduce the reach and power of the worst forms of propaganda we need to have just this kind of clarification of issues and viewpoints.

Before concluding this chapter, I would like to draw attention to one of Jacques Ellul's most important contributions to the study of propaganda. This is the idea that propaganda is facilitated by the existence of myths in human consciousness. By "myth" he means an unchallenged, deeply held interpretive picture of the world that forms the basis of a person's world outlook and colors all of that person's beliefs about what is good and valuable. Here is how he explains the relevant idea of myth. It is "an all-encompassing, activating image: a sort of vision of desirable objectives that have lost their material, practical character and have become strongly colored, overwhelming, all-encompassing, and which displace from the consciousness all that is not related to it. Such an image pushes man to action precisely because it includes all that he feels is good, just, and true."[28]

Examples of such myths, applicable at various times and places to people in different countries, are myths of Race, the Hero, the Führer, the Proletariat, the Nation, the Worker, Progress, History, Communist Society, Youth, Productivity, and the State. Eventually, he says, the myth takes possession of a person's mind so completely that his or her life is consecrated to it. "But that effect can be created only by slow, patient work by all the methods of propaganda, not by any immediate operation."[29] Maybe today we could add to that a myth of Success that seems to underlie some of the worst Wall Street excesses, as well as crooked local politics.

If Ellul is right, it is myths that allow the state or other power-wielders to mobilize populations to engage in war. They are the buttons that are pressed by the relevant authorities, whether in Communist, Fascist, Theocratic, or Democratic states. Again, if Ellul is right, that should lead us to seek to try to counter the conditions that make possible immoral reflex actions, the immorality of which the actor is not conscious because he or she is guided by an all-encompassing myth that excludes such considerations. Even though the excessive devotion to a narrow form of patriotism might seem harmless under most circumstances, it should still be resisted as something that under other conditions could be used to engage in shameful violations of human rights.

In conclusion, the way of reducing the reach and scope of the worst forms of propaganda will require responses at many different levels: general education, knowledge of specific propaganda techniques, and awareness of the different levels that can affect propaganda messages, such as the structure of media, the impact of law, and the kinds of myths that make the manipulation of people easily carried out. It will require constant vigilance and organization by well-intentioned people with the courage to stand up to threats and the patience to keep up the struggle for the rights and decency of all people and other living creatures on this planet, including future generations.

Notes

1. In the Roman Forum one can see inscribed on the Arch of Severus, built in 203, the words *ob rem publicam restitutam imperiumque populi Romani propagatum,* referring to the propagation of Roman imperial rule. As the gerundive, "propaganda" means simply "things to be propagated." Nancy Snow's working definition of propaganda is neutral: "Propaganda is source-based, cause-oriented, emotion-laden content that utilizes mass persuasion media to cultivate the mass mind in service to the source's goals. Its utilization is not good or bad as all social institutions (government, commercial, citizen-based) use propaganda for their own purposes. The ethical questions associated with propaganda involve its means/ends agreement or lack thereof and its asymmetrical exchange of information that always favors the sponsor of propaganda. At its best, propaganda involves pro-social causes that do not stray too far from the truth; at it worst, propaganda serves strictly a pro-source function that uses whatever means necessary to fulfill its goals." See also Philip M. Taylor, *Munitions of the Mind,* 3rd ed. (Manchester, England: Manchester Univ. Press, 2003), 6–8: "Essentially, propaganda is really no more than the communication of ideas designed to persuade people to think and behave in a desired way."

2. Such a propaganda institution can be in the service of war or peace, commercial and private or government and public ends. Moral judgments matter, but means and methods of such institutions and the intentions and goals of the propagandists serving such institutions are more the focus here.

3. "All propaganda is lies" has been attributed to George Orwell, but in searching for the reference the closest I have been able to find is in his essay "Looking Back on the Spanish War," where he writes about government information concerning internal affairs: "It is all, from whatever source, party propaganda—that is to say, lies." From George Orwell, *Homage to Catalonia and Looking Back on the Spanish War* (Harmondsworth: Penguin Books, 1966), 233. Calling all party propaganda lies is not the same as calling all propaganda lies. Orwell self-avowedly engaged in his own form of propaganda (see "Why I Write," in

George Orwell, *Collected Essays* [London: Mercury Books, 1961], 425). I doubt therefore that Orwell would agree with Dan Kuehl's assertion that he argued that "propaganda is inherently immoral, regardless of who is using it or for what purpose, because propaganda possesses immutably evil characteristics." The case of Jacques Ellul is more complicated, because he does have a thoroughly negative view of "total propaganda," which he regards in some places as the only genuine propaganda. But he realizes that ordinary usage of the term is not so restricted, and he regularly uses "propaganda" in a broader sense, where its use may be necessitated and not a matter for unqualified condemnation.

4. G. K Chesterton: "Tennyson put it very feebly and inadequately when he said that the blackest of lies is the lie that is half a truth. The blackest of lies is the lie that is entirely a truth. Once give me the right to pick out anything and I shall not need to invent anything" ("Distortions in the Press," *Illustrated London News,* November 6, 1909). As examples, Chesterton indicated how misleading it would be to characterize the nineteenth century only by reference to Jack the Ripper and a notorious fraud, Whitaker Wright.

5. Edward S. Herman and Noam Chomsky, *Manufacturing Consent: The Political Economy of the Mass Media* (New York: Pantheon Books, 1988), 1–35.

6. Jacques Ellul, *Propaganda* (1965; translation from original French, New York: Vintage, 1973), 62–70.

7. See on this John J. Mearsheimer, *Why Leaders Lie: The Truth about Lying in International Politics* (New York: Oxford Univ. Press, 2011), 56–57. Experts opposed to government propaganda may be intimidated by fearmongering designed to mobilize the general public against dissenting intellectuals (sometimes designated by the derogatory "pointy-heads"). "They would then be isolated and feel suspect, and maybe even worried about their careers, which would then make them more likely to temper their criticisms or remain silent, or maybe even shift gears and support the government's policy." Mearsheimer underwent fierce attacks for his book, *The Israel Lobby and U.S. Foreign Policy,* coauthored with Stephen M. Walt (Toronto: Viking Canada, 2007). I would imagine him to have had personal experience of such pressures.

8. Editor's note: Fox News Channel is not considered respectable cable news to most moderates and liberals, but some conservatives and Republicans might find it to be a "fair and balanced" answer to the liberal-leaning mainstream media agenda offered up by other cable networks, like MSNBC and CNN as well as the Big Three over-the-air legacy networks of ABC, CBS, and NBC.

9. Wendell Potter, *Deadly Spin* (New York: Bloomsbury Press, 2010).

10. Mickey Huff, *Censored 2013: The Top Censored Stories and Media Analysis of 2011–2012* (New York: Seven Stories Press, 2012). Carl Jensen at Sonoma State University founded the news-monitoring project in 1976, and New York-based Seven Stories Press has published the yearbook of the top twenty-five underreported stories since 1994. Nancy Snow has been a longtime Project Censored judge. See also http://www.projectcensored.org.

11. Joel Bakan, *The Corporation: The Pathological Pursuit of Profit and Power* (New York: Penguin, 2004).

12. 2011 Breaux Symposium report, *In the Name of Democracy: Political Communication Research and Practice in a Polarized Media Environment* (Baton Rouge, La,.: Reilly

Center for Media and Public Affairs, Manship School of Mass Communication, 2011), 52. See also W. Lance Bennett, "Toward a Theory of Press-State Relations in the United States," *Journal of Communication* 40, no. 2 (1990): 103–127.

13. *Associated Press v. United States,* 326 U.S. 1 (1945).

14. The Ontario Press Council is supported financially by contributions from member newspapers, through an assessment based each year on the circulation of a given newspaper compared with total circulation of all member newspapers.

15. *Schenck v. United States,* 249 U.S. 47 (1919).

16. Supreme Court of Canada, R v. Keegstra [1990] 3 S.C.R., 714. per Chief Justice Dickson.

17. John B. Whitton and Arthur Larson, *Propaganda: Towards Disarmament in the War of Words* (Dobbs Ferry, N.Y.: Oceana Publications, 1964).

18. Michael G. Kearney, *The Prohibition of Propaganda for War in International Law* (New York: Oxford Univ. Press, 2007), 249.

19. See George Lakoff, *The Political Mind* (New York: Penguin, 2008), for an introduction to his thinking, as well as his best-selling *Don't Think of an Elephant!* (White River Junction, Vt.: Chelsea Green, 2004). Lakoff's commentaries frequently appear on the Internet and are easily accessible.

20. See the excellent video *Lobbying for Lives: Lessons from the Front,* 1988, distributed by MediCinema.

21. For more on the problem described here, see James L. Turk, ed., *Universities at Risk: How Politics, Special Interests and Corporatization Threaten Academic Integrity* (Toronto: James Lorimer, 2008).

22. I have argued elsewhere that the highly propagandized environment in which wars are started without adequate knowledge and consent by the citizenry should lead us to have, at least *prima facie,* a favorable attitude toward the WikiLeaks project, despite the obvious possibilities it poses for causing harm as well as good. See "Propaganda and the Ethics of WikiLeaks," *Global Media Journal,* Australian ed., 5, no. 1 (2011): 1–13.

23. Larisa Breton and Adam Pearson, "Contextual Truth-Telling to Counter Extremist-Supportive Messaging Online: The Wikileaks 'Collateral Murder' Case Study," *Small Wars Journal* (November 6, 2010), http://smallwarsjournal.com/jrnl/art/contextual-truth-telling-to-counter-extremist-supportive-messaging-online.

24. Cited as congressional testimony in May 1963 when Murrow was director of the U.S. Information Agency, in Dan Kuehl, "Propaganda Defined: How Should We Define Propaganda in the Digital Age?" paper presented at the 2012 Breaux Symposium, March 29, 2012.

25. Richard Clarke, *Against All Enemies* (New York: Free Press, 2004), 32–33.

26. Joseph C. Wilson, "What I Didn't Find in Africa," *New York Times,* July 6, 2003.

27. "Let them hate us, so long as they fear us." U.S. diplomat John Brady Kiesling criticized this attitude in a very articulate letter of resignation to Secretary of State Colin L. Powell. His text was printed in the *New York Times* on February 27, 2003.

28. Ellul, *Propaganda,* 31.

29. Ibid., 31–32.

CONTRIBUTORS

★ ★ ★ ★

GARTH S. JOWETT is professor of communications at the University of Houston. He is coeditor with Victoria O'Donnell of *Propaganda and Persuasion*, 5th ed. (Thousand Oaks, Calif.: Sage Publications, 2012), and *Readings in Propaganda and Persuasion: New and Classic Studies* (Thousand Oaks, Calif.: Sage Publications, 2006). His book *Film: The Democratic Art* (Boston: Little, Brown, 1976) is widely acknowledged as one of the most significant contributions to the emergence of the study of motion pictures as a social and cultural factor in American life. His later book with Ian Jarvie and Kathryn Fuller, *Children and the Movies: Media Influence and the Payne Fund Studies* (New York: Cambridge Univ. Press, 2006), is considered to be the definitive examination of the Payne Fund Studies and their important place in American cinema history.

DANIEL KUEHL is an associate professor in the Institute for Intelligence Studies at Mercyhurst University. He is the former director of the Information Operations Concentration Program at the National Defense University in Washington, D.C. He retired as a lieutenant colonel in 1994 after nearly twenty-two years of active duty in the U.S. Air Force. He lectures and publishes widely on information power, information operations, and cyberwar. His current research focuses on the relationship between the information age and national security.

MORDECAI LEE is professor of governmental affairs at the University of Wisconsin–Milwaukee. He is author of *The First Presidential Communications Agency: FDR's Office of Government Reports* (Albany:

State Univ. of New York Press, 2005) and *Congress vs. the Bureaucracy: Muzzling Agency Public Relations* (Norman: Univ. of Oklahoma Press, 2011) and coeditor of *The Practice of Government Public Relations* (Boca Raton, Fla.: CRC Press, 2012). His most recent book is *Promoting the War Effort: Robert Horton and Federal Propaganda, 1938–1946* (Baton Rouge: Louisiana State Univ. Press, 2012).

RANDAL MARLIN is an adjunct professor of philosophy at Carleton University, where he has taught since 1966, specializing in existentialism, phenomenology, and philosophy of law. In 1979–1980 he won a Department of Defense Fellowship to study in Bordeaux, France, with *Propaganda* author Jacques Ellul, returning to teach a full-year course, "Truth and Propaganda," which he continues to teach in semi-retirement. In 2013 he was elected vice-president of the International Jacques Ellul Society. He is the author of *Propaganda and the Ethics of Persuasion* (Orchard Park, N.Y.: Broadview Press, 2002).

ASRA Q. NOMANI is a former veteran reporter for the *Wall Street Journal* and the author of several works, including *Milestones for a Spiritual Jihad: Toward an Islam of Grace* ([Kalamazoo, Mich.]: Fetzer Institute, 2010), *Standing Alone: An American Woman's Struggle for the Soul of Islam* (New York: HarperSanFrancisco, 2006), and *Tantrika: Traveling the Road of Divine Love* (San Francisco: HarperSanFrancisco, 2003). She is an adjunct professor at Georgetown University's School of Continuing Studies and codirects the Pearl Project, a faculty-student investigation into the murder of *Wall Street Journal* reporter Daniel Pearl.

ANTHONY PRATKANIS is professor of psychology at the University of California in Santa Cruz, California. An expert on economic fraud crimes, terrorist and dictator propaganda, marketing and consumer behavior, and subliminal persuasion, Dr. Pratkanis's books include *Age of Propaganda* with Elliot Aronson (rev. ed., New York: Holt, 2001), *The Science of Social Influence* (New York: Psychology Press, 2007), and *Weapons of Fraud* with Doug Shadel (Seattle, Wash.: AARP, 2005). He is the founding editor of *Social Influence,* a journal from Psychology Press.

NANCY SNOW is professor of communications at California State University, Fullerton, who holds adjunct professor appointments at the USC Annenberg School for Communication and Journalism and the Interdisciplinary Center Herzliya Lauder School of Government, Diplomacy and Strategy. She is the author of *Propaganda, Inc.*, 3rd ed. (New York: Seven Stories Press, 2010), *Information War* (New York: Seven Stories Press, 2004), *The Arrogance of American Power* (Lanham, Md.: Rowman and Littlefield, 2006), coeditor with Philip M. Taylor of the *Routledge Handbook of Public Diplomacy* (New York: Routledge, 2009), and coeditor with Yahya M. Kamalipour of *War, Media, and Propaganda* (Lanham, Md.: Rowman and Littlefield, 2004). Other works include *Citizen Arianna* (Ann Arbor, Mich.: Nimble Books, 2011) and *Persuader-in-Chief* (Ann Arbor, Mich.: Nimble Books, 2009). Her 2013 book, *Truth Is the Best Propaganda* (McLean, VA: Miniver Press), spotlights the speeches and rhetoric of Edward R. Murrow as director of the U.S. Information Agency.

J. MICHAEL SPROULE is emeritus professor of communication studies at San Jose State University and past president (2007) of the National Communication Association. His work focuses on rhetorical history and propaganda studies, including such books as *The Rhetoric of Western Thought*, 10th ed. (Dubuque, Iowa: Kendall/Hunt, 2011), *Propaganda and Democracy* (New York: Cambridge Univ. Press, 1997), and *Channels of Propaganda* (Bloomington, Ind.: ERIC/EDINFO Press, 1994). His current work centers on nineteenth-century media and social influence, as represented by his most recent publication, "Inventing Public Speaking: Rhetoric and the Speech Book, 1730–1930," *Rhetoric and Public Affairs* 15 (2012): 563–608.

INDEX

ACLU, 42
Act of Valor, 175
Ad Age, 141
Adams, John, 25n25
adversary model of influence, 45–48
advertising: and celebrities, 123; and consumerism, 120–23, 131–35; Creel on, 128; as negative propaganda, 144; on Obama versus Bush, 141–42; and older male lifestyle brands, 134; of prescription drugs, 131–33; of sports consumer products, 134; statistics on, 122; during Super Bowl, 24n18, 123; by tobacco industry, 43, 185, 189, 193–94; U.S. invention of, 135; and youth market, 133–34
Afghanistan: civilian casualties in, 21; news media's coverage of war in, 159, 161, 180; opposition to war in, within U.S., 189; public support for invasion of, in U.S., 137; U.S. Marines urinating on corpses in, 19, 20, 164, 198; violence against women in, 164; war in generally, 94. *See also* Taliban
Against All Enemies (Clarke), 197
Age of Propaganda (Aronson and Pratkanis), 32, 44, 57
Agha-Soltan, Neda, 19, 20
Agriculture Department (USDA), 118n44
Aidid, Mohamed Farrah, 163
Ailes, Roger, 82–83
airline industry, 151
Al Jazeera, 16, 18, 27n40, 162, 165–66, 180–81, 183n25
Al-Hasawi, Mustafa, 164–65
Al-Qaeda, 76, 149, 157, 160, 162, 164
Albany Business Review, 85
Ali, Ali Abdul Aziz, 162
Alinsky, Saul, 45–48, 59, 60
Allport, Gordon, 52
Alter, Jonathan, 180
Amedore, George, 85
American Revolution, 14, 25n25
"American way of life," 129–36
Americans for Prosperity Foundation, 89
Angle, Sharron, 83
anti-Semitism, 154, 171–74. *See also* Nazis
Antigone (Sophocles), 33
"Arab Spring," 21
Arab world. *See* Al Jazeera; Iraq War I; Iraq War II; Islam; Middle East
Aristotle, 33, 53, 57, 89
Arnett, Peter, 18, 27n39
Aronson, Elliot, 32, 44
Assange, Julian, 195
Associated Press, 163, 190
Assyrians, 13, 14, 17–18
(Astro) Turf Wars, 189
Auer, J. Jeffrey, 38
Austen, Jane, 58
autocracy, 54–56
automobile industry, 37

Bachman, Michele, 81, 91n28
Bakan, Joel, 189
Baker, George, 44, 59, 67n15
Baker, Ray Stannard, 126
Baker, Sherry, 68n15
"banal imperialism," 125
Barney, Coleman F., 66n15
Barry, John, 100
Battleship Potemkin, 14–15, 25n28
Bauman, John, 159
Baxter, Leone, 143
BBC, 18, 27n40
Beck, Glenn, 81
Beecher, Henry Ward, 44, 59
Beers, Charlotte, 140
Bell, Alexander Graham, 17
Bell, Ulric, 173
Berger, John, 120
Bernays, Edward L., 5, 79, 126
Beyoncé, 123
Bhutto, Benazir, 161
Bin Laden, Osama, 162, 164, 182
Black Hawk Down (battle), 163
Black, Hugo, 190
Black, Jay, 44
Blitzer, Wolf, 161
Blum, John Morton, 104
Bolin, Diana, 36, 37
Bolton, John, 83
Boston Phoenix, 149
Brace, Paul, 52
Brachman, Jarret, 162–63
Braden, Waldo Warder, 67n15
Brands, H. W., 103, 106
Breaux, John, 64
Breaux Symposium, 1–2, 4, 64, 189
Brembeck, Winston L., 43, 44, 67n15
Breton, Larisa, 195–96
Brewer, Susan A., 100
Brickman, Philip, 36, 37
Britain, 19, 76, 87, 113, 163, 172, 176, 187–88
Brokaw, Tom, 103
Brown, Willie, 131
Bryant, Kobe, 134
bunglers and influence, 34–35
bureaucrats versus politicians, 112–16
Bush, George H. W., 82
Bush, George W.: compared with Obama, 141–42; and embedded journalists program, 161; firing of federal prosecutors by, 76; and Iraq War II, 109, 115, 131, 137–40, 180, 196–97; and political campaign of 2004, 109; promotion of education policies of, 191; and War on Terror, 96, 138, 140
Butt, Tariq, 154–55

Cable News Network. *See* CNN
Caesar Augustus, 14
Campaigns, Inc., 143
Campt, David, 67n15
Canada, 191, 192, 193–94, 202n14
Capra, Frank, 56, 169
Carey, Alex, 121–22, 129
Carlson, Les, 49
Carter, Jimmy, 49, 76
CBS Corporation, 124
CBS News, 149, 159
celebrities, 122–23, 127
censorship, 47, 95, 100, 107, 109, 189, 201n10
Center for Media and Democracy, 188
Center for Responsive Politics, 127
Chandler, Harry, 86
"Changing Minds Winning Peace," 140–41
Channels of Propaganda (Sproule), 125
Chesterton, G. K., 184, 201n4
China, 16, 20, 134, 135–36
Chomsky, Noam, 122, 126, 151, 187, 189
Choudhary, Khalid, 157–58
Christianity. *See* religion
Christie, Chris, 83
Churchill, Winston, 15
CIA, 160, 197
Cialdini, Bob, 34–40

Citizens United v. Federal Election Commission, 86, 88–89, 127
civil rights movement, 15–16, 50, 51
Civil War, 10, 40, 50, 56
Clarke, Arthur C., 16, 26n37
Clarke, Richard, 197
Clarke, Victoria, 161
Clay, Henry, 50, 59
climate research, 79–80, 189
Clinton, Bill, 81, 141, 142, 197
CNN, 16, 20, 26–27nn38–40, 80–81, 83, 161, 179, 180, 201n8
CNN Effect, 26n38
Colbert, Stephen, 43
Cold War, 11, 12, 15–16, 21, 53, 94, 181–82. *See also* Soviet Union/Russia
"Collateral Murder," 21–22, 196–98
commercial/cultural American propaganda, 120–37
Commission on Freedom of the Press, 190–91
Committee on Public Information (CPI), 97–103, 105–6, 127–28
community organizing, 45–48, 194
Compromises of 1850 and 1876, 50
Conserva, Henry T., 38, 39
consumerism, 39, 131–35, 176–77. *See also* advertising
Conway, Erik M., 189
Cooper, Anderson, 81
Cooper, Thomas, 66n15
copyright law, 83–85
corporate propaganda, 82, 86–87, 124–25, 151–52
Corporation, The (Bakan), 189
Coughlin, Father Charles, 38
CPI. *See* Committee on Public Information (CPI)
Creel, George, 99–101, 127–28
Cronkite, Walter, 180
Cuba, 178, 183n19, 197. *See also* Guantanamo Bay; TV Martí
cultural American propaganda, 120–37
cultural imperialism, 135–36
Current TV, 183n25

Daily Beast, 164
Daily Mail, 188
Dauber, Cori, 19
Davis, Elmer, 106–7
Davison, W. Phillips, 121
De Caro, Chuck, 27n41
Dear John, 175
Declaration of Independence, 130, 131
Deen, Paula, 132
Defense Department, U.S. (DOD), 10, 12–13, 24–25n19, 152, 161, 162, 164, 197
democracy: democratic persuasion, 52–56; and democratic virtù, 48, 60–64; Ellul on, 24n13, 120; Entman on "democracy without citizens," 44; influence in, versus autocracy, 54–56; Marston on, 56; rational free choice for individuals in, 42; and rule of law, 75; two-way symmetrical model and, 50
Democratic National Convention protests, 27n40
democratic virtù, 48, 60–64
Dewey, Tom, 110
Diggs, B. J., 66n15
digital age, 11, 13, 17–22, 23n3, 27n41, 121, 123–24. *See also* information and communication technologies (ICT); Internet
Digital Millennium Copyright Act (1998), 84–85
Digital Theft Deterrent Act, 84
DiMaggio, Anthony, 189
Discourses on Livy (Machiavelli), 61
Division of Information (DOI), 97, 98, 105–6
Djerejian, Edward P., 140–41
Dobson, Sebastian, 23n2
DOD. *See* Defense Department, U.S. (DOD)
DOI. *See* Division of Information (DOI)

Don't Think of an Elephant! (Lakoff), 142
Douglass, David, 53
Douglass, Frederick, 51
Drudge Report, 81
Du Maurier, George, 57
Dudley, Drew, 128
due-process clause, 84
Duke, Charles, 49
Durant, Michael, 163

Eastern Europe, 27n40, 181–82
Eastern Mennonite University, 60
Edelman, Richard, 124, 145n14
Ehrenfeld, Rachel, 76
Ehrlichman, John, 119n46
Eichmann, Adolf, 37
Eisenstein, Sergei, 14–15
Ellsberg, Daniel, 198
Ellul, Jacques, 4, 7, 11, 24n13, 120–22, 185, 187, 199, 201n3
Emanuel, Rahm, 142
emotions, 43–44
Encyclopedia Britannica, Inc., 35
England. *See* Britain
entertainment. *See* motion pictures; television
Entman, Robert, 44
environmental issues, 79–80, 175, 185, 189
Environmental Protection Agency (EPA), 80
ethical effects-reasoning matrix, 49
ethics of influence and propaganda. *See* influence and persuasion
Ewbank, Henry Lee, 38

Facebook, 20, 85, 121, 129, 150, 164, 188
Farmer, John, 76
Farrell, Leah, 162
FBI, 118n43, 148, 153, 156–58
Federal Communications Commission (FCC), 77–78, 82
Federal Election Commission, 86, 88–89
Federal Trade Commission (FTC), 35, 39
Feffer, John, 136–37
Fifth Amendment, 84
Fight for Freedom, 173
films. *See* motion pictures
First Amendment, 42, 46, 47, 100, 190, 192. *See also* freedom of speech; freedom of the press
"First They Came" (Niemöller), 60–61
Fisher, Roger, 49
Fitzgerald, Cantor, 162
Fleming, Thomas, 104
"flog" ("fake blog"), 124
FNC. *See* Fox News Channel (FNC)
Foner, Eric, 96
Foreign Affairs, 175–76
Foreign Policy in Focus, 136–37
Forrest Gump, 18
Fox News Channel (FNC), 77, 80–83, 85, 124, 180, 188–89, 197, 201n8
"Fox News Effect," 83
Free and Responsible Press, A, 190–91
freedom of speech, 3, 42, 46, 47, 59, 88, 110, 173, 190–94
freedom of the press, 77, 173, 190
Friedman, Hershey H., 67n15
Friedrich, James, 53
Fryburger, Vernon, 38
FTC. *See* Federal Trade Commission (FTC)
Fulbright, J. William, 138

Gaddafi, Muammar, 182
Gandhi, Mahatma, 161
GAO. *See* Government Accountability Office (GAO)
Garber, William, 40
Garrison, William Lloyd, 51
Gawker (blog), 83
Geisel, Theodore, 175
genocide, 185, 192
Germany, 12, 15–17, 26n36, 171–72, 176, 177. *See also* Holocaust; Nazis
"Getting to Yes" approach, 49

Gettysburg Address, 40, 56
Gingrich, Newt, 83
Glassman, James, 140
Glick, Jeremy, 189
Global War on Terror, 94, 96, 137–40, 182. *See also* terrorism
Godin, Seth, 36–38
Goebbels, Joseph, 11, 15, 56
good propaganda. *See* influence and persuasion
Gorbachev, Mikhail, 16
Gore, Al, 79, 183n25
Government Accountability Office (GAO), 139, 191
Gowing, Nik, 18–19
Graebner, William, 32
granfalloon tactic, 56
Gray, Giles Wilkeson, 67n15
Great Thaw Trial, The, 169–70
Greatest Generation, The (Brokaw), 103
Green Zone, 175
Greenwald, Robert, 189
Grove, Stephen, 49
Grunig, James, 48–49
Guantanamo Bay, 148–49, 152, 157, 162–65
Gulf Wars. *See* Iraq War I; Iraq War II
Gutenberg, Johannes, 17

Haiman, Franklyn S., 41–45, 67n15
Hamlin, Janet, 162, 164
Hand, Learned, 46, 190
Hard Measures (Rodriguez), 160
Hardy, Thomas, 57
Harlow, Rex F., 106
Harvard Negotiation Project, 49
Hassan, Abdullah "Firimbi," 163
hate speech and hate propaganda legislation, 59, 192
Hays, Will, 173
Hearst, William Randolph, 86, 120
Hedges, Chris, 141
Herman, Edward S., 122, 187
Hezbollah, 21
Hinckley, Barbara, 52
Hippler, Fritz, 56
Hitler, Adolf, 10–11, 26n29, 40, 128, 169, 171–72, 185. *See also* Nazis
Hobbes, Thomas, 33, 46–47
Holmes, Oliver Wendell, 192
Holocaust, 60–61, 185
Holocaust Memorial Museum, 11, 23n4, 26n33
hormone replacement therapy, 78
Horton, Robert, 105–6
Howell, William, 43, 44
Huckabee, Mike, 83
Huff, Mickey, 189
Huffington, Arianna, 81
Huffington Post, 85, 121
Hughes, Karen, 140
Hume, Brit, 82
Huntington, Henry, 44, 59, 67n15
Hurt Locker, The, 175
Hussein, Saddam, 161, 197
Hutchins, Robert, 190
Huxley, Aldous, 121–22

"I Have a Dream" (King), 40, 56
ICCPR, 192–93
ICT. *See* information and communication technologies (ICT)
Iglesias, David C., 76
In the Company of Men (Durant), 163
India, 81, 91n28, 153–54, 164, 176, 179
influence and persuasion: Alinsky's adversary model of, 45–48, 59, 60; in autocracy, 54–56; and Beecher on effective preaching, 44; and bunglers, 34–35; and Cialdini's truthfulness, 34–40; debate over morality of, 29–32; definition of good propaganda, 44; democratic persuasion, 52–56; and democratic virtù, 48, 60–64; and emotions as component of persuasion, 43–44; and Haiman's reasoned discourse, 41–45;

influence and persuasion (*continued*)
Institute for Propaganda Analysis (IPA) on taboo tactics in, 4, 6, 38–41; Lewin on democratic influence, 31, 32; list of ethical principles regarding, 66–68n15; and meaning of "good," 33–34; mutuality of, among stakeholders, 48–52; partisans' approach to, 29–32, 59–60; purists' approach to, 29–32, 59–60; and rules for appealing to emotions, 44; and sleuths, 34–36, 40; and smugglers, 34–38; taboo tactics in, 4, 6, 38–41; Ten Commandments of Good Influence and Propaganda, 34, 38, 41, 44, 48, 52–54, 56, 58–61; as tool, 56–60; trade-offs in, 58–60; uneasiness about use of, 29; weapon metaphor for, 57, 58; White on democratic persuasion, 53, 54; Zimbardo on, 31. *See also* propaganda
information and communication technologies (ICT), 9, 10, 14–17, 23n3, 89–90. *See also* digital age; Internet; Twitter
Insider, The, 188–89
Institute for Propaganda Analysis (IPA), 4, 6, 38–41, 52, 57
insurance industry, 188
International Criminal Court, 193
Internet: and "Arab Spring," 21; and "Collateral Murder," 21–22, 196–98; and copyright law, 84–85; growth of, 9, 19–20; limitations on access to, 76–78; message-dense environment of, 43; and net neutrality, 77–78; news sites on, 85, 121, 188; Obama on, 5; and propaganda, 11, 19–20, 121, 123–24; and social media, 20, 85, 121, 124, 129, 150, 164; video of Pearl's murder on, 159, 166; and videos by "citizen journalists" on, 18–20, 181, 182; videos on, "going viral," 19, 22. *See also* digital age; Facebook; WikiLeaks; YouTube
IPA. *See* Institute for Propaganda Analysis (IPA)
Iran, 19, 164
Iraq War I, 16, 18, 26–27nn39–40, 94, 179–80
Iraq War II: and "Collateral Murder" incident (2007), 21–22, 196–98; impact of, on Iraqis, 193; justification for, 196–97; and killing of Blackwater guards, 164; motion pictures on, 175; propaganda on, 98, 108–10, 115–16, 137–39; and public diplomacy, 140; television coverage of, 180–81; Use of Force Resolution (2002) for, 94, 108
Islam, 21, 137, 140–41, 152, 160–61, 164, 166
Israel, 154

Japan, 23n2, 171, 182
Jefferson, Thomas, 48, 60, 61, 62, 64, 126–27, 131
Jensen, Carl, 201n10
John Paul II, Pope, 20
Johnson, Lyndon B., 96, 109
Johnson, William, 127
Jordan, Eason, 161
Journal of the American Medical Association, 78
journalism. *See* news media
Jowett, Garth S., 5–6, 39, 165, 168–83, 203
"just plain folks" technique, 124
Justice Department, U.S., 76, 161

Kanetkar, Jay, 159
Kansas-Nebraska Act, 50
Kant, Immanuel, 33
Karim, Fazal, 155–57
Kasich, John, 83
Katsner, Rudolf, 37, 38
Kearney, Richard, 193
Keith-Spiegel, Patricia, 66n15
Kelleher, Tom, 66n15
Kennedy, John F., 16, 26n36
Key, Wilson Bryan, 40
Khalid Sheikh Mohammed (KSM), 148–49, 155–65

Khan, Fayyaz, 155
Khan, Kamran, 154
Kiesling, John Brady, 202n27
King, Martin Luther, Jr., 32, 40, 51, 56, 161
Koch, Charles and David, 89
Koch, Ed, 136
Koocher, Gerald P., 66n15
Koppel, Andrea, 20
Korean War, 94
Kreider, Eugene C., 67n15
Krugman, Paul, 80
KSM (Khalid Sheikh Mohammed), 148–49, 155–65
Kuehl, Dan, 5, 9–28, 131, 137, 139, 195–99, 201n3, 203

Lagone, Michael D., 67n15
Lakoff, George, 142, 193
Larson, Arthur, 193
Larson, Lars, 175
Lasswell, Harold, 11
law: for combatting propaganda, 190–94; hate propaganda legislation, 192; ideological use of, 75–76; international law for combatting worst propaganda, 192–93; and prosecutorial error, 76; rule of law, 75. *See also* lobbying
Lebanon, 21
Lee, Mordecai, 7, 94–119, 203–4
Lee, Stan, 60
Leff, Arthur Allen, 53
Lemnitzer, L. L., 197
Lessig, Lawrence, 85
Letterman, David, 85
Leviathan (Hobbes), 46–47
Lewin, Kurt, 31, 32, 49, 53, 54
Lewis, Gordon, 68n15
"libel tourism," 76
Liberia, 59
Libya, 182
Liebling, A. J., 77
Limbaugh, Rush, 44, 79, 81
Lincoln, Abraham, 40, 44, 51, 52, 56, 97
Lincoln Group, 138, 140
Lindbergh, Charles, 174
Lippmann, Walter, 80, 126
Litfin, A. Duane, 67n15
lobbying, 47, 89, 105, 125, 137, 194
London subway bombings, 19
London *Times*, 187–88, 190
Lorax, The, 175
Lords of the Press (Seldes), 86
Los Angeles Times, 86, 138–39
Louisiana State University Breaux Symposium, 1–2, 4, 64, 189
Lucas, George, 25–26n29
Luntz, Frank, 142
Luther, Martin, 161
Lynch, Jessica, 197
Lysenko, Trofim, 41

Machiavelli, Niccolò, 45, 48, 61–62
MacLean, Eleanor, 38
mainstream media. *See* motion pictures; news media; radio; television
Malik, Veena, 164
Mandela, Nelson, 51
Manning, Bradley, 195
Manufacturing Consent (Chomsky and Herman), 122
Marconi, Guglielmo, 17
Marines, U.S., 19, 20, 164, 198
Marlin, Randal, 5, 7, 143, 184–202, 204
Marston, John, 56
Martinson, David L., 68n15
Mass Effect (video game), 77
mass media. *See* motion pictures; news media; radio; television
May, Rollo, 30
McCarthy, Joe, 81
McClure's magazine, 126
McNamara, Robert, 197
Mearsheimer, John J., 201n7
media. *See* motion pictures; news media; radio; television

"media barons"/media oligopolies, 86–87, 124–25, 187–88, 190
medical research, 78–79
Mellett, Lowell, 105
Merah, Mohamed, 165–66
Merchants of Doubt (Oreskes and Conway), 189
Merton, Robert, 52–53
Mesopotamian empires, 13–14, 17–18
Messina, Alex, 66n15
Mexico, 179
Miami Herald, 152, 162
Michelangelo, 14
Middle East, 21, 140–41, 154. *See also* Iraq War I; Iraq War II; Islam
Midway Airlines, 151
military/governmental American propaganda, 137–44. *See also* wartime propaganda
Mill, John Stuart, 33
Miller, Richard, 36, 37
Milton, John, 187
Ming, Yao, 134
Minnick, Wayne, 38, 40
Missouri Compromises of 1820, 50–51, 52, 58–59
Mnookin, Robert, 37
Moore, Michael, 136, 190
Morse, Anne Nishimura, 23n2
Morse, Samuel, 17
Mossad, 154
motion pictures: audience involvement in, 174–75; *Battleship Potemkin*, 14–15, 25n28; *Black Hawk Down*, 163; for exposure of propaganda, 188–90; Fox News Channel documentary *Outfoxed*, 81–82, 85, 189–90; on Iraq War, 175; *The Lorax*, 175; Nye's attack and U.S. Senate subcommittee hearings on, 170–75; propaganda function of, 11, 14–15, 18, 169–76; *Triumph of the Will*, 11, 15, 18, 23–24n5, 25–26n29, 169; *Wall-E*, 175; and World War I, 100; and World War II, 103, 169, 172–73; worldwide circulation of, 175–76. *See also specific films*
MoveOn.org, 82
Moyers, Bill, 56
MSNBC, 80, 83, 175, 201n8
Mugabe, Robert, 20
Mulligan, John, 157–58
Munitions of the Mind (Taylor), 3, 7–8
Munson, Gorham, 4
Murdoch, Rupert, 82–83, 85–87, 124, 187, 188, 190
Murrow, Edward R., 11, 12, 15, 24nn6–7, 131, 196, 198
Muslims. *See* Islam
mutuality of influence, 48–52
Muzzamil, Muhammad, 156
myths in human consciousness, 199–200

"Nashi" movement, 21
"Nasrak Haz el Deni" ("Our Victory"), 21
National Bureau of Economic Research, 83
NATO, 12
Nazis: Hollywood movies with anti-Nazi focus, 172; and Holocaust, 60–61, 185; propaganda by, 10–11, 15, 23–24nn4–5, 37, 38, 51, 56, 169; and *Triumph of the Will*, 11, 15, 18, 23–24n5, 25–26n29, 169
net neutrality, 77–78
New England Journal of Medicine, 78
New York Herald Tribune, 174
New York Post, 86
New York Times, 4, 85, 124, 137, 141, 143, 163, 188, 197
News Corporation, 82, 86–87, 124
news media: bias of, 80–83, 85–87; business model of, 80; and "indexing" of mainstream newspapers, 190; on Iraq War II, 138–39, 180–81, 197; and journalists as propagandists, 148–66; and media oligopolies, 82, 86–87, 124–25, 187–88, 190; and military's embedded

journalists program, 161; and professionalization of journalism, 101; public opinion on credibility of, 2; television news reporting, 177–82; and videos by "citizen journalists" on Internet, 18–20; and Vietnam War, 16, 180; during World War II, 104–5, 107–8. *See also* Al Jazeera; television; *and specific newspapers and television networks*
News of the World, 87, 188
Newsweek, 163, 180
Niemöller, Martin, 60–61
Nixon, Richard, 82, 109, 116n4, 118–19n46
No Labels, 64
Nomani, Ansa, 153–54
Nomani, Asra Q., 6–7, 148–67, 204
nonviolence, 32, 60
North Korea, 9, 11
Northcliffe, Lord, 187–88
Northwest Airlines, 151
Novo Nordisk, 132–33
Nye, Gerald P., 170–74

Obama, Barack, 5, 81, 91n28, 133, 141–43, 178
O'Donnell, Victoria, 5, 39, 165, 168
Office of Government Reports (OGR), 105, 106
Office of Price Administration (OPA), 104–5, 107
Office of War Information (OWI), 97, 98, 106–7
Oldham, Taki, 189
oligarchy, 89
Olympics, 165
OPA. *See* Office of Price Administration (OPA)
O'Reilly, Bill, 189
Oreskes, Naomi, 189
Orwell, George, 11, 12, 14, 200–201n3
Outfoxed, 81–82, 85, 189–90
OWI. *See* Office of War Information (OWI)

Packard, Vance, 38, 67n15
PACs, 82, 127; Super PACs, 88–89, 127, 129
Pakistan, 152–61, 164
Palestine: Peace Not Apartheid (Carter), 76
Palin, Sarah, 83
Parsons, Patricia, 68n15
partisanship, 29–32, 59–60, 63–64, 78–80
PATRIOT Act, 108–9
Patton, Bruce, 49
Paul, St., 89
peace propagandists, 8, 60
Pearl, Daniel, 7, 148–49, 152–60, 166
Pearl, Mariane, 152–53, 158–60
Pearson, Adam, 195–96
Pearson, Ron, 67n15
Pellegrino, Frank, 148–49
Peloponnesian War, 39
Pentagon Papers, 198
Perelman, Chaïm, 42
Pericles, 39
Persians, 13–14
persuasion. *See* influence and persuasion; propaganda
Persuasion (Austen), 58
pervasive propaganda: and advertising, 24n18, 120–23, 128, 131–34, 141–42, 144; and "American way of life," 129–36; and "banal imperialism," 125; commercial/cultural American propaganda, 120–37; and cultural imperialism, 135–36; Davison on, 121; and media oligopolies, 82, 86–87, 124–25, 187–88, 190; military/governmental American propaganda, 137–44; negative traits of, 143–44; and public diplomacy, 139–40; and Wall of Propaganda, 125
Pew Research Center for the People and the Press, 2
Pfizer, 79
pharmaceutical industries, 78–79, 131–33
Pickett, Gregory, 49
Plame, Valerie, 197

Plato, 31
Political Action Committees. *See* PACs
political campaigns, 2–3, 5, 83, 110, 127, 133, 143
political consultants, 143
politics-administration dichotomy, 111–13
Postman, Neil, 125
Potter, Wendell, 188
Powell, Colin L., 202n27
PR Watch, 188
Pratkanis, Anthony, 6, 29–74, 143, 204
presidential appointments, 112, 118nn42–43
presidential approval ratings, 51–52
Prince, The (Machiavelli), 45, 61
Progressive era, 99–101, 111, 126, 170
Prohibition of Propaganda for War in International Law (Kearney), 193
Project Censored, 189, 201n10
propaganda: as amoral and value-neutral, 3, 11, 32, 184, 200n1; Breaux Symposium on, 1–2, 4, 64, 189; cognitive impact of, 21–22, 23n3; commercial/cultural American propaganda, 120–37; connectivity for dissemination of, 19–21, 23n3; corporate propaganda, 82, 86–87, 124–25, 151–52; creation of content of, 17–19, 21, 23n3; dangers of intersections between public discourse and, 75–90; definitions of, 9–13, 32, 96, 168, 184–85, 200; in digital age generally, 5, 17–23; and entertainment, 168–82; intention behind, linked with value judgments, 3–4; journalists as propagandists, 148–66; military/governmental American propaganda, 137–44; and myths in human consciousness, 199–200; negative traits of, 143–44; peace propagandists, 8, 60; as pejorative term, 1, 3–4, 8, 9, 10–13, 29, 32, 184; pervasiveness of, 120–44; reform of worst propaganda, 186–200; sociological propaganda, 185, 187; taboo tactics in, 4, 6, 38–41; three C's of, 17–22, 23n3; visual propaganda, 13–17, 22, 23n2, 25n27, 28n61; workings of, 186–87; "worst forms" of, 185–86. *See also* advertising; influence and persuasion; reform of worst propaganda; wartime propaganda
Propaganda (Ellul), 7, 120
Propaganda: Towards Disarmament in the War of Words (Whitton and Larson), 193
Propaganda and Persuasion (Jowett and O'Donnell), 165
propaganda and public discourse, dangers of intersections between: and *Citizens United v. Federal Election Commission*, 86, 88–89; and ideological use of the law, 75–76; and limitations on Internet access, 76–78; and manipulation of copyright law, 83–85; and Murdoch scandal in Britain, 85–87; and news bias, 80–83, 85–87; and science used for institutional or partisan gain, 78–80; signals of, 75
Propaganda, Inc. (Snow), 3
"propagation of the faith," 10, 128
Protagoras, 46
public administration, 111–15
Public Citizen's Commercial Alert campaign, 136
public diplomacy, 139–41
public discourse. *See* propaganda and public discourse, dangers of intersections between
Public Opinion (Lippmann), 126
purist's approach to influence, 29–32, 59–60
Putin, Vladimir, 21

radio, 10, 14, 121, 173, 178, 181, 183n19, 185
Ramaphosa, Cyril, 51
rationality, 41–44

Reagan, Ronald, 16–17, 82, 131, 139, 141
reasoned discourse, 41–44
reform of worst propaganda: by community organizing, 194; by enlightening people about forms of propaganda, 187–89; by exposing devices of propaganda, 186–87; and Government Accountability Office (GAO) reports, 191; and hate propaganda legislation, 192; and international law, 192–93; legal routes for, 190–94; and media oligopolies, 187–88, 190; and myths in human consciousness, 199–200; and problem of perspective, 195–99; regulation of news media for, 190–91; and whistleblowers, 188–89, 194–95
Rehman, Attaur, 155
religion: in America, 79, 129, 133; Beecher on preaching, 44; Christian teachings on God and normative system of ethics, 53–54; Christian teachings on wealth, 89; and Jefferson's definition of virtù, 62; "propagation of the faith" in Roman Catholic tradition, 10, 128; Ten Commandments of Moses, 58. *See also* Islam
Rendon Group, 138, 140
Reuters, 21
Revere, Paul, 14, 25n25
Rickey, Branch, 51, 52
Riefenstahl, Leni, 11, 15, 18, 23–24n5, 25–26n29
Robinson, Jackie, 51
Rodriguez, Jose, 160
Rogers, Carl, 31
Roman Empire, 14, 200n1
Romney, George, 143
Roosevelt, Franklin, 40, 51–52, 97–98, 102, 104–7, 110, 170, 174
Rosenberg, Carol, 152, 162
Routledge Handbook of Public Diplomacy (Taylor and Snow), 3
Rove, Karl, 76
Russia. *See* Soviet Union/Russia
Rwanda, 185

St. John, Burton, III, 101
Sandage, Charles, 38
Santorum, Rick, 83
Saving Private Ryan, 103
Schiffman, Stephen, 49
Schirch, Lisa, 67n15
school boards, 114–15
Schramm, Wilbur, 66n15
Schrier, William, 40, 43, 56, 57, 68n15
Schudson, Michael, 81
Schwarzenegger, Arnold, 80, 134
Schweitzer, Albert, 67n15
science, 78–80, 194
Seldes, George, 86
Seuss, Dr., 175
Shahid, Shaikh, 157
Sharf, Frederick A., 23n2
Sharp, Gene, 32
Sharp, Granville, 51
Sheikh, Omar, 155
Shridharani, Krishnalal, 32
Silver, Nate, 143
Skinner, B. F., 31
slavery, 50–51
sleuths and influence, 34–36, 40
Smiley, William, 67n15
Smith, Adam, 42
Smith, Kate, 52
Smith-Mundt Act (1948), 25n21
smugglers and influence, 34–38
Snow, Nancy, 1–8, 11, 51, 120–47, 184, 187, 200n1, 201n10, 205
social media, 20, 85, 121, 124, 129, 150, 164
Society for the Psychological Study of Social Issues (S.P.S.S.I.), 52
sociological propaganda, 87, 185
Socrates, 31
"SOFTWAR," 17, 27n41
Somalia, 163

SOPA. *See* Stop Online Piracy Act (SOPA)
Sophists, 31, 45–46
Sophocles, 33
SourceWatch, 188
Soviet Union/Russia, 15–17, 18, 20, 21, 23n2, 27n40, 27n43. *See also* Cold War
Spector, Phil, 125
Spielberg, Steven, 103
Sproule, Michael, 6, 38, 39, 61, 75–93, 125, 205
S.P.S.S.I., 52
Stalin, Joseph, 18
Star Wars, 25–26n29
State Department, U.S., 13, 138–40, 158
Steele, Richard W., 101
Steinem, Gloria, 161
Stelter, Brian, 85
Stevens, Ted, 76
Stone, I. F., 189
Stop Online Piracy Act (SOPA), 85
Super PACs, 88–89, 127, 129; PACs, 82, 127

Taliban, 19, 30, 157, 164. *See also* Afghanistan
Tarrouche, Zied, 165–66
Taylor, Philip M., 3–4, 7–8, 11, 184, 200n1
Tea Party movement, 79, 89
television: and Cold War propaganda, 11; de Caro as technical advisor for, 27n41; German use of, 15, 26n33; and Gulf War, 16, 18, 179–80; and Iraq War II, 180–81; *Law & Order* on, 114; morning talk shows on, 131–32; Murrow on, 15, 24n6, 131; news reporting on, 177–82; on Pearl's kidnapping and murder, 159–60; prescription drug advertising on, 131–34; propaganda function of, 176–82; satellite television, 16–17; soap operas on, 179; Soviet use of, 15; Super Bowl commercials on, 24n18, 123; in Third World countries, 176–77; TV Martí, 178, 183n19; and Vietnam War, 16, 180; wartime coverage on, 16. *See also* news media; *and specific television networks*
Ten Commandments of Good Influence and Propaganda, 34, 38, 41, 44, 48, 52–54, 56, 58–61
Terminator movies, 26n37
terrorism, 19, 21, 26n38, 27n40, 94, 96, 131, 137, 148–49, 152–65. *See also* Global War on Terror
Tess of the d'Urbervilles (Hardy), 57
Thaw, Harry K., 169–70
Thistlethwaite, Donald, 43
Thomas, Cal, 103
Three C's of propaganda, 17–22, 23n3
Tillman, Pat, 197
Time magazine, 163
Time Warner, 86, 124, 183n25
tobacco industry, 43, 185, 189, 193–94
Tolstoy, Leo, 32
tool metaphor for influence, 56–60
Toulmin, Stephen, 42
Trilby (du Maurier), 57
Triumph of the Will, 11, 15, 18, 23–24n5, 25–26n29, 169
Trudeau, Pierre, 191
Truman, Harry, 97
truthiness, 43, 44
Turner, Marlene, 54–55
Tutsis, 192
Tutwiler, Margaret, 140
TV Martí, 178, 183n19
Twitter, 20, 124, 129, 150, 188
two-way symmetrical model of influence, 48–49
2001: A Space Odyssey, 26n37

Ubuntu, 42, 53, 59
Ul-Haq, Siraj, 156–57
Ulpian, 54
United Nations International Covenant on Civil and Political Rights (ICCPR), 192–93
U.S. Information Agency (USIA), 51

U.S. Information Center, 105, 107
Ury, Bill, 49
USDA. *See* Agriculture Department (USDA)
USSR. *See* Soviet Union/Russia

Viacom, 124
Victoza, 132–33
video games, 77
Vietnam War: Gulf of Tonkin Resolution on, 94, 108, 197; international opinion of, 139; and Pentagon Papers, 198; propaganda on, 16, 94, 96, 98, 108–10, 138, 180; protests against, 130–31; television coverage of, 16, 180
virtù. *See* democratic virtù
visual propaganda, 13–17, 22, 23n2, 25n27, 28n61

Wakefield, Robert I., 66n15
Walden Two (Skinner), 31
Wall Street Journal, 86, 124, 148–52, 160, 188, 190
Wall-E, 175
Wallace, Amy, 123
Wallace, Karl, 53
Walmart, 124
Walt Disney Company, 86, 124–25
Walter, Otis M., 67n15
Walton, Douglas, 42–43
Wanger, Walter, 175–76
War on Terror. *See* Global War on Terror
War Powers Act (1973), 94, 110
Warner, Harry, 172
wartime propaganda: definition of, 96; and Gettysburg Address, 40, 56; and Gulf War, 16, 18, 179–80; historical lessons on, for contemporary America, 108–10; and Iraq War II, 94, 98, 108–10, 115–16, 137–39; and military's embedded journalists program, 161; narrative of U.S. domestic war propaganda, 96–99; by Nazis, 10–11, 15, 23–24nn4–5, 37, 38, 51, 56, 169; and Peloponnesian War, 39; proposal for domestic propaganda in undeclared war, 110–16; and Russo-Japanese War, 23n2; by U.S. during Constitutional versus non-Constitutional wars, 94–96, 110; by U.S. during World War I, 97–103, 105–6, 120–21, 127–28; by U.S. during World War II, 4, 40, 97–99, 103–8, 169, 170; and Vietnam War, 16, 94, 96, 98, 108–10, 138, 180. *See also specific wars*
Washington Post, 105, 153, 154, 156, 174, 197
weapon metaphor for propaganda, 57, 58
Weapons of Fraud (Pratkanis and Shadel), 57
Weiman, Henry Nelson, 67n15
Whately, Richard, 43
Wheeler, Burton K., 172
When Media Goes to War (DiMaggio), 189
whistleblowers, 188–89, 194–95
White, Ralph K., 40, 53
White, Stanford, 169
Whitton, John B., 193
Why We Fight films, 169
Wigand, Jeffrey, 189
WikiLeaks, 20–22, 28n58, 195–99, 202n22
Wilberforce, William, 51
Williams, Armstrong, 139, 191
Willkie, Wendell, 173
Wilson, Joseph C., 197
Wilson, Woodrow, 97–101
Word of Mouth Marketing Association (WOMMA), 124
Words That Work (Luntz), 142
World War I: Committee on Public Information (CPI) during, 97–103, 105–6, 127–28; compared with World War II propaganda, 96–99; Congressional declaration of war for, 94; origins of propaganda during, 10, 120–21; and Wilson, 97–101

World War II: bond drive during, 52–53; compared with World War I propaganda, 96–99; Congressional declaration of war for, 94; dissatisfaction with, in U.S., 103–8; Division of Information (DOI) in, 97, 98, 105–6; and isolationism in America, 51–52, 170–74; memorial to, 103; Munson on propaganda during, 4; news media during, 104–5, 107–8; Office of War Information (OWI) during, 97, 98, 106–7; and Roosevelt, 51–52, 97–98, 104–7, 174; *Why We Fight* films during, 169. *See also* Nazis
WPA, 62–63
Wyeth Pharmaceuticals, 78

Yoder, John Howard, 32
YouTube, 85, 150, 188

Zanuck, Darryl F., 172, 173
Zarefsky, David, 68n15
Zimbabwe, 20–21
Zimbardo, Phil, 31